D0676968

# ALFRED EINSTEIN

ALFRED EINSTEIN was born in Munich in 1880 and received his doctorate in musicology at the University of Munich in 1903. He became editor of *Zeitschrift für Musikwissenschaft* and was also music critic of the *Münchener Post* and the *Berliner Tageblatt*. He was the author of *Geschichte der Musik* and edited a new edition of Riemann's *Musik-Lexikon,* and became widely known as a musicologist to musicians and scholars throughout the world. He was forced to leave Germany in 1933, eventually settled in the United States, and was appointed professor of music at Smith College. His published works in English are: *A Short History of Music, Greatness in Music, Music in the Romantic Era, Mozart, Schubert,* and his definitive writing on the Italian madrigal, published in three volumes. He also edited the third edition of the Köchel catalogue of Mozart's works. He died at the age of 71 in 1952. This volume of essays, assembled by Paul Henry Lang, displays the great breadth of Dr. Einstein's interests and the variety of the man.

# ESSAYS
# ON
# MUSIC

## Alfred Einstein

The Norton Library
W · W · NORTON & COMPANY · INC ·
NEW YORK

TABOR COLLEGE
LIBRARY
HILLSBORO, KANSAS

COPYRIGHT © 1956 BY HERTHA EINSTEIN

FIRST PUBLISHED IN THE NORTON LIBRARY 1962

W. W. Norton & Company, Inc. is also the publisher of current or forthcoming books on music by Howard Boatwright, Nadia Boulanger, Manfred Bukofzer, Alfred Einstein, Richard Franko Goldman, Donald Jay Grout, Charles Ives, Paul Henry Lang, Joseph Machlis, Arthur Mendel, Douglas Moore, Carl Parrish, Vincent Persichetti, Marc Pincherle, Walter Piston, Gustave Reese, Curt Sachs, and Arnold Schönberg.

PRINTED IN THE UNITED STATES OF AMERICA

# Contents

# Introduction

I**N FEBRUARY, 1952**, a great scholar departed from us, still animated, at three-score-and-eleven years, with such plans and projects as had characterized a busy and fruitful life. Now comes posterity, Alfred Einstein's heir, to take official inventory of the substantial estate in the shape of great books, admirable essays, and some unpublished manuscripts. The books are in the library of many devoted students and lovers of music, they are fascinating and invaluable guides for all of us. The articles, many of them, are accessible in well-known musical journals; but others are hidden in learned professional periodicals, some of which are foreign to the English-speaking world; while a number of the manuscripts patently demand the printer's ink.

My long-standing friendship with my honored colleague, as well as the confidence of Mrs. Einstein and the Publishers, assigned to me the difficult task—and the privilege—of selecting from this estate a sheaf of papers to be gathered into a volume, a sort of salute to this rare connoisseur of music and its ways. Shall I make a list, add, subtract? My hands move hesitatingly among the papers; there can still be felt on them another hand's warmth, a noble, friendly hand, and the steady charm of a personality is everywhere. How does one arrive at a decision as to what to choose and in what order?

Musical historiography is the youngest of the modern humanistic disciplines; therefore its precepts and findings are rapidly changing. Einstein was only two generations removed from the founders of musicology, but he himself contributed generously to its rapid progress. He completely reshaped the monument of Mozart research, Köchel's celebrated *Verzeichniss*, and he opened an entire new Renaissance wing in the museum of music with his great work on the Italian madrigal. His long tenure as editor of one of the most distinguished journals of musicology, *Zeitschrift für Musikwissenschaft*, spanned a brilliant era of scholarship, of discoveries, of the coming of age of a host of young scholars, all of whom were helped and encouraged by the unselfish and dedicated editor. Reviewing his career, one comes to realize that beyond favoring his main fields of interest, any specific alignment in the selection of Einstein's articles is of no importance. Seeing them one next to the other, the reader will feel that they belong together, for they convey the manifestations of a globe-trotting spirit acquainted with every path on the musical sphere.

Nor was it necessary, with a very few exceptions, to document and annotate these essays. As with Ambros, it is the insight and imagination as well as the vivid personal presentation that will keep Einstein's writings forever fresh; a few changed data, or even the results of more recent investigations will not alter these essential traits. His writings do not resemble waves which disappear in order to cede their place to the next ones, but rather are like bricks which gain in value with every additional brick placed upon them.

Alfred Einstein was a born scholar for whom scholarship

was bread and vocation, and this scholarship was truly creative —and musical. Many an idea may have come to him as a dry echo from his four book-lined walls; but by the time it was elaborated and committed to paper it always breathed a musical atmosphere. And he was a real humanist, interested not only in musicological detail but in everything contributing to a style and to a man. He could devoutly immerse himself in philological minutiae, stop at a chord or at a word and analyse it with patient solicitude; but even in this painstaking quest he showed superiority over the raw materials of the scholar's métier. Furthermore, this zeal for the musicological procedure did not prevent him from seeing the essence. On the contrary, the greatest virtue of his sharp eye and intellect lay in his ability to espy in a rich and complicated fabric—such as the Renaissance madrigal—the fundamental, the primeval element; or in lifting from the maze of the nonessential the common unifying traits. This scholarly synthesis is at the same time literature, not only by reason of the excellence of its style, but because it is a true history of ideas.

Einstein looks askance at illusions. His method of writing shows periods and individuals from their own point of view, it helps to peel off acquired bias, and it traces the birth of styles and ideologies and demonstrates their interrelationships. He can show the beauty of ideas, but also the corruption of noble intentions, the peculiar scales of human greatness and frailty, the slow and inexorable maturing of fateful conditions, as for instance when he deals with the figures of Mozart or Schubert, or with the Enlightenment.

Musicology today is not rich in literary qualities. The oldsters stiffly guard their "scientific" style, while the younger generation, competent in method and technique, seems to have no use for the music of a literary prose. They forget that the word is the key to truth, and that it is with the aid of the word that we elucidate and organize existence, that the word is a force which empowers us to seize the past and, at our will, make it the present. Einstein could use the right word in the right place, and through his words there speaks to us the whole man, whose intelligence was free, whose judgments were clear and positive. His style is the lively style of the spirited critic; he wore his great learning lightly and always tempered it with wit and sarcasm; yet even his playful asides and puns are always logical and to the point.

It was his erudition and wide acquaintance with the cognate and auxiliary fields that made him the logical person to be sought out and entrusted with the modernization of both Riemann's famous *Musiklexikon* and the revised and enlarged German edition of Eaglefield-Hull's *Dictionary of Modern Music and Musicians*. His intimate knowledge of literature and the fine arts more than once offers competition to the music he deals with. He loves to draw parallels and to quote illustrative concordances. Yet he was a musician of the line, even disdaining the use of modern clefs. When I remonstrated with him that the scores in his monumental *The Italian Madrigal* would cause difficulty to many of his readers because of the old clefs, he was astonished: "Why, it is so much easier to read such scores with all the parts neatly within the staves!" He was indeed happy with his scores, many of which he edited for practical use, and nothing caused him more pleasure than such events as the performance of five little-known symphonies by Haydn which he had edited for The New Friends of Music.

For many years Einstein was chief critic and music editor of the leading Munich and Berlin newspapers. In spite of the alert and vivid style of his critiques, here too were the scholar's standards. In his judgments he always took as a point of departure the narrow premises of the subject and the outward forms and phenomena. Then he gradually smuggled in the philologist's interest in accuracy and detail, compassion for the human element, and an esthetic evaluation which often broadened to an examination of the genre itself. And for his judgments he was ready to take the field, always with an open visor.

There is still another aspect of this remarkable man's career, his editorship of the leading German musicological periodical. Editorship of a great scholarly journal is a difficult thing and is entirely different from the activity of the creative writer or critic. A critic can be subjective and can with fighting spirit represent a powerful individual tendency or taste in the musical world. The editor must deny himself, he must see with the eyes of many people at the same time, and, like the good *concierge*, must watch every door. Einstein's wide schooling, his self-discipline, modesty, candor, and friendliness made him an ideal editor. The conservatism he inevitably brought with him from the turn of the century when the guards were changed mixed happily with the inner necessities of newer music and musicology. As editor he could be severe with the pruning shears, but just as frequently he offered himself as a stake for tender plants sent to his journal.

In the center of Einstein's musical experience and faith are the Italian Renaissance and eighteenth-century classicism. That his first writings belong in nature and scope to the traditions of nineteenth-century German musicology is natural; but he soon turns to the Muse of lyricism, to that very particular thinking Muse of the Renaissance, as the immense treasure of the madrigal opens to him. It was on a comprehensive essay on the relationship of words and music that he was working when death overtook him. It must have been this predilection which also led him to Gluck, Mozart, and Schubert.

A very attractive trait in the elderly scholar was his love for the youthful and the fresh. He was like a gardener to whom the first buds are dearer than the full bloom, like the vintner to whom the new wine causes more joy than the aged treasures of the cave. How he liked to discuss the young Mozart, or the young de Rore! To the uninitiated all this is lost, for the bud has no leaves and casts slight shadow, its verdure cannot be seen from a distance. But he who loves and understands the buds can see the coming garden.

One hesitates to rake up the coals of the past. Time fortunately buries the conflicts, but it must be said that the wounds received when he was compelled to flee his native land to which his work had brought honor never healed, and left their mark on the remaining two decades of his life. Einstein did not "defend" himself and did not humiliate himself; there was in him the pride of a retiring nature, and he was lacking in the parvenu's clinging to his station. Though at first a little forlorn, he lived happily among us here in the United States in the congenial atmosphere offered him by Smith College, universally admired and loved, struggling a bit with a strange language, but with a quiet dignity triumphing over the awkwardness of the impediment.

When I first received a letter from him, in his neat, almost eighteenth-century hand, I felt as if a distinguished older brother had spoken to me. Many more letters came across the years, always warm and helpful, for Einstein was an extraordinarily understanding and enthusiastic colleague who rejoiced in his younger confrères' work.

There is among laymen a rather widespread notion that the scholar's thoughts are cold in contrast to the artist's warmth of feeling, and for that reason inferior. But they forget that the scholar's thoughts likewise spring from his experience, from his brushes with the world and with himself. These essays are the fruit of their author's inner life, of his mind and heart together.

Paul Henry Lang

*※》 *》》 *《《· *《《

# Sources and Acknowledgments

Acknowledgment is hereby made to the journals in which a number of the chapters in this book first appeared: *Acta Musicologica:* Vol. 9, 1937 (Chapter XVI). *Drei und Zwanzig:* No. 31/33, 1937 (Chapter I). *Journal of the American Musicological Society:* Spring, 1948 (Chapter XI). *Journal of the Warburg Institute:* Vol. 1 (Chapter VII). *Kirchenmusikalisches Jahrbuch:* 1911 (Chapter IX). *Monatshefte für Deutschen Unterricht* (Chapter XIV). *Monthly Musical Record:* Vol. 64, 1934 (Chapter XXI); Vol. 65, 1935 (Chapter XII); Vol. 68, 1938 (Chapter XXII); Vol. 69, 1939 (Chapter XX). *Music and Letters:* Vol. 19, 1938 (Chapter XVII); Vol. 22, 1941 (Chapter II); Vol. 25, 1944 (Chapter VIII). *The Music Review:* August, 1946 (Chapter XV). *The Musical Quarterly:* Vol. 20, 1934 (Chapter IV); Vol. 23, 1937 (Chapter V); Vol. 40, 1954 (Chapter VI). *Neue Musik-Zeitung:* Vol. 49, 1927–28 (Chapter X).

# Essays on Music

# I

# Fictions That Have Shaped
# Musical History

Some time ago an essay of mine appeared which met with
warm approval in some quarters and equally strong
condemnation in others. This article, entitled "Rest
and Movement in Music," called attention to the fact that
music, like the other arts, does not always directly express
the spirit of its time by having, so to speak, the same positive
and negative characteristics as that spirit; but rather may
represent its contradiction, the image of a desired ideal, the
flight into antithesis.

This sounds paradoxical, and those who opposed the idea
insisted that art must always be a direct reflection of life.
But it often happens that it is not the obvious perceptions,
but the paradoxical ones, which are right. It is not necessary
to prove that art is the exact image of the culture of an age;
that is a truism. A proof would be interesting only if it
showed when and why such a literal reflection comes about.

3

Even the images in a mirror reverse the right and left sides of what they reflect; and art is more rarely a mirror image than is generally supposed.

It is an old and often corrected error to believe that art has its prototype in nature. For art, nature is no more than material without intrinsic form. In any case, our concept of nature conforms to art, for it has been shaped by great artists. No doubt Rubens in sensual Flanders found a number of different female types to choose from; but he preferred one particular type for certain psychological reasons, and since then we have had women of the Rubens type. Ever since Rembrandt saw a room in half-light in a Dutch windmill and painted it, there is a room in half-light everywhere in the world. The English landscape may always have looked as Constable depicted it; but Constable's paintings have made it the more difficult for us to see it any other way. Only a still greater artist could make us see it differently. We become aware of natural things only when a great artist has first seen them for us and has given them the form that we see.

A most overwhelming example of the fact that whole centuries have seen, because of art, not reality but a fiction, is the figure of the peasant in both painting and poetry. (People may have seen the reality apart from the artistic fiction, but did not take it for truth.) In reality the peasant has always been doomed to heavy labor in the fields, in every sort of weather, and has possessed whatever more or less desirable attributes are connected with life on the soil. When the peasant was given any attention in earlier art, especially the Netherlands school from Breughel to Teniers and Brouwer, he was portrayed, to the amusement of the bourgeois class, as a figure of fun, a simpleton, boorish and clownish. Never shown at his work, he was depicted at his crude revels, dancing, feasting, smoking, and carousing until he made himself sick. This was the case until the end of the seventeenth century, up to the time of Watteau with his Paris gentry dressed in country costume. Then, in the nineteenth century, Millet and Segantini depicted the heroic peasant. No longer a roisterer, the peasant was seen at his labors, which were treated as a form of divine worship. But in reality the peasant is neither comic nor heroic.

In poetry there was another fiction about the peasant, which prevailed for centuries and was derived from classical antiquity, from Theocritus and Vergil, Longus and Horace. This was the pastoral tradition of the peasant as shepherd, pious and innocent, owning his land and tending his flocks with the blessing of the gods. The shepherd was always simple and good, a model to be contrasted with the corrupt city dweller. In youth the shepherds were Daphnis and Chloë, in old age they were Philemon and Baucis. This fiction was firmly rooted, and in the sixteenth century became a fashion, almost a disease, which afflicted all Europe: in Italy, through poets from Sannazaro to Guarini and Marino; in Germany, as a silly and pedantic pastoralism; in England, where Shakespeare finally raised it to an enchanting arabesque; and in Spain, where Cervantes tried vainly to cure it. The disease remained alive and virulent, assuming all possible forms, until it was brought to an end by the French Revolution. Or rather, it was almost brought to an end. For in the nineteenth century, the fashion of sentimentalism created the Swiss idyll, which has as its opposite the harsh naturalism of Zola, equally unrealistic in essence. The only writer in the nineteenth century who knew the peasant and portrayed him as he was, was Jeremias Gotthelf, and even he wrote as somewhat of an "uplifter." Gotthelf was a genius, but he was denied international recognition because he was a regional writer limited to Bern, and in fact dealt almost exclusively with the Emmental.

Is a fiction the same as falsehood? Yes and no. One can neither create art nor invent falsehood without the aid of imagination; thus art and untruth are intimately related in their origin. The whole pastoral world is as unreal and untrue as possible, but it would be absurd not to recognize that it is owing to this fiction that such a work of art as Torquato Tasso's *Aminta* was possible. Fictions are fruitful, for they create art. This is true for music also, and here we come back to our original point. There are times when art directly represents the spirit of the age. Perhaps—only perhaps—this is most likely to be true in archaic epochs, when art still has the function of worship. But even prehistoric man scratched the outlines of buffalo, stag, and antelope on the walls of his cave in order to exorcise the spirits of the game he hunted. The Egyptian chiseled and painted for the same reason he embalmed, in order to extend life into eternity. The Greek created an ideal world of light, because in actual life he suffered too passionately. There are other eras when art forms the counterimage of the times; this may happen in latter epochs which are able to look back on the distant perfection of olden time. There are also ages in which art is bipolar, at once the expression of the times and the flight into the ideal, both healthy and diseased, positive and negative. In such a disunity and dualism we have been caught since the beginning of the nineteenth century.

I am convinced that medieval polyphony is the product of a fiction. It is not correct to say that the so-called "latent feeling for harmonic relationships" led to writing for many voices. Polyphony and harmony have originally nothing whatever to do with each other. What occurred was that in certain monastery schools there was an attempt, not to find a new melody appropriate to one already known, but to combine existing melodies. Religious and mystic concepts most certainly played a role in this. Polyphony did not come from the people or the folk tradition, but was invented. Regarding this, as is true for so many artistic occasions, one may say that things develop after they have been produced, not the other way around; just as a folk song, for instance, grows only after some individuals have created it. Only after the principle of polyphony had been invented and the crude combination of melodies had been accomplished with increasing success, did a feeling develop for the harmonic relationships between these melodies. One could represent the whole history of medieval music as the history of the weakening, reduction, and repression of the polyphonic principle in favor of the harmonic. It is a battle between intellectual, mystic, abstract polyphony and sensuous harmonic sonority. The whole history of music is a stream flowing back and forth between these two poles. And this fluctuation does not by any means always correspond to the ebb and flow of the cultural, political, and general currents of the age.

I have said already that art is not imitation of nature, but a shaping and forming of nature. In music, fortunately, there can be no question of imitating nature; music is autonomous, belonging to another intellectual world, another sphere of the imagination than all the other arts. Yet in music the notion of *imitazione della natura* has played an extraordinary role, and this notion is a genuine fiction. This watchword or dogma arose in the sixteenth century, and like all the artistic teaching of the Renaissance, it was influenced by Antiquity. Music was supposed to "imitate," to afford an image in the manner of painting, the more direct and naive the better. Everyone who knows something of madrigals knows to what fantastic extremes of "depiction" the music of that time could go and with what seemingly childish musical "painting" the composers were occupied. In the second half of the sixteenth century, people began to regard these literal depictions as puerile and demanded a new and different "imitation of nature," namely the imitation of various mental states and processes. But the taste for pictorial music could not be wholly eradicated, and over the centuries the fiction retained its animating and creative force. The whole art of the cantata as practiced by Johann Sebastian Bach, and even a large portion of his instrumental compositions, would be inconceivable without this fiction of "painting in music." And I fear that we today, in this age of aesthetic purism, wrongly characterize as symbolic or mystic what Bach naively intended to be pictorial.

The most striking demonstration that art, at least the art of music, is no copy, no direct expression of life, is perhaps the music of the Renaissance. In life, as distinguished from art, the age was one of powerful tensions. The discovery of America filled the old world with mounting unrest; the battlefield between the great political powers, France and Spain, was prepared, and from the battle England emerged as the real victor. The world of feudalism gave way to that of the middle class with its money economy. Social tension had its counterpart in an all-encompassing religious tension: no one was certain of physical security, and all were facing spiritual crisis.

Nothing of this appears in the music. The final balance between polyphony and harmony was achieved apparently without struggle, certainly without convulsion. In this violently agitated world, a kind of music arose which evidently had no other aim than the attainment of sonority, the soothing of all passions, the resolution of all discord in blessed harmonies. Like a procession of angels music hovered above earthly things. (Perhaps "Saint Cecilia" by Raffaello Santi in the Bologna gallery is less pleasing to us as a painting than it was to our grandfathers; nevertheless, the idea of the picture corresponds to the feeling of the age.) This music was undramatically perfected in an age that was filled with drama to the point of explosion. It was a long while, almost an entire century, before an element of unrest made its way into Renaissance music; the smooth surface, heretofore moved only from the depths, was finally disturbed by a strong gust of wind as Renaissance music became Baroque music. Unrest in music began only when the political and spiritual tensions of the century had been mitigated. By then the Counter Reformation had taken up its position against the Reformation—that is, against the religious aspects of the movement; Europeans had regained a measure of security through the victory over the Turks at Lepanto, and they were still enjoying a brief period of civil peace before the storms of the seventeenth century.

The great example of the fruitfulness of a fiction is the history of opera. The Florentine dilettantes who wished to revive the ancient music drama knew as good as nothing about this form of Greek drama. Because of this very ignorance, they helped to bring to birth a genuine modern creation. But in this they served only as midwives; for the greater the artist who occupied himself with their ideas, the more he departed from them. After only a few decades of experiments a living opera had come into being, chiefly in Venice, and this no longer had any connection with the aesthetic or archeological specter that haunted the minds of the Florentine camerata. That philological ghost, which can also be called the Platonic Ideal of ancient music drama—and hence a fiction—was recurrently to interrupt or inspire the development of opera, generally doing both at once. The so-called reform opera of Gluck certainly does not resemble its fictive prototype or Ideal any more than an opera of Scarlatti or Rameau or Piccinni. Nietzsche has suggested that Piccinni may have been in the right as opposed to Gluck. And certainly *opera buffa*, which never harked back to the antique, was just as opposed to *opera seria*—Rossini's *Barber*, say, in contrast to Spontini's *Vestale*.

What an evil for creativeness this fiction of antique drama has been in the history of opera. Even Wagner was to fall victim to it. Perhaps this fiction is the origin of all that Wagner's opponents regard as his "falseness." In all his operas, not only in *Die Meistersinger*, Wagner treated middle-class conflicts: in *Lohengrin* the impossibility of marriage between the man of genius and a woman who wishes to penetrate the "mystery" of this genius; in *Tristan* a fairly common story— the tragedy of adultery; in the *Ring* the curse of unlawful possession. Wagner clothed these stories in heroic garb, raising them to the level of legend or myth, because middle-class conflicts are unsuited for heroic music. But behind this enhancement of the material lies always the fiction of antique drama and particularly the fiction of its effect: the religious unification of an audience by means of art. In the nineteenth century, after a hundred years of Rationalism, a work of art was supposed to exercise its religious function as it had done 2300 years before: this can well be termed the triumph of a fiction. Wagner's supporters and detractors will never come to an agreement. One side sees in his work the fulfillment of this fiction—namely the renewal of antique drama in the "spirit of Germany," a new Olympia in Bayreuth. The other side can admire only the most personal, most peculiarly Wagnerian aspect of his work.

Wagner is the typical representative of the Romantic movement. But for the Romantics, art, especially music, was the medium of a two-fold fiction, at once the expression and the denial of an age. Romanticism was bipolar. It was essentially false in its use as an organ of life, for in the nineteenth century art was no longer a natural blossoming of culture but something at the second remove, cut off and separated—a fictive world above the real and secularized existence of individual and nation. This did not prevent the individual artist from producing a wondrous and even a great work of art. But when art becomes the personal concern of the artist, it tends frequently to become a flight from reality. Wagner's *Parsifal* is the most perfect example of this bipolarity. Flight from the senses! The ideal of asceticism preached from the operatic stage! The teachings of St. Francis offered to the jaded, industrialized, newspaper-reading man of the nineteenth century! Art as a new form of religion! Nothing could more clearly demonstrate the fictive role of art in the nineteenth century.

Our "new music" too is largely the product of an imagined ideal or of a fiction. Let us put aside the fact that art in the twentieth century is an even more artificial, rootless affair than in the nineteenth, and that its whole existence has become more fictive. How could we be able to create a true expression of the times? Artistically we live on an enormous legacy from the past. Modern creation clings to the legacy like a tiny baby clinging to a mighty father, grandfather, great-grandfather, and so on. The worst of it is that, as it is in all good families, so it is here; what great-grandfather, grandfather, and father say is regarded as true, good, and beautiful, while baby presumably can produce only Dadaism, if not worse. The only true expression of our times is, perhaps, dance music, which is exactly like us so we will not praise it. We have not developed from it anything worthy of mention, perhaps because we have always regarded it as a baby deserving only contempt. And the essence of the "new music" is wishing, not the achievement of simplicity, truth, and realism. It is merely a counterattack on the Romantic movement, but an attack that by no means overcomes Romanticism. How could it be possible to conquer the Romantic movement? Are we not ourselves burdened by even more of the past than were our fathers? Are we not still more restless, divided, and even diffused? Our music too is not a complete, veracious reflection of expression symbolizing the spirit of our times. Rather it is the image of our unfulfilled wishes. But perhaps even this image, as has happened so often in the past, will one day possess creative power.

⋙ ⋙ ⋘ ⋘

# II

# The Mortality of Opera

IN THE January 1940 number of *Music and Letters* appeared a contribution on "Operatic Mortality" by H. G. Sear—an essay on the various modes of death in the last acts of tragic operas, modes of death well calculated to astonish those learned in human pathology. Death in opera, indeed, rarely has anything in common with normal demise: operatic truth obeys its own laws.

At the first glance I misunderstood the title of Mr. Sear's attractive and entertaining article, for it made me think, not of death in opera, but of the mortality of opera itself. Well, that too is matter for speculation. It may not be so amusing a subject as that dealt with by Mr. Sear: rather it is often tragicomic, if not positively depressing; but it is no less instructive.

Opera has been, at any rate since the middle of the nineteenth century, the most exacting of all musical works of art. The midwifery and surgery it requires before it can be brought to life runs to a hundred assistants at least, and if a few choral and orchestral works, such as those by Berlioz,

for example, demand an equally numerous participation, they
do not ask for the help of stagecraft, nor for the collaboration
of so many branches of art. But these pretensions, these efforts
to impart life to the monstrous baby, stand in inverse ratio to
its vitality. It ought to promise a longer life, not to say a fair
chance of immortality; but that immortality presents a sorry
spectacle, the more so when it is compared with that of works
belonging to other categories of music which are much older
than opera, whose history after all comprises barely three centuries and a half.

Nowhere else in music does the idea of immortality change
more quickly. Giuseppe Carpani, the Italian translator of
*The Creation*, an honest essayist who was greatly vexed by
that unscrupulous and thick-skinned plagiarist, Monsieur
Bombet, *alias* Stendhal, *alias* Henri Beyle, once enumerated the
immortal works of the "golden age of music," the eighteenth
century, in his *Le Haydine*.[1] They are, next to Haydn's
*Creation*, Pergolesi's *Stabat Mater* and *Serva padrona*, Paisiello's
*Barbiere di Siviglia* and *La Frascatana*, Cimarosa's *Orazii e
Curiazii* and *Matrimonio segreto*, Mozart's *Don Giovanni*,
Salieri's *Axur*, Sarti's *Giulio Sabino*, Gluck's *Ifigenia*, Sacchini's
*Oedipe à Colone*, Jommelli's *Miserere* and *Veni Sancte
Spiritus*, Zingarelli's *Giulietta e Romeo*, Cherubini's *Due
giornate*, Naumann's *Pater noster* (Carpani calls him Neu-
mann!), Guglielmi's oratorio *Debora e Sisara* and Graun's
*Passion*.[2]

Now, with the exception of *The Creation* and *Don Giovanni*, and possibly Gluck's *Iphigénie en Tauride*, what an

[1] Second edition, 1823, p. 164.
[2] For the sake of completeness I have enumerated the oratorios and church
music as well as the operas.

array of tombstones is here! Every name is an epitaph, and that is true not only of the operas mentioned by Carpani. One may admit that in place of Pergolesi's *Stabat Mater* and Graun's *Passion* a few other works have retained the radiance of immortality, quite apart from Handel's oratorios, which Carpani does cite with some respect as the model for Haydn's: Bach's Passions, *B minor Mass* and *Magnificat*, and a few more of Mozart's operas. History's choice is far more severe and selective than the Italian's generous enthusiasm. It was Ibsen who, asked about the probable length of life for a dramatic work, estimated it at thirty, possibly forty and at the most fifty years, which was only too true of his own plays. It is said, however, that Verdi, on hearing this dictum, asked angrily: "E il mio Rigoletto?"; and there was truth in that too, for *Rigoletto* is nearly ninety years old and shows no signs of celebrating its hundredth birthday with any particular appearance of decrepitude.

There are few operas which have grown so aged within that space of three and a half centuries that one may grant them immortality, doubtful and relative though that concept may be; but on the whole, opera is a frail creature, destined in most cases to a very early death, if indeed it ever comes to birth at all—that is to say, if it ever reaches the stage. For it is the creature of contradiction and dissension, the object of the eternally undecided contest between the conflicting demands of poetry and music, the victim of an everlasting dependence on singers, conductors, producers and designers—in short an "impossible work of art." Today it dies in the mother's womb more often than not and remains entombed in the desk of its progenitor, the composer.

It was different when opera first appeared. A musical work

for the stage was not engendered by an inner urge on the composer's part, and hardly with any thought that immortality or even survival might be claimed for it. It was commissioned for a definite place and occasion, and for artists chosen in advance. It was at first purely an occasional piece for performance at court. If it was printed at all, permanence was thus given to it with an entirely different object from that which attached to the publication of an operatic score in the nineteenth century. Altogether, in the sixteenth century the printing of secular works was only partly intended, as it was later and still is today, to allow it to circulate among more or less extensive groups of musicians and amateurs who wished to perform it. Another and almost as important a purpose was merely to produce a souvenir of some festive occasion, usually a wedding or some princely visit, worth no more than the descriptions of such festivities by stewards, emissaries or literary men, descriptions which often went into several editions. One of the earliest publications of this kind is connected with a dramatic performance at a wedding: the *Musiche fatte nelle nozze dello illustrissimo duca di Firenze il signor Cosimo de' Medici*, dating from 1539, about the artistic side of which we are informed by Vasari's life of Bastiano di Sangallo. It would be a mistake to suppose that this music was printed for the purpose of being performed elsewhere, even though it was brought out in part-books, not in score.

It was for similar reasons that such works as Peri's *Euridice*, Gagliano's *Dafne* and Monteverdi's *Orfeo* were printed. The last-named's *Arianna* was probably not deemed worthy of this honour simply because it had been decided to print the *Dafne*, performed on the same occasion, and because, unlike Florence, Mantua possessed no musical press. A few cardinals emulated the ostentation of the Medici and Gonzaga families by publishing the operas performed at their palaces; but when opera migrated to Venice, publication ceased, owing to the jealousy among the patricians, which made any such enterprise impossible. No Venetian opera was printed, and it was only in Paris, under Louis XIV, that the publication of all operas performed at the Académie Royale became a custom, for the same reason as it had been at the Italian courts.

There were repeat performances, however. Peri's *Dafne* was repeated at Florence during a visit from the Duke of Parma in 1604; his *Euridice* was revived for Louis XIII. Nothing was so fit to stagger one's guests with as opera, the new sensation. Monteverdi's revivals of *Arianna* at Venice in 1639 and 1640, probably in a form very different from that of 1608, on the other hand, were quite another thing. There it was actually the fame of a work which called for its resuscitation. Nor is this the only event of the kind in the seventeenth century: the same master's *Incoronazione di Poppea* of 1642 was given again in another Venetian operahouse four years later; Cavalli's *Giasone* of 1649 was repeated in 1664 and 1666, his *Serse* of 1654 in 1663 and 1666; Cesti's *La Dori*, the most successful opera of the century, was brought out, after its production at Florence in 1661, at Venice in 1663, 1666, 1667 and 1671, at Rome in 1672 and at Munich in 1680. That was the first international success.

But these are exceptions, appearing the more rare when the enormous wealth of operatic writing is considered. Operas were ephemera. People wanted to hear something new, because above all they wanted to *see* something new. It has often been said, and rightly, that in the operatic hierarchy of the first hundred years the machinist stood in the front rank; the singers, that is to say the *prima donna* and *primo uomo*, stood after him; and only then came the composer at a long distance, followed, still farther behind, by that miserable menial, who was made to clean everybody's boots, the librettist—for "poet" was too good a name for him.

This order of precedence has changed more than once in the course of musical history. It was a long time before the musician came to hold the front place he has kept, as we know, to the present day. The next to advance, oddly enough, seemed to be the librettist, in the case of Zeno and Metastasio. It seemed so, I say, for in reality it was the *prima donna* and *primo uomo* who predominated, while the machinist fell back to second place, or shared it with the composer. The reasons why Zeno and Metastasio again secured for the librettist the honourable rank he had occupied at the time of Rinuccini and Chiabrera need not be discussed here: they were many, chief among them being the secret beginnings of purism and classicism in the eighteenth century. Their vogue as poets, however, made opera more impermanent than ever. The poet remained, the composer vanished. Of Zeno's more successful libretti, such as *Merope*, each would on an average be set ten times; of Metastasio's, as for instance *Didone, Alessandro nell' Indie, Artaserse, Adriano in Siria, Ezio, L'Olimpiade, Demofoonte, Serse,* or *Semiramide,* each would be used by some forty composers. It was in turn another triumph for the composer that the public should wish to hear the words of the same arias sung to new melodies again and again; but at the same time this is only another proof of the insatiable desire on the part of the Venetian, Roman, and Neapolitan operatic publics to hear new music, or rather of their insurmountable reluctance to listen to what was familiar. The consequence was an ever-increasing mass of production, resulting inevitably in its growing more and more shallow and conventional.

This routine did not fail to provoke opposition, the most familiar manifestation of which, though not the earliest, is Benedetto Marcello's *Teatro alla moda* of 1720, directed in the first place against Antonio Vivaldi—to whom Marcello was not fit to hold a candle. We are in the eighteenth century, the century of æsthetic reasoning. The humdrum goings-on of opera were unfavourably compared with the dignity of antique drama, and the final result was what has been called the Gluckian operatic reform. Oh no, the Gluckian reform did not do away with operatic laxity, least of all in Italy; but it suddenly created a species of opera which claimed international success, permanence, and, if possible, perpetuity. There had been no such thing before, although Venetian opera had for a time been exported to Paris and at all times to the German courts, especially in Vienna, Dresden, and Munich, and although the works of men like Agostino Steffani were performed not only at Hanover, but also at Brunswick and Hamburg. For the first time an opera— Gluck's *Orfeo*—was given not only in Italian, but also in French, and *Alceste* not only in Italian and French, but even in German. For the first time a libretto was closely associated with its music, so that Ferdinando Giuseppe Bertoni, who was foolhardy enough to set *Orfeo* again, failed lamentably with it. *Ezio* and *Artaserse* were Metastasio's *Ezio* and *Artaserse; Orfeo* and *Alceste* were Gluck's *Orfeo* and *Alceste.*

To name these two is to name the earliest operas which claimed a so-called immortality-value. True, there is an earlier work—not an opera, but merely an intermezzo too modest to make any such claim, which goes on proving its puppet-play

TABOR COLLEGE
LIBRARY
HILLSBORO, KANSAS

29522

vitality: Pergolesi's *Serva padrona*. Vitality—the opposite of mortality. But mortality remains the rule for operatic babies, even after Gluck. Few composers ever thought, like him, of any lasting future for their works. Success for them meant applause at the first production and repeat performances during a season; the sale of the score to more than one impresario and performances on more than one stage meant an exceptional success. Mozart never expected more, and he would have been greatly surprised had he been told that *Don Giovanni* or *The Magic Flute* would still be sung after a century and a half, for all that he was well aware of his worth and of the value of these and other works of his.

This conception is still current in Italy and in countries influenced by Italian conditions. Operas there are not written for eternity, but for a season, and even now they are intended for particular singers. Goodness knows why one work is a fiasco and another makes a triumphal progress through Italy and beyond. Rossini had as great hopes of *Aureliano in Palmira* and *Sigismondo* and *Adelaide di Borgogna*—not to mention the works of his youth—as of *Tancredi*, *Elisabetta*, *regina d'Inghilterra* and *Mosè*, which happened to be successes. Nor did the initial failure of the *Barbiere* disturb his equanimity—another *opera buffa* could, after all, be written in three weeks!

Verdi's case was hardly different. He too, up to about 1860, was capable of turning out an opera, not in three weeks, it is true, but well within six months, and if a *Stiffelio* did not have the success of a *Trovatore*, it could not be helped. Sometimes, as in the very case of *Stiffelio*, Verdi tried to mend matters by a new version; if that only made them worse, he would dismiss the work with a shrug of the shoulder. It was to be very different later on, to be sure; but *Aida*, *Otello* and

*Falstaff* merely showed that Verdi's sense of responsibility towards himself had grown. It was no pose for him to say that he had written *Falstaff* for himself.

Success, permanence, perpetuity—these things are incalculable. Nobody knows why some operas die of diphtheria, scarlet fever, or some other childhood disease, while others remain perfectly healthy. Curious cases are to be observed among the works of Mascagni, Leoncavallo and Puccini (whose *Manon Lescaut* is vastly superior, in my opinion, to *Bohème*, and certainly better than Massenet's *Manon*). Non-Italian operas too are apt to show puzzling signs of vitality at times. In Germany, where a system of permanent opera forces managements to keep a large repertory going, a series of operas of the first half of the nineteenth century (apart from Wagner, Verdi and a few other works still capable of attracting) is maintained which remains only just acceptable. Munich in the days of my youth had perhaps the most extensive repertory of some sixty to eighty different works, for here was a city with half a million inhabitants forced to offer more change in order to fill its theatre night after night than a place of the size of Berlin, where the same works could be more often repeated. Among German operas (for the repertory was international) Lortzing's *Waffenschmied* and *Zar und Zimmermann* were constantly given, but the best work by this composer (whom friend Dent, by the way, treated with bitter injustice [1] by comparing him to Herr von Flotow), *Der Wildschütz*, was done only intermittently. A feeble, sickly, blue-eyed opera of the Biedermeier period, Conradin Kreutzer's *Nachtlager von Granada*, kept itself before the

[1] Edward J. Dent, "A Best-Seller in Opera," *Music & Letters*, XXII (No. 2, April, 1941).

public with a tenacity for which no good reason was to be discovered. On the other hand nothing was known of *Boris Godunov,* or indeed of any Russian opera. Nowadays this nucleus of works dating from the years between *Fidelio* and *Lohengrin* has presumably dwindled to an infinitesimal residue, and since more recent times have provided few substitutes, the German operatic situation too is becoming more and more precarious. But more of that later.

The claim to permanence dates from the romantic period, which indeed began to make many unhealthy claims upon art. Beethoven transformed *Leonore* into *Fidelio,* and the revision was a very different thing from Mozart's revision of *Don Giovanni* for Vienna or from his second Vienna *Figaro,* undertaken merely to please the new singers. Beethoven's revision was one made for artistic reasons, at any rate in part. Weber took nearly three years over the composition of *Der Freischütz.* The huge national success of this work saddled Weber with a new responsibility, and *Euryanthe* thus became a work done according to plan and calculated to meet with a much more than ephemeral success: its failure must therefore have hurt Weber the more deeply.

Operatic composition became more and more of a perilous venture, most of all in the case of Wagner, whose later *Gesamt-Kunstwerk* was a gamble with eternity. Even to the operas which prepared the ground for his later works— *Tannhäuser* and *Lohengrin*—Wagner deliberately imparted a "deeper significance," a philosophical interpretation, for the simple purpose of keeping them aloof from current operatic affairs and raising them to a higher status. It is amusing to reflect that Wagner's least tendentious work—*Tristan*— should now seem his most full-blooded and permanent.

We have arrived at the opposite pole of the original purpose of operatic production: in the place of the intention to write for the day, for a single festive occasion, we find an urge to secure musical stage works for all time, and if possible for all nations. The difference may be seen expressed even in the outward appearance of a work—the composer's manuscript: compare the original score of Monteverdi's *Incoronazione*, with its notation on two staves, with the wonderfully complex image of a Wagnerian score, in which the minutest detail is despotically laid down, to be obeyed by the remotest posterity. Such a score, clearly, could only have been written by one who was convinced of its permanence, its immortality.

The misfortune was, though, that after Wagner nearly every German and Germanically-influenced composer tried to write operas that pretended to this immortality. And immortality's capital was usually invested, so to speak, in a detailed elaboration of the orchestral share in the work rather than in opera as such—namely in that remarkable, highly-wrought, and, in successful cases, fascinating organism in which scenic, dramatic, and musical values are ideally balanced. However, we are not concerned with operatic æsthetics at the moment. All we need establish is the fact that even the most successful composers have suffered their failures. Puccini had his *Fanciulla del West* next to *Bohème, Tosca,* and *Madama Butterfly,* Strauss his *Frau ohne Schatten* and *Aegyptische Helena,* to say nothing of many another fiasco, next to *Rosenkavalier* and *Salome.* As for the later and younger practitioners, it may fairly be said that for each birth they have a tombstone to show. The inscriptions on these tombstones more often than not inform us of the operatic baby's death immediately after birth, or at least in the first bloom of its youth. Infant mortality rises to 100 per cent for some years in the operatic department. The epidemic is a tragic, indeed a catastrophic one, if one reflects that the gestation of these babies took as a rule longer than that of a young elephant.

Should the period of that gestation be shortened? Should not opera once more become a less pretentious form of art, as it was in the seventeenth and eighteenth centuries, when its miscarriage or death was fraught with less tragic consequences? This would mean a smaller risk for the impresario, less hard labour for the conductor, singers, and orchestra, a more light-hearted response on the part of the public, and a less heavy responsibility for the critic. An attempt of this kind was made in Germany before 1933, but it was strangled because it originated with "culture-bolshevists." Italy still shows an astonishingly large annual production of new operas, but the lighter ones among them are not written by the more responsible people. In countries that have as yet no established operatic cultivation—like that in which this essay is being written—the only chance is to create *light* operas, even if it has to be done in some operatic Hollywood. No operatic culture can thrive on import. *Grand* opera, the super-national opera of the past in Italy, Germany, France, and Russia, would mean stagnation and no more vitality than we find in a museum.

But is not opera as such dead already? Does it not present a mere appearance of life nowadays? An artistic life, of course, it never showed at all consistently, for it was from the first a product of luxury and has always relied, like the cuckoo in the strange bird's nest, on unwilling foster-parents: princes, states, cities or communities. The more still-born or short-lived children are brought into its world, the more mummified must be its appearance. It is so complex an organism, so dependent on a hundred economic, political, and social conditions, that its future may be foretold with as little confidence as a "military expert" of today may feel about the next event of the war or a meteorologist about the weather conditions in August, 1999. The great unknown quantity will always be the artist, who not only makes the best of the given circumstances, but may create new conditions for himself. The prospects for the immortality of opera are gloomy; all the same, the species cannot yet be said with certainty to have made its *exitus letalis.*

# III

## Early Concert Life

IT WOULD be a very interesting task to write a book about the development of the concert audience, its beginnings and changes, the differences between centuries and between nations. A musical audience in the modern sense has existed for opera perhaps only since the foundation of the Venetian opera houses, which were built, of course, for the aristocracy of Venice and their many noble and wealthy visitors. The concert audience came into existence with the oratorios and concerti grossi and organ concertos of Handel; in the field of opera Handel was still merely a purveyor of music for a part of the English aristocracy, and the importance of his determination to write for another and greater public can hardly be overemphasized.

In earlier times there was no audience in the modern sense. The church was the only place where a musician was able to reach a fairly large audience—but it cannot be said that the congregation was a real audience with an interest in musical and esthetic values. A church musician serves the church.

A churchgoer is there for edification and music is only a means to an end; in the Protestant church the worshipper takes an active part in the service, not as a musician but as a believer. In the past it was very difficult to listen to music just for enjoyment, as a "connoisseur."

The topic can also be studied from the point of view of the musician of the past. How was the musician to earn his living? The "free musician" was unknown, although after the fifteenth century, there was the "virtuoso," the successor to the medieval minstrel or jongleur. We understand the connection between them when we read of Conrad Paumann, organist at the cathedral in Munich, who not only played the organ, but also the lute and violin and several wind instruments; about 1470 he paid a professional visit to some Italian courts— Milan, Mantua, Ferrara—where the princes and courtiers admired his technical skill, and he was remunerated as a minstrel, with clothes, with pieces of silk and velvet, and a sword. During the sixteenth century the virtuoso was a virtuoso on only two instruments: the viola and the lute; at first in connection with improvisation and singing, and a little later on the instruments alone. Such improvisers and instrumentalists went from court to court and were sometimes generously and sometimes poorly remunerated; therefore, except for a few born "bohemians," they felt a need for a regular salary, a steady job.

In general, the musician was a church musician and was appointed by the chapter of a cathedral or monastery, by a prince who loved pomp or splendor in the divine service, or by a government like the Venetian Republic. First of all he composed church music; if he were commissioned, he composed secular pieces too. He was never impelled by his own "genius." We must not forget that until the end of the eighteenth century the great musicians were only artisans, members of a craft; that they were also great musicians is only incidental. But during the fifteenth and sixteenth centuries a difference becomes apparent between essentially "ecclesiastical" and essentially "secular" composers. There are musicians who never wrote a single secular piece, as for example Tomás de Victoria; of Gombert or Morales we know only one or two madrigals. We are accustomed to think of Palestrina as a church composer in spite of the fact that he composed many madrigals. On the other hand, there are composers who decidedly had an inclination for secular art. The Florentine musicians of the *trecento* were secular musicians, they composed not for the church, but for the cultivated society of the town. Luca Marenzio is a secular composer in spite of the fact that he also composed some motets—although never a Mass. And so, after the beginning of the sixteenth century, there are several musicians whom we may call secular musicians: they either had no opportunity to find church positions, or had no inclination to compose church music. By the end of the fifteenth century and the beginning of the sixteenth, the musicians at the court of Mantua of Isabella and Francesco Gonzaga were secular musicians: we know of a few laude by Tromboncino and Cara besides their frottole and strambotti; but laude do not really belong to church music.

The question arises, who paid these secular musicians? How did they earn their livings? A negative answer is: not by publishing their works. There is no history of musical copyright; but we do know that the musician or author was always the last one to be protected. The composer had no legal rights at all. Before Petrucci published his editions, he procured for himself the privilege, first from the Venetian Republic, then from the Pope, that nobody should print polyphonic music for twenty years except himself. His attempt at monopoly was unsuccessful, because the Pope gave Andrea Antico permission to print organ music, and Antico printed polyphonic music too. And, of course, Petrucci did not give Josquin or Mouton or de La Rue a single soldo. No publisher did.

In most cases the composer undertook the expenses of printing himself, hoping to be compensated later by the man to whom he dedicated his work; or he sent copies to princes or wealthy people. The compensations varied according to the quality of the gift and the degree of generosity of the recipient. We know that Giaches Wert, after sending a book of madrigals to the Duke of Bavaria, received fifty ducats. The Imperial Court had its rate for single pieces, church or secular music, and whole books. If a book of Masses, motets, or madrigals was a success, the composer did not gain anything from it. The publisher reprinted it to his own advantage; and rival publishers issued editions without any consideration for the composer. And the profit cannot have been small. The editions were larger than we think; for instance, we know that the first edition of Boiardo's great romance, *Orlando Innamorato* (1495), ran to 1200 copies, not one of which has been preserved. You see: the situation of the creative musician was not a very happy one during the sixteenth century either, although not so bad as that of a modern composer—except in a few cases.

A great help for the "secular" musician of the *cinquecento* were the musical academies—*le accademie*. The academy in general is a characteristic institution of the Renaissance, or—if we want to avoid this term—of Humanism. The first one was the "Platonic Academy" in Florence; some cultivated men from the circle of Cosimo de Medici, the most important one of whom was Marsilio Ficino, met in the afternoons and evenings in the Villa Careggi and discussed the problems of Platonic philosophy. They must have started about 1460. By the end of the fifteenth, and throughout the sixteenth, century all sorts of academies were being founded for scientific, archeological, and literary purposes. There was no city in Italy without its academy, and the larger cities had several. Most of them had strange names: the *Desios* (The Desirers) in Conegliano; the *Spennati* (The Featherless) in Faenza; the *Insensati* (The Insane) in Perugia; the *Erranti* (The Erring) in Brescia; the *Intrepidi* (The Fearless) of Ferrara; and so on. The most famous academies were the *Accademia della Crusca* (The Academy of Bran) in Florence, whose aim, as its name indicated, was to purify the Italian language by removing the husks of vulgar usage, and whose members edited the first important Italian dictionary; and the *Accademia dell' Arcadia* in Rome, whose members modeled themselves on Theocritan shepherds. Each member of an academy had a nickname; Gluck, for example, who was an Arcadian in the eighteenth century, used the nickname Olindo Treppanio.

Some of the academies were exclusively musical. Most of the names I have just mentioned were musical clubs. They were often less intellectual than social; music was not a matter for speculation, but for entertainment. We can easily imagine the beginnings. Some young gentlemen prepare a festivity in Florence—a wedding, let us say. They meet to discuss the matter, hire a poet, musicians, and a painter, and sometimes keep their association up after the festivity. We possess a report on such a group in Venice in the chronicle of Marin Sanuto. He writes (November 20, 1504): "Recently some young patricians, thirteen in number, founded a new society with the name *I contenti* [The Happy] and that for the wedding of one of them, namely Sier Sabastian Cantarini. . . ." We do not know whether this society was continued. Three years later, on October 24, 1507, he says: "This morning a company of young men was founded, all about eighteen years old, all very wealthy, under the name of the *Immortali* [The Immortals], thirteen in number. They elected a princi- pal, or president for the period of a year and they want to arrange a festivity immediately, first the principal, then all the others. . . . They went to Mass in the church of the Madonna di Miracoli, visited San Marco afterwards . . . and they call themselves the 'Immortals'—so now we have in this city four societies of a similar name, the *Semprevivi, Perpetui, Eterni,* and now these *Immortali.* NB: other societies of today are, *Puavoli, Felici, Principali, Liberali, Sbragenzai, Fraterni, Potenti.*" Certainly all these societies needed music and musical entertainment. Even academies with literary and philosophical aims did not disdain musical entertainment; we know this from the biography of Serafino Aquilano, writ- ten by his friend Vincenzo Calmeta and published in 1504. About 1485 Serafino returned to Rome in the company of his patron Ascanio Sforza, and there founded a club in the house of a young nobleman, Paolo Cortese; where, Calmeta reports, every day "assembled a great number of cultivated spirits," scientists, poets, philosophers; and Serafino "with the harmony of his music and the wit of his strambotti very often brightened the severe discussions of the literary men."

The change in musical style was responsible for purely musical academies. The new polyphonic music, especially the new madrigal, induced the music lover not merely to listen to music but to take a part in producing it himself; music became much more of a social institution than it had been before. During the first half of the sixteenth century noblemen began to study singing and the playing of instruments, and a knowledge of music became one of the requirements in the education of a courtier. There is a famous passage in Castiglione's *The Courtier*, published in 1528, about singing and playing the viola in society.

In 1543, one of the first purely musical academies, the *Accademia Filarmonica de Verona*, was established. The founders were a few young men of the noble families of Verona and some artists—two painters, a poet, and a musician. The purpose of the *Filarmonica* was to cultivate and to perform music. Only later, in 1547, did the members come to recognize that poetry was also necessary, to supply the texts they needed. All members had to pay an annual fee (12 mocenigos-ducats); they elected a *principe*, a *governatore*, and four other members to their board. The anniversary of the founding was a day of special solemnity and festivity: in the morning there was Mass in one of the churches of Verona— a musical Mass, different every year; and in the evening there was a banquet.

At the end of 1546 the members decided to hire a "*maestro di musica*" to teach singing and playing; and a few months later they engaged a Netherlander, Metre Jan (or Giovanni) Nasco, who had formerly been in the service of a *condottiere* in Vicenza, Paolo Naldi. Nasco had composed a "Song of the Nightingale" for the Academy before 1546, which was not printed until 1554. The members had a choice among three candidates: Vincenzo Ruffo, Gabriele Martinengo, and Metre Jan—and it is significant that they elected not one of the two Italians, both Veronese, but the "*maestro fiammingo*." Nasco received a salary of 30 ducats a year and lodgings in the building of the Academy; he had to be at the disposal of the members as a teacher every afternoon, and all his compositions became the property of the Academy. He also had to compose to any text the members wished. In the mornings Nasco was free to give instruction to nonmembers, but not in the rooms of the club. The Academy was proud of Nasco, and its president, Brusasorci, the painter, painted his portrait, which is now in the Museum di Castelvecchio in Verona. Nasco was a sociable fellow; he liked a good drink, and in 1548 he and some other members of the club made fun of Vincenzo Ruffo—and all of them had to pay for kicking over the traces a little.

Nasco remained maestro of the Academy until the end of 1551, and left his position only because his financial situation was bad and the 36 ducats he was by then getting were not enough. He became *maestro di cappella* at the Cathedral of Treviso; but he always remained on good terms with the Academy, sending religious and secular compositions for the first of May and for the Carnival. Nasco died in 1561. His widow dedicated a book of Lamentations by him to the Academy.

The *Accademia Filarmonica* remained in existence for a long time and possessed a few excellent masters, the best ones being Lambert Courtois, a Frenchman, and Vincenzo Ruffo. But during the second half of the sixteenth century the glory of the *Filarmonica* was overshadowed by the private academy of a Veronese Maecenas, Mario Bevilacqua, of whom we shall speak later. In 1564 the *Filarmonica* joined the *Accademia della Vittoria*— a sign that it was no longer strong enough to support itself.

In the meantime, many other chiefly musical academies were founded: the *Unisoni* in Perugia; the *Filomusi*, *Filaschisi*, and *Filarmonici* in Bologna (Mozart!); the *Intronati* and *Filomeni* in Siena; the *Elevati*, *Umidi*, and *Fiorentini* in Florence. The most important was the *Umidi* in Florence, whose members preferred the performance of comedies with music. Some of this music is still extant—for instance, the music to the comedy *Il furto* (*The Theft*) by Franceso D'Ambra, performed in 1544 in the rooms of the Academy, and the intermezzi composed by Corteccia, who was court composer to Cosimo I, and choirmaster of San Lorenzo. The members of the academies loved music in a dramatic mood and in pastoral disguise. Nasco and Ruffo are the most important forerunners of the cantata-composers of the seventeenth century. They had already set to music true cantata texts.

Nasco, Ruffo, Corteccia and others were church composers, or choirmasters. A musician who served the academies throughout his whole life was Francesco Portinaro of Padua. In 1557 he dedicated madrigals to the *Academici Costanti* in Vicenza and during the same year he was appointed choirmaster to the newly founded Paduan *Accademia degli Elevati;* in 1560, he dedicated madrigals to its "fathers," "presidents," and "gentlemen." The Academy of the Elevated was organized on the model of the *Filarmonica* of Verona: the members were interested in Latin and Italian poetry, mathematics, rhetoric, and music; the club meetings were a mixture of erudition and art and before and after each lecture, music was played. But unlike the *Filarmonica*, not all the members were experienced musicians. Portinari already had some musical companions with whom he played concerts. But for special evenings the four were not sufficient, and Portinari had to hire a few more. The musical zeal of the gentlemen themselves does not seem to have been very great. The Academy of the Elevated was replaced by a new academy in 1573, the *Rinascenti*, which also engaged Portinari; another academy, the *Animosi* was shortlived because in 1576 a pestilence raged in Padua which claimed 12,000 people. In any case, Venice was too near and the academies in Padua could not compete with hers. In the academies one may observe the change from the gaiety of the Renaissance to the severity, the darkening of the minds, of the Counter Reformation. Portinari was a composer of commissioned pieces; and in examining his works one sees the whole local history of music in Padua between 1550 and 1580.

A knowledge of the academies is useful in understanding some—perhaps many—compositions of the sixteenth and seventeenth centuries. An example: in Domenico Megli's *Musiche* (1602) there is a madrigal beginning

> Com'esser puo che sia
> Si ACCESA l'alma mia. . . .

which is a tribute to one of the most famous singers of that time, Isabella Andreini, who as a member of the *Accademia Intenta* in Reggio had the nickname *L'accesa*.

The *Accademia Filarmonica* in Verona existed until the end of the sixteenth century. But it had a formidable rival in the private academy or *ridotto* (weekly party) of Count Mario Bevilacqua, one of the famous patrons of the arts in his time. *Ridotto* or *ridutto* was the name given to clubs smaller than academies; and many musicians founded or entertained such *ridotti*, as for example Canon Spirito Pratoneri of Reggio, whose club was called a *ricettacolo sempre de virtuosi*—an "eternal shelter of virtuosos." Count Bevilacqua's group was not a small one. Bevilacqua belonged to a noble Veronese family; born in 1536, he became *provveditore di Verona*, warden or governor of the city, in 1576, in the service of the Republic of Venice. He built a magnificent palace, designed by Michele Sanmichele, filled it with sculptures, pictures, and tapestries, and gave musical and dramatic performances. We know that around 1590 he was also a patron of the *compagnia degli comici Uniti*. Almost every great musician of that time dedicated a work to him except Monteverdi; and Monteverdi did not because there was jealousy between Bevilacqua and the Dukes Guglielmo and Vincenzo at the Mantuan court. But Lasso, Merulo, Monte, and Vecchi did; and a few young musicians, like Stivorio, confessed that they owed their whole musical and artistic education to the evenings in Bevilacqua's *ridotto*. Another musician, Leoni Leoni, tells us that Bevilacqua loved him like a son, "*come figliuolo amato*."

It has been proved that Bevilacqua hired some accomplished musicians for his *ridotto*, among them a professional organist, Paolo Masnelli. The greatest glory of his *ridotto* lies in the fact that Luca Marenzio composed and dedicated to him a book of madrigals. Marenzio tells us that he composed this book in an entirely new manner, and that "*per l'imitazione delle parole*," and the "*proprieta dello stile*," he had aimed at a certain "*mesta gravita*," a mournful dignity; and that while composing it he always had the Count and the *littani* of his circle in mind.

And this is the real importance of the musical academies. The composer was able to write for them without giving thought to the general taste of the time, or to the commissioners of music. Music written for academies was art for art's sake. One has only to remember the work of Gesualdo, with its harmonic experiments, its utter boldness—it was not written for the great public. Gesualdo was a prince; and in the same style in which he had privately murdered his wife and her lover, he likewise created privately, writing compositions, for himself, for his chamber, for his *ridotto*. And in writing for Bevilacqua's *ridotto*, Marenzio, too, composed a book of— so to speak—inconsiderate compositions.

Bevilacqua died in 1593. During the last years of his life another *ridotto* of the greatest historical importance was formed, that of Count Bardi of Florence, the so-called *camerata fiorentina*. It was a genuine, a typical Florentine club. A few aristocrats, a few musicians, a few scientists—all a little highbrow or *bel esprits*. Their one and only aim was a new realization of the miraculous effects of the Greek drama, about which they knew only from heresay; and they created the opera. The opera is not the only product of an academy; Monteverdi's creative output also depended upon the academies. He was a member of the *Invaghiti* of Mantua and his academic name was "l'Ottuso." The *Orfeo* was performed in the *Accademia degl' Invaghiti*. Monteverdi dedicated the fourth book of his madrigals (1603) to the *Accademia degli Intrepidi* in Ferrara, founded in 1601, and it is significant that all the numbers of the book were familiar to the members of the Academy, as Monteverdi says in the dedicatory letter. The

Duke of Mantua was the *principe*, the president, of the *Accademia degli Intrepidi*.

And thus it is obvious that anyone who would write a history of the development of the concert audience will have to start with the history of the Italian academies.

# IV

## Opus I

WE HAVE no intention of writing a learned or elaborate treatise on when, where, and how musicians began to number their compositions. It was probably in Italy, during the sixteenth century, that certain musicians first grouped single works of theirs into series: masses, motets, madrigals. Where such series ran parallel, the total number of individual pieces was often quite high. From Philippe de Monte we have as many as eleven books of six-part, not less than twenty-nine books of five-part, and four books of four-part madrigals, besides ecclesiastical works. If you add these, you get the respectable sum of about fifty works, or fifty opera, of which the majority contain as many as twenty or even thirty single pieces. The early usage continued into the twentieth century; it is found in the tendency of even quite modern composers to gather under one opus number several works, or to bind them into one sheaf. We still have, for instance, "song albums" which are a sign of continuing creative overabundance, _vide_ Max Reger's Op. 76, _Schlichte Weisen_, which contains sixty songs.

By the beginning of the seventeenth century, the designation of compositions by opus numbers had become firmly established. The procedures differ: one musician counts only his instrumental works, another only his vocal ones; still another mingles vocal and instrumental works, counting them in the order of their appearance or publication; and, again, some composers give opus numbers also to unpublished works. We find that with some the figures mount considerably; Biagio Marini, in the first half of the seventeenth century, reached his fifty-fifth opus. In many cases, the numbering is the only indication we have of how many of a man's works were saved and how many were lost. Different manners of counting were adopted, and several of them continued simultaneously.

Essays and books have been written in late years on the "last face" or death mask, the last letter, the last work. And the last work, finished or unfinished, is always a summing up, and even more than a summing up. The journey is at an end; one looks back and looks into the unknown, the unknowable, the infinite. The last work sheds light upon the whole journey, its duration, its ascent and descent. And upon the last work falls light from a beyond that inspires us with awe. Need I cite examples? The _Art of Fugue_ of Bach, unfinished, to be sure, even with Bach's choral _Vor deinen Thron tret' ich hiemit_, a pious conclusion appended by the son and editor?— a conclusion which must not, as was the case with the recent "revivals" of the work, be misused for melodramatic ends. Or shall we take Handel's _Jephtha_, with the pathetic note in the manuscript stating on what day the composer was struck with blindness and had to interrupt his work? Or take Mozart's mysterious *Requiem?* Shall we add to these examples Beethoven's last quartets, Wagner's *Parsifal*, Verdi's *Falstaff*, the Adagio of Bruckner's Ninth Symphony, and the *Vier ernste Gesänge* of Brahms? The minor composer writes his last opus number, the great composer writes his last work. The difference is probably not fortuitous.

With the "first work," fortuity is more apt to intervene. The beginning is equally important, equally characteristic of the time and personality. Opus I is never identical with the first work. Weber is said to have remarked to Schubert once, "The first litter of dogs and the first opera should always be drowned." Opus I is always the work with which a musician is intent upon introducing himself to the public, with which he wishes to prove his legitimate claims. I am not endeavoring to be all-embracing; not even every one of the great masters can be considered here, nor shall I attempt to go into the last philological details, although naturally I should like to avoid misstatements or serious omissions. My aim is not that of the bibliophile or antiquary; what I wish to stress is merely what is typical or characteristic of a composer, as it appears in his Opus I.

## BACH

Bach was forty years old when a work of his was first published on his own initiative: in 1726, he issued the E major Partita. It constituted the first part of the *Klavierübung* to which he added, one a year, five more Partitas, so that, strictly

speaking, his Opus I was not finished until 1731. This was not
the first work of his to be printed. That honor belongs to a
composition published some twenty years previously, to the
so-called *Mühlhauser Ratswechsel*-Cantata of 1708 (*Gott ist
mein König*). This work does not bear an opus number. It
owed its publication not to Bach himself, but to the town
council of Mühlhausen. The motive that prompted the council
was not esteem for the then twenty-three year old organist
of St. Blasius' Church, but self-esteem for its own august body.
Bach himself may have engraved his own Opus I or may have
had it engraved by his son Carl Philip Emanuel to judge by the
primitive nature of the engraving. The modesty of the title
and outward appearance are in striking contrast with the
inner significance. We can best measure this significance if we
consider that the man who wrote the work had already composed, but refrained from publishing, his Inventions and Orchestral Suites, his *Well-Tempered Clavier*, his Coethen Solo
Sonatas, and hundreds of other works that he alone, in his own
time, was able to evaluate. This Opus I, at least, the composer
wanted to insure against the mercies of careless copyists.
Bach's Partitas are the supreme specimens of their kind. They
represent the summit of all Bach's dance suites; they surpass
those of Bach's suites that preceded them, even the French
and English, which in themselves seem unsurpassable. Yet
Bach did not publish these latter sets of suites. If he issued the
Partitas he must have had a special reason. And that reason
must have been more than to prove his supreme musical
craftsmanship.

Indeed it seems to me that in these Partitas he planned and
accomplished the fusion of the Italian, French, and German
"gusto"; that he planned and achieved such fusion deliber-

ately. His suites are German, because they are Bach's. What his contemporaries, even the most eminent among them, such as Georg Philipp Telemann, strove for was at best an adaptation or imitation of the Italian and French manner. Bach retains the titles that reveal the origin of the different pieces: *Preludio, Sinfonia, Ouverture;* he distinguishes between *Corrente* and *Courante*. But he imbues them with a uniform style, which is his own. Considered from the musical standpoint, this is no small feat, comparable only to an attempt at uniting the various creeds (an idea which haunted the noblest spirits of his time, such as Leibnitz). Or comparable, in our age of nationalism, to the realization of a United States of Europe. Bach is the patron saint of music and musicians. His Opus I should preserve him as the patron saint of a far distant European future. Bach was fundamentally religious; he could instil religion even into Partitas, pieces ordinarily counted as worldly and "gallant."

## HANDEL

Bach has often been compared, or rather contrasted, with Handel. As far as the age at which they published their first opus is concerned, they closely resemble each other. Handel was all of fifty years old before he published his first work with an opus number, an age at which he already had a long string of important compositions to his credit. In all his lifetime he did not get beyond his Opus VI, because, like Bach, he numbered only his instrumental music. But unlike Bach, he chose only instrumental ensemble works with a *basso con-*

*tinuo;* that is, he did not count works for keyboard instruments alone.

Handel's Opus I comprised twelve Chamber Sonatas, some for flute, recorder, oboe, or violin. They were published in 1724 by Witvogel in Amsterdam. Later they were reprinted in English editions and were greatly augmented, until finally this Opus I comprised fifteen sonatas. This enlargement was not a part of Handel's original plan. I have before me an English edition of *ca.* 1733, published by John Walsh, which bears the inscription "more Correct than the former Edition" (and the edition is really better than Chrysander's in the "complete works"); this Walsh edition contains only those twelve sonatas that form a homogeneous unit.

The twelve sonatas might serve as a "school" of melody-writing. They are not well known or often played; only the one in A major, for the violin, enjoys a certain popularity, and occasionally receives the attention of one of our virtuosos. Hitherto neither the historical nor the artistic importance of these sonatas has been sufficiently stressed. Nowhere do I find a reference to the relation of certain of their movements to the Organ Concertos and to the Concerti grossi, Opus VI. These sonatas are proof that neither Handel's music nor his personality are as fully known and understood as they should be. Handel is the greatest *Italian* musician of his time. By birth a German, he was the greatest Italian musician of England. All that the Italian solo sonata produced is represented in his Opus I and is brought into relation with England. One should scrutinize these sonatas for their indebtedness to the old masters of Bologna or Venice. The Allegro of No. 8, for oboe, is descended from Legrenzi. The A major sonata curtsies to Corelli. No. 5, for flute, is typically English:

it pays tribute to the chief ingredient of the old English Chamber Sonata, the "Canzon," and at the same time pokes gentle fun at it. This Opus I, if analyzed in detail, might go a long way towards giving us a better knowledge of Handel.

## HAYDN

Everything in Haydn's Opus I is new and personal, except one point: it adheres to the custom of tagging several compositions with the same number. The opus comprises six string quartets. But does it not seem like preordination that he should begin precisely with a form of composition which owes practically to him alone its peculiar development? To it he remained true, to it devoted his last, his very last effort. Great masters are privileged in their seeming immunity to mere accident.

A characteristic difficulty is presented by the "philologic" and bibliographic problems of this Opus I. For there are several *opere prime* by Haydn, of differing content. His whole life long, Haydn was, and continued increasingly to be, a victim of publishers. No matter how carefully he strove to protect his new works in authorized editions, in Paris, as well as in London, genuine and spurious "Haydns" were printed and offered for sale under arbitrary opus numbers, so that often the same opus number appears on different works.

In the Pleyel edition of 1803, which represents Haydn's definitive version of his Opus I and therefore has always been regarded as standard, No. 5, the Quartet in B major, is nonetheless extraneous. It has a totally different form and structure and was evidently written later than the other five quartets.

It is simply an Italian opera-*sinfonia*, and indeed appears as such in publishers' catalogs of the period, with the addition of two French horns. It does not really belong to this series of Haydn's quartets.

The actual Opus I, No. 1, of Haydn is a Quartet in E-flat major which is the first quartet published by Huberty in Paris; it was twice reprinted in 1932, on the occasion of Haydn's centenary, by Miss Marion M. Scott in London and Mr. Karl Geiringer in Vienna. In 1803 Haydn had not forgotten it, only it escaped his memory that once upon a time it had been printed: he designated it as "a Quartet not yet engraved." It fits perfectly into the framework of Opus I. Since Huberty's catalog was sold to another Paris publisher in 1761, Haydn's Opus I must have been printed before that year. Neither Griesinger, who places this composition in the year 1750, nor others who have assigned it to 1765, are right. It must have been written in 1755, when Haydn was twenty-three years old.

Of late there has been a tendency to deny a proper quartet-character to Opera 1 and 2 and to maintain that they resemble too much the old Vienna Cassation, the Quadro, the Suite, or those types of pieces still conceived primarily for performance in the open air. It is claimed that Opera 1 and 2 do not yet attain to true "chamber" style. To be sure, Opus 3 goes a long step beyond the first twelve quartets. But already Opus I bears Haydn's personal stamp. Above all things, it is typically Viennese, carefree and artless—for Haydn wrote as naturally as the bird sings. At the same time it points to the future and to Haydn's position in a new century of music. Indeed, the core of his first Quadri lies in the Adagios which are Ariosos in the old style. They are still steeped in opera and

stage music. Even the *ritornello* maintains a rudimentary existence. The old "echo" effect is heard again (in No. 4). There
is the Italian *cantilena*, but it already bears intimate and personal traces.

Haydn's real self is disclosed in the Minuets (of which each
of these quartets contains two that flank the middle movement); or in the short-phrased opening and final movements,
all of them in quick or quickest tempo. Practically everything
that later developed is found here in germ: a mixing, even
though not a complete amalgamation, of motival work and
violinistic technique, of *cantilena* and virtuosity, of the dialogue between violin and viola; the humor, the freshness, the
wit; the vigorous two-part writing in the minuets; the irreg-
ularity in the melodic line, the contrasts within the smallest
space. To analyze the work completely would mean writing
a book.

But it is not analysis that we are after. The important thing
is to recognize the wonderful economy and modesty of
Haydn, who writes Quadri as a hundred other Viennese musicians might have written them, who does not wish to strut,
but cannot avoid manifesting his originality. He will continue
to write as modestly, quietly, unobtrusively, and logically as
he began. He will sit in Eisenstadt and Esterház, far from the
madding crowd, and nevertheless glory will surround him
in the end such as no master before him achieved.

### MOZART

Mozart made an early start, for the Fates had decreed an
early end for him. None of our great masters wrote his Opus 1

at an earlier age, or rather none was subjected so early to publication. His ambitious and enterprising father presented the
infant prodigy at all the courts, in all the capitals of Europe, as
a virtuoso and also as a composer. Creative ability at so tender
an age is even a greater miracle than a precocious talent for
the piano and the violin. Late in 1763 Father Mozart came to
Paris with his two children. At the end of January, 1764, he
published four sonatas for piano, with violin *ad libitum*, that
the boy had written. The first two sonatas were published as
Opus I and were dedicated to Madame Victoire of France,
the second daughter of the King.

We need not discuss these works in detail. That has been
done conscientiously by St. Foix and Wyzewa. This music
reflects all the impressions that the boy received in Paris, together with recollections of Salzburg and Vienna. And yet,
here and there, we find traces of that indescribable quality for
which we have found but the one word "Mozartean."

In his childhood Mozart had already used four opus numbers. Later on he became more sparing with such numbering,
and he never went beyond Opus 17 or 18. The six great
quartets of 1785, dedicated to Haydn, bear his Opus No. X;
the C minor Fantaisie and Sonata for piano bear the number
XI; it is doubtful whether he himself gave numbers to any of
the later works. He had no time to count; the time to create
was too short and precious. He always seized an opportunity
and, like Goethe, was always ready to write "occasional
pieces." When fifteen years after his first visit to Paris he returned there, he had evidently forgotten his childish "indis-
cretions" and published, with Sieber, another set of sonatas
for piano and violin which he designated as Opus I. There are
six of them (Köchel Nos. 301–306) dedicated to the Princess

Marie Elizabeth. Later Artaria in Vienna, undoubtedly with
Mozart's consent, published another series of piano and violin
sonatas as Opus 2 (Köchel Nos. 376, 296, 377–380). Therefore we have two different Opera 1 and Opera 2 of Mozart. It
does not often happen that a composer gives the same opus
number to different works.

Eventually Mozart discovered the necessity of keeping a
register of his compositions. On February 9, 1784, he began
to enter into a little green notebook everything that he wrote,
with the date, the title, and the opening phrases of the music.
The first entry was the Piano Concerto in E-flat major. But
he forgot to make some entries, and much of his work continued to be of the "occasional" type: upon the heels of the
great C Major Symphony, the "Jupiter," there followed the
song *Beym Auszug in das Feld*. If these are "occasional pieces,"
the occasions were made rare and wonderful by some mysterious power of which only Mozart had the secret.

## BEETHOVEN

Beethoven is the first composer whose opus numbers we
learn to remember and are apt to know. Thus, in thinking of
his string quartets, we have a definite idea of what is represented by Opus 18, Opus 59, Opus 74, 95, 127, etc.; or, in
thinking of the piano sonatas, by Opus 106 and 111. These
figures have a meaning for us. They tell the initiate about the
origin and character of the works. To be sure, many of these
numbers would mislead anyone who makes from them de-
ductions about the date of the works to which they are affixed.
The order of Beethoven's opus numbers is not chronological.

Beethoven published later much that was written before his Opus I, such as his preludes for piano, Opus 39; the songs, Opus 52; the variations for piano, Opus 44; the octet, Opus 103; etc.—works that originated during his youth at Bonn. It might have been preferable if he had so designated them or if he had published them without opus numbers. But in spite of his greatness, he was a little mercenary, and saw no fault in fooling his publishers now and then; nor was he under any obligation to inform posterity exactly when each work had been composed.

Prior to Beethoven's Opus I, he produced rather lavishly, recklessly, chaotically. When Beethoven came to Vienna in 1792, he paid little attention to this early production. Indeed, after he had gone back to "school" with Albrechtsberger, he began all over again. Among his lessons for Albrechtsberger are sketches for the three piano trios in E-flat, G, and C minor, and these three he united under one opus number. In May, 1795, he gave them to a publisher, in July they were delivered to the subscribers, and on October 21, they were placed on public sale. They are dedicated to Count Lichnowsky. As late as 1817, Beethoven arranged the third trio as a string quartet.

It is this third trio against the publication of which the older master, Haydn, is said to have counseled the younger Beethoven. The story is not absolutely proved, and there are chronological discrepancies; for in the beginning of 1794 Haydn had returned to London for his second visit. But nevertheless the story is not impossible. For this young musician was rather weird. He indulged in strange antics. He did not follow the footsteps of Haydn and Mozart, but went ways of his own. In the *Coda* of the first movement of the Trio,

No. 1, he plays one trump card after another. In the *Adagio cantabile* he indulges in an explosion, something unthinkable with any of the older masters. In Mozart we find surprises of wit, taste, depth; in Haydn we encounter humor and sparkle—but no explosions. And no Scherzos with quite such deceptive beginnings. The *Finale* of 1790 resembles Haydn, and yet Haydn would never have written a second theme so frankly vulgar as the following:

Especially not with such a sudden entrance of a triplet accompaniment. The Allegro is a mixture of songfulness, capriciousness and learnedness, such as did not exist before Beethoven. The *Largo con espressione* is a hymnus *alla* Haydn—but how agitated, restless, excited! And the second theme belongs decidedly to the nineteenth century; it anticipates the whole romantic and neo-romantic school.

In the G major *Scherzo* the middle section is in B minor. We can easily guess what horrified Papa Haydn in the C minor Trio: it was the *Finale*. It opens with a brutal crash, which is followed by a trivial theme. This no longer has anything in common with "art" or "style"; it is pure naturalism. It would have been impossible for Haydn to tolerate it. He would have had to jump out of his own skin. A new era had begun.

### SCHUBERT

Schubert was not a "superchild," but a superman. Mozart was both. But Schubert's productiveness was even more prodigious, considering that he was destined to die even younger than Mozart. On May 1, 1810, he wrote his first extended composition; on October 2, 1814, he wrote *Gretchen am Spinnrad;* in 1815 he composed not less than 146 songs, in addition to operas, masses, symphonies, string quartets, piano sonatas, and other compositions of every kind and description. In the winter of 1815 he wrote his "Opus I": his first setting of Goethe's ballad, *The Erlking*. His friend, Josef von Spaun, surprised Schubert in his paternal house in the *Himmelpfortgrund*, in the act of jotting down the first notes inspired by Goethe's poem. The same evening, in the Vienna *Convikt*, the new work was heard for the first time and created more headshaking and astonishment than the admiration it deserved. It was Josef von Spaun once more who, on April 17, 1816, wrote to Goethe that Schubert intended to publish eight books of songs of which the first and second were to be exclusively devoted to verses of the great poet. The letter was accompanied by the manuscript of the first book of songs, among which was *The Erlking* with a simplified piano accompaniment: eighth notes replaced the triplets, for Goethe's accompanist was not to be frightened and was to have an "easy job" of it. But all was in vain, Goethe paid no attention to letter or music. In the spring of 1817 Schubert offered *The Erlking* to Breitkopf & Härtel in Leipzig as Opus I, but the famous publishers likewise ignored it. Not until 1820, or probably more correctly, not until January 25, 1821, did *The Erlking* receive its first public performance. In February, 1819, Schubert had made his first bow to the public as composer of songs, whereupon the *Leipziger Allgemeine Musikalische Zeitung* referred to him, not unjustly, as "a talented young man." And owing only to the renewed intervention of his friends did *The Erlking*, six years after it was written, finally appear in print. It was first put on sale on March 31, 1821, by the publishers Cappi & Diabelli, "am Graben in Wien," for 2 Gulden, Vienna currency, designated as Opus I, and respectfully dedicated to "Musikgraf" Moritz Dietrichstein. Not that Cappi & Diabelli had actually taken the work into their catalog. That would have been too much of a risk. No, they merely took it "on commission." Only with later editions did they acknowledge themselves as "publishers" and, like other clairvoyant members of their industry, admit that there was a fairly good business to be done with *The Erlking* and other songs of Schubert.

## SCHUMANN

If we consider that in 1830, when he published his Opus I, Schumann was not yet a real musician in the fullest sense of the word, the venture was an extraordinarily early one. He was still a dilettante pianist who shortly before as a student in Heidelberg had for the first and only time appeared in public, playing the Moscheles Variations on the "Alexander

March." His piano-playing, in the beginning, was only a means to improvisation; later on it rather hampered his improvisation. And improvisation was, with him, a form of poetic creation; for his musical roots were sunk in poetry, and Jean Paul influenced his musical creation more than did Beethoven and Schubert and Weber, or all the minor gods of the romantic Olympus put together. Only later on, perhaps to his detriment, did he turn composer; and from the composer's standpoint he himself passed incredibly severe and sharp judgment upon one of his most original works, the *Carnaval*. He was more lenient towards his Opus I, as we may gather from a letter addressed to his mother from Leipzig on September 2, 1831:

> For the present I am not going to Weimar. For very shortly I expect to become father of a healthy, flourishing child that I hope to hold over the baptismal font in Leipzig. The child will be published by Probst, and may Heaven grant that you will understand its first childish stammerings and signs of budding life. If you but knew how keen they are, these first joys of authorship; they are hardly less wonderful than the bridal state. And so at present the whole heaven of my heart is filled with hope and anticipation—I am as proud as the Doge of Venice when he weds the sea. For the first time I embrace that greater world which comprises in its wide expanse the world and home of the artist. Is it not a beautiful and comforting thought that this first drop may evaporate into the infinite ether and fall upon some wounded heart, to ease its sorrow and heal the wound?

We see that he is very much in earnest, as well as incorrigibly "romantic," about his Opus I. He reproaches old fogey Fink, czar of the *Allgemeine Musikalische Zeitung*, for not having reviewed the work; he tends to his newly born in a more prosaic manner by sending two copies to Heckel in Mannheim, home of the young lady identified by the mysterious dedication and the mysterious theme *a b e g g*.

What are we to think of this truly extraordinary Opus I? It contains the most daring, capricious, original variations imaginable, even though they show the influences of Moscheles and Hummel in matters of technique. "Giovanni Minotti" (*Zeitschrift für Musik*, Vol. 94) has offered a solution for the odd letter-puzzle of the "name theme," of the picture or portrait, of the two imaginary countesses as represented by the waltz motive of the first section and the reversion of it in the second. He makes the mistake of characterizing Schumann, the frolicsome, as a "buffoon of genius." We remain as ignorant as before of what is really intended by these variations: by the first, which hovers between virtuosity and polyphony; by the second, with its "speaking" bass (*il basso parlando*); by the third, which turns into pure imagery; or by the finale "alla Fantasia." It is an episode in musical tones that might have been taken from a novel of Jean Paul, an intimate ballroom scene, such as the one in Berlioz's *Symphonie fantastique* is not, and much more original than Berlioz. Who will solve the puzzle of Schumann's music, not merely that of the letter-puzzle?

## CHOPIN

We have Schumann's opinion of Chopin's Opus I, the Rondo in C minor, dedicated to Madame von Linde, wife of the friend and colleague of Chopin's father, Rector Dr. Samuel v. Linde. Schumann wrote on June 11, 1832, to Friedrich Wieck:

Chopin's first composition (I surely believe that it must be at least his tenth) is now in my hands. A lady would say that it is rather nice, rather piquant, almost Moschelesian. But I think you will want Clara to study it; because it is full of *esprit* and not very difficult. I respectfully submit, however, that between this and Opus 2 there must lie at least two years and twenty compositions.

How keen, how correct! Chopin was indeed influenced by Moscheles, and in 1825 he publicly performed the first movement of one of Moscheles' concertos. This is the same year in which this Opus I was written, the work of a boy of fifteen, and published in Warsaw. Schumann was right in his assumption. We know of unpublished four-hand pieces of Chopin; waltzes, mazurkas, variations, and polonaises, written before and after his Opus I. And with what subtle instinct had Schumann gathered from this Opus I that its creator would some day be the darling and confidant of so many fair ones, with all their avowed and unavowed dreams and aspirations. This merely means that this Rondo already contains something of the genius Chopin, who was a musical brother of Heinrich Heine, and even more. There is the rigor of discipline and the freedom of improvisation—an only apparent freedom; the wide circle of soft or brilliant tonalities, such as a combination of E major and D flat major; the Italian ornaments—in Poland, too, Rossini was idolized; the Polish and heroic elements. In this pupil of the Warsaw Lyceum, who wrote the Rondo, we have already the whole Chopin. He does not have to disavow his Opus I.

## BRAHMS

"The young people of today are in such a hurry to have their unfinished stuff performed and published." Thus Brahms exclaimed; and he added "what a holy fear I had of printer's ink! I still have the sheet of paper on which Schumann and Joachim indicated those of my youthful compositions that I was to publish. And still, only a few of them got into print." This is literally true. No other musician shared the fate of Brahms: he was introduced and announced to the world by a great and recognized master, as one of the chosen, as "one who is called ideally to give the highest expression to the spirit of the times," before the world had heard a single note of these works. Nor did the world ever hear most of these early compositions of Brahms. On Schumann's recommendation, Breitkopf & Härtel were ready to accept unseen anything by Brahms. Schumann decided that the following works of Brahms should be brought out: one String Quartet, Opus 1; one book of Six Songs, Opus 2; one Grand Scherzo for Pianoforte, Opus 3; another book of Six Songs, Opus 4; and a Grand Sonata in C major for Pianoforte, Opus 5. Three weeks earlier, Schumann had made a totally different choice: a Fantaisie in D minor for Piano Trio, Opus 1; a book of Songs, Opus 2; a Scherzo in E-flat minor, Opus 3; a Sonata in C major, Opus 4; a Sonata for violin and piano in A minor, Opus 5; and a book of Songs, Opus 6.

We know that things turned out totally different. The Fantaisie, the String Quartet (it was not in B minor) disappeared. Brahms burned them. The Sonata in A minor vanished; the violin part, in 1872, still existed in Bonn. Perhaps the work may yet be discovered.

Brahms chose as his Opus I the C major Sonata for piano, and followed it with the one in F-sharp minor. In the meantime he had read Schumann's glowing tribute *Neue Bahnen*, published in the *Neue Zeitschrift für Musik* of October 23, 1853. He immediately realized what terrific responsibility Schumann's trumpet blast had laid upon him. It was no small matter to be proclaimed before the world as the coming genius, in a time when so many spurious geniuses disported themselves, and at the very moment when Wagner, in Zürich, was quietly preparing for the revolutionary creation of his "Music of the Future."

Someone else might have been deterred from stepping forward, or might have deferred the step. Brahms dared to make it; he knew that his Opus I would stand the test. He wrought it as well as he could. Therein lies his greatness: that from the beginning to the end, with each subsequent opus number, he realized his responsibility to his own time and to eternity.

## WAGNER

From Wagner we have two opus numbers, and no more. Opus I is a Sonata in E flat for piano solo; Opus 2 is a Polonaise in D major for piano, four-hands. Both were written in 1831 and were published by Breitkopf & Härtel for the Easter Fair in 1832. The first was priced at 20 Groschen, the second at 8.

This Opus I, too, was not the composer's first work. While a student in Leipzig, Wagner wrote an Overture in C major, and a four-hand Sonata in B-flat major, which he arranged for orchestra. Then there was an Overture in B-flat major which his friend and later enemy, Heinrich Dorn, publicly performed at Christmas, 1830; an Overture to Schiller's *The Bride of Messina*, another composition inspired by Goethe's *Faust*. Only after having written all these works did Wagner begin serious study with Theodor Weinlig and set out to write fugues. In his autobiography Wagner says:

> In order to bring me completely under his friendly and soothing domination, Weinlig had at the same time asked me to write a sonata which, as a proof of my friendship to him, I was to construct with the simplest harmonic and thematic material; as a model he recommended to me one of the most childish sonatas of Pleyel. Whoever knew my recently written overtures certainly must have been astonished that I brought myself to write this sonata which, through an indiscretion of Messrs. Breitkopf & Härtel, has been newly reprinted. As a reward for my abstinence, Weinlig gave himself the pleasure of having my trivial composition put in print by these publishers.

Well, this is merely one of the many trifling or serious inaccuracies in Wagner's autobiography which we are able to charge him with on the strength of his own letters. On March 3 (21), 1832, he wrote to his sister Ottilie: "Another piece of news—this week a piano sonata of mine, which I have dedicated to Weinlig, has appeared in print. I have received for it 20 Thalers' worth of music . . . the piece is not very difficult . . . I shall be very glad if you like it."

We see that young Wagner views his Opus I not very tragically, but quite seriously and does not disavow it. But the Wagner who dictated his autobiography to Cosima was perhaps not so intent upon the truth as he was upon making an impression on her; yet he was right when he repudiated this "youthful error." Of his Opus 2 he, who was so ready and eager to rake up the past, made no mention at all. He might have continued this series of opus numbers with a Piano Fantaisie in F-sharp minor, three Overtures, and a large C major Symphony which shortly before his death he had performed for him in Venice, an Aria for soprano and orchestra, the *Glockentöne* by Apel, the introduction to *Die Hochzeit*, and so forth. His *Flying Dutchman* would have been about Opus 20 and *Parsifal*, perhaps, his Opus 40.

May I be forgiven my flippancy: opus numbers, in the later work of Wagner, would have been an absurdity. He wrote only major works, and his minor works are so entirely minor, that they do not count at all. His really creative life begins with his operas, and his operas do not require to be tagged with numbers. They are colossal monuments of a colossal musical potency.

These examples of Opus I must suffice. I do not intend to carry the reader farther forward into a more recent past. It might prove interesting to consider the Opus I of such radicals as Strauss (a totally insignificant military march), of Debussy (still steeped in Massenet), of Scriabin (unblushingly Chopinesque), or of Schoenberg (leaning on Wagner and Mahler). But I should like to add a few general reflections on one of the fundamental problems presented by all musical "first offenses": the question of originality, and of the significance and value of such originality. It is clear that there are differences. (Bach and Handel do not come into this consideration, since they were ripe and finished masters at the time when their Opus I was published.) If we examine their real beginnings we shall find that they are rooted in the tradition of their times, or that they are simply imitating earlier models. Before the beginning or the middle of the eighteenth century, the conception of "originality" could hardly be said to have existed. During the Renaissance, we meet with a few masters who—although they are not intent upon originality or, to use a classical phrase, *"rerum novarum cupidi"*—seek to explore unknown regions of expression. No one will claim that Marenzio, or Gesualdo, or Monteverdi, or Schütz, were "original" in our sense of the word. They did not possess true "spontaneity," they did not boldly strike a special or personal note. The first who may be said to have done so was Domenico Scarlatti, who, in his entire work from beginning to end, sounded a personal and unmistakable note, whose music had infinite and constantly renewed charm, although it cannot be placed side by side with that of Bach or Handel, and not even beside that of Domenico's wholly "unoriginal" father, Alessandro.

Among the composers whom we have reviewed, the truly original ones are Haydn, Chopin, Schumann, and possibly Brahms. Beethoven is a special case. Decidedly unoriginal are Mozart and Wagner. Chopin remains original his whole life long. Except for a few of his earliest works, he exhibits personal traits and a craftsmanship which would make it very difficult to establish the chronological order of his compositions—if we did not fortunately know it. Of Mozart, on the contrary, one might say that he was so much subjected to influences of others, or was (to put it bluntly) so unoriginal that we have been able, from these influences, to establish the chronology of his compositions with almost absolute certainty. Schumann sprang into being possessed of a prodigious amount of originality; and in fact it is only his earlier works, the compositions for piano and the songs, that remain most alive. As he progressed, he retrogressed; he lost his freshness, became weak, developed mannerisms, was shorn of his spontaneity. He ceased to be original. But this is probably the only case in which originality and quality are so closely linked.

In general, originality and greatness have little or nothing in common. Can one call Beethoven truly original? Undoubtedly not, as far as so-called "invention" is concerned. If we look at Beethoven's work, we see that he was not intent upon being "different" from his predecessors or contemporaries, but that he tried to surpass them in magnitude. He has to give more than the others, qualitatively and quantitatively. There are some characteristic remarks of his on that subject. In his work, too, we can detect the models that served him; to be sure, they are not so much models as starting points, or springboards which facilitate his upward leap. His originality does not reside in his melody, rhythm, or harmony, however personal these may be; it resides in the power of his temperament, in the discipline of his mind with which he illumines the night of his emotions, in the exuberant play of his forces.

"However personal these may be"—here we have the key: originality is not the decisive factor, but personality. In his last quartets Beethoven grows more and more simple in his invention, but even the simplest is wholly personal. It would be insulting the sublimity of these works if we were to call them original. In the end, one may *become* original. Wagner is an example (Debussy, Scriabin, Schoenberg are others). In the course of his development, Wagner grew to be more and more personal and original. Until the very end of his creative life Wagner became an ever greater "inventor." And because he was a man of such extraordinary intelligence and mental discipline, he was able to rule the musician in him, to develop and even overpower him. If we compare one measure in *Parsifal* or *Tristan* with *Rienzi* we must marvel at the growth in the quality of his invention, which does not represent a "condensation" but, in spite of a relationship with this concept, represents something totally new. Wagner was not original, but became so. It may sound like a paradox to say: as one may lose one's originality, one may also acquire it.

In the life of a young composer, his Opus I is always a great event. It should be viewed in a friendly light. If the composer is original, his originality will unquestionably elicit praise. If he is not original, and is taken to task for it, let him find consolation in the examples of Wagner or Mozart. And the critics? Let them be tolerant in judging any Opus I; and if they cannot be tolerant, let them learn by the experience of others and at least be—careful.

# V

# Opus Ultimum

THERE is always the danger of approaching a composer's Opus Ultimum—that is, his last work—in a journalistic vein. The last work is apt to stir the listener to maudlin comment, whereas the "last face," the death mask, generally leaves the beholder silent. Death masks are not popular unless surrounded with a romantic aureole, and, strangely enough, the most popular "death mask" of a musician, that of Beethoven, was in reality a life mask; the real death mask, made too late after the *post mortem*, awakens horror. I shall not dwell here on "last thoughts," such as those attributed to certain romantic composers, as, for instance, Weber, Schubert, or Chopin. There is also a subtle difference between the last work upon which a composer was engaged and his last Opus. The last creative effort is not always the last Opus.

But what is the last Opus? Is it the one that rounds out the work of a lifetime, that concludes the *Gesamtwerk*? Is it a matter of fulfilling a destiny? We are in a position to survey the entire lifework of a great master and to arrange it into an organism, the sum of his artistic creation. We can scarcely do otherwise: we can conceive of biography—in fact, of all history—only in a certain order, sometimes an arbitrary one. We cannot imagine *Figaro* without *Don Giovanni* (and *vice versa*), or Beethoven's *Missa Solemnis* without the Ninth Symphony, or Bach's later *Passion according to St. John* without the earlier *Passion according to St. Matthew;* they seem to supplement and complete each other, and we are apt to forget that Bach composed two more Passions that are lost to us. If one were found again, our musical scholars would immediately recognize and prove it to be a "necessary link" in the chain of Bach's works. After ten years no one would be able to imagine his work without it. How slowly and late were the last touches added to the picture of Schubert's creativeness! Can one imagine that years had to pass before the great C Major Symphony was discovered, and decades before the "Unfinished" revealed new heights and depths in Schubert's soul? Almost every creative artist is haunted by the fear of dying before his work has reached completion. The creator sees with his mind's eye his unborn work completed, but he knows that only after it is born can it lead a life of its own and bear witness of him.

Some of our greatest musicians have lived to be very old or have died very young. Those who have strangely and mistakenly been called "frühvollendet" ("too early completed") have either received from Fate an astoundingly early maturity with no further development in later years, or, more often, have had to pay for this early maturity with early death, as did Purcell, Pergolesi, Mozart, Weber, Schubert, Mendelssohn, Chopin. The melancholy, extremely pessimistic Grillparzer did not believe in the so-called "completion" when he wrote the inscription for Schubert's gravestone: "Music entombed here a rich possession, but still much brighter hopes." Still brighter hopes! If we let our imagination roam, it is difficult to conceive what might not have happened in the realm of music if Mozart had lived beyond the age of thirty-five, or Schubert beyond thirty-one. Mozart, who learned from Haydn only to be outlived by him and to teach the teacher; Mozart, only fourteen years older than Beethoven, whom he normally could have outlived! Schubert only sixteen years older than Wagner, dead when Wagner was fifteen years old! There is no end to the possibilities. But it is better to leave the general aspects until the end and to proceed immediately to particular cases.

## BACH

The theme is inexhaustible. We must begin somewhere and end somewhere. And we begin with Bach.

In Bach's case there is a last composition and an Opus Ultimum, and it is or was not certain which was the Opus Ultimum. Bach died on Tuesday, July 28, 1750, a blind man who had recovered his sight only a few days before his death. The Chevalier John Taylor, Court Oculist to the English king, George III, had operated on him late in 1749 and had discovered the symptoms of an earlier stroke. The same doctor had by strange coincidence operated on Handel a few years before, and described the unsuccessful operation in his *History of the Travels and Adventures of the Chevalier John Taylor* (1761, Vol. I, p. 25). A few days before his death, Bach was still working with his son-in-law Altnikol, dictating to him a chorale prelude on the melody and text of *Vor deinen Thron tret' ich hiemit*. It was his last piece of work, the continuation and conclusion of a revision of a long series of chorale preludes known by every organist, the so-called "Schübler" Chorales. A curious story attaches to this last prelude, which is really a conclusion in that, from the ultimate and unimaginable heights of accomplishment, Bach returns in it to his earliest youth, to the form of Pachelbel's organ chorales from which he had begun. One can only begin to speak of these few measures, in which severity and highest fancy are united, in which the last awe before things earthly melts into the first awe inspired by the vision of things divine.

That this ineffable piece has for a long time been regarded as Bach's "last thought" is due to the original edition of his last opus, *Die Kunst der Fuge*. This was begun in 1749. Before Bach died, the greater half had already been engraved under his supervision by a still unidentified publisher. More recent Bach research has pointed out, but not for the first time, in what a deceptive form the work appeared after Bach's death. The unknown publisher ended it with this "last" chorale prelude so that the buyer would not feel he was getting a bad bargain owing to the incompleteness of the last fugue. For the book was dear: the price was five thaler, and later Carl Philipp Emanuel had to reduce it to four. And when we perform *The Art of Fugue* today, we still often end it with the chorale that has organically not the slightest connection with the work. I have always found this ending, to put it mildly, melodramatic. "Here the Composer put away his pen. . . ." Surely one cannot stop an unfinished triple fugue at the 239th measure. It should be given an ending adapting it for practical performance, as was attempted by Busoni in the three different versions of his *Fantasia Contrapuntistica*. Or one should leave it out. In no case should we, after listening to Bach's "Opus Ultimum," which is impregnated with his musical greatness and sublimity, be presented with his "last piece of work." The autograph manuscript of the *Kunst der Fuge*, which contains seven more measures of the triple fugue than does the engraved edition, carries this Observation, added by Carl Philipp Emanuel: "N.B. While at work on this fugue, where the name B A C H is brought into the countersubject, the composer died." Incidentally, even this unfinished fugue is written strongly and clearly, and shows traces of the growing eye trouble only in the ever diminishing size of the writing. Bach bends lower and lower over his music paper.

It was uncertain for a long time whether this triple fugue belonged to the *Kunst der Fuge* or not. If not, as Wilhelm Rust and Philipp Spitta thought, then the *Kunst der Fuge* is a complete work. If it did, then the composition must be counted among the great torsos, in which the works of our great musicians are all too rich. It was Gustav Nottebohm who established the relationship of this fugue to the whole work, when he linked its three themes to the main theme of the *Kunst*.

It is neither my intention nor my task to treat the *Kunst der Fuge* here as a work in itself—that would require a separate article. I shall only mention its meaning as the ending of Bach's creative work.

The *Kunst der Fuge* as a living work of art has been rediscovered for us after it had been revealed to the nineteenth century, through Nägeli's reprint at Zürich, as an abstract or pedagogical work. Even for the generation immediately before ours it was mostly a sort of manual, intended to serve purposes of instruction. Today it is considered by many to be the pinnacle and crowning achievement of Bach's whole art. And who can deny this? A time may come when our successors will prefer to recognize the culmination of Bach's creative activity in the works of the first decades at Leipzig, or in the instrumental pieces of the Cöthen days, or perhaps even in his earliest efforts. But it is undeniable that in the aging Bach ancient springs begin to well up again— springs which two hundred and fifty years before had been streams, works in which the constructive, the abstract, cele- brated their greatest victory, and in which the Middle Ages showed themselves at their most glorious in their music. And the throwback into mystic forms and spaces appears in Bach at a time when the world around him is turning towards "gallantry," when all polyphony is being stamped with the sign of erudition—in other words, of archaism and death. No- where could it be made clearer that a genius like Bach does not create for the world and its wants, but must acquit an obligation to himself and follow an inner law.

But we should not make too much of this throwback. It is true that the symptoms present themselves early. Let us survey the succession of works of Bach's last decade. The third part of the *Clavierübung* closes with the fugue on the Communion Hymn, *Jesus Christus under Heiland*, and next follow the four duets, in one of which (i.e., in the middle movement of the Duet in F) Spitta "forgives with difficulty a strong scholastic savor." Then come the so-called "Schübler" Chorales; the canonical variations on the Christmas song, *Vom Himmel hoch da komm' ich her*. Next is the *Musikalisches Opfer*—an echo of Bach's visit to Potsdam in May, 1747—that remarkable mix- ture of musical "gallantry" and learning, in which the latter outweighs the former because, for the bearer of the dedication, Frederick the Great, it was the learning of "old Bach" that was astonishing and precious. But in this succession of abstract pieces stands the *Aria mit 30 Veränderungen*, in which learning bows to gallantry and completely loses itself in it. The worldly and the ecclesiastical, the abstract and the sensuous Bach are all one. No one side is preponderant. It is possible that, at the end of his life, Bach considered a part of his ecclesiastical works too worldly, too much a *biblia pauperum* in music. To be sure, it is not difficult to trace, in Bach's complete works, the Baroque as well as the Gothic filiation. No one knows whether Bach tried to preserve a balance between the Gothic and the Baroque; no one understands the secret ways of development and fulfillment. Bach's *Kunst der Fuge* resembles Dante's *Divina Commedia*, which the poet's contemporaries and even the men of the later Renaissance regarded admiringly as the sum of mediæval knowledge, as an encyclopædia of learning, rather than as a work of poetic art. But creations of this sort—testaments of their creators—always possess a greatness that transcends the limits of the time of their origin and reaches far out into the future.

### HANDEL

The alleged similarity of the two great contemporaries who are often regarded as the Siamese twins of music seems to apply even to their deaths. Six months after Bach's death, Handel met the fate of blindness. We know the touching note he set down on the manuscript of *Jephtha* at the end of the chorus that closes the second act:

*biss hierher kommen den 13. Febr. 1751*
*verhindert worden wegen relaxation,*
*des Gesichts meines linken Auges*

*so relaxt.*

Came this far 13th Febr. 1751
Was prevented on account of the relaxation
of the sight of my left eye

so relaxed.

**But after ten days he could write on the following page:**

*den 23ᵗ dieses etwas besser worden*
*wird angegangen*

On the 23ʳᵈ this has become somewhat better
work goes on.

And he succeeds in finishing the composition on August 31,
1751. It took him longer than any of its companions. Then
comes complete or almost complete darkness. Handel still
writes new arias for new performances of old oratorios, for
*Susanna, Samson,* and others. In 1757 he even revises his old
*Triumph* (whose text, by Panfili, had been newly translated
for him by Morell) to such a degree that it can be considered
a partly new composition. But *Jephtha* remains his last Opus.

What does this last Opus mean in relation to the whole of
Handel's output? It is the culmination of a series attaining a
uniformly high level, surpassed only by the *Messiah*. However
gloomy the end of Handel's life may seem, the end of his work
is perfectly harmonious and representative of himself and of
his time. He presents the sharpest possible contrast with Bach.
The customary parallel between Bach and Handel is a fallacy.

They are contemporaries; but otherwise they have nothing in common, least of all counterpoint; all their conceptions of melody, harmony, and rhythm are different. Handel's nearest musical kin are the Italians of the late seventeenth and early eighteenth century. Measured by them, he stands as a giant. An art historian, one of those who have recognized the (unfortunately undeniable) superiority of historical research in the fine arts over musical research, has said that in the history of music parallels with other arts do not coincide in time: musicians do not belong to a century, but to a millennium. Schubert is not the contemporary of the pleasant Viennese painter Moritz von Schwind, but of Giorgione. Thus, Bach completes not only the Age of the Baroque in music, but also that of the Gothic, each within the other. Handel rounds off the age of Carissimi: the classic Italian Sonata, the classic Italian Cantata, the classic Italian Oratorio. He closes the seventeenth century; he is as a musician neither German nor English, but Italian.

## HAYDN

Joseph Haydn is an example of a rare case, that of a master who of his own free will puts an end to his creating, or, shall we say, who sorrowfully recognizes the decline of his forces and resignedly yields to it. Haydn outlived his creative ability, not his fame, which in his failing years climbed to its peak and was attested by countless honors. He himself had often bewailed the beginning and the cause of this growing weakness: the composition of the *Seasons*, the first performance of which, on April 24, 1801, exhausted his powers. He had overtaxed himself. He had had to struggle too much with Van Swieten's miserable text. "But there are too few words! . . . I have had to plague myself whole days over one place,—then—no, you won't believe how I have tortured myself." To such a high and mighty librettist he had not dared to make his needs and wishes as a musician detailed and clear enough. On June 5, he made his will. But then new plans were made for three new oratorios of which two had subjects that would lie very close to the heart of an old, religious man: *Das jüngste Gericht* and *Die letzten Dinge*. In the summer, still another Mass came forth, the so-called *Schöpfungsmesse*, also a few three- and four-part songs; and in 1802 Haydn wrote his last music for the Church, one more High Mass, the *Harmonie Messe*. When he was asked to write a new piano sonata for the wife of General Moreau, an invitation that could not be ignored, he practised a little deception and sent a piece he had written long before.

But in 1803, in his seventy-first year, he began his last work, a quartet. Since he began with quartets, he wanted to end with one. Two movements were completed, an Andante Grazioso and a Minuet and Trio. He did not have the strength to add the other two movements. In 1806, he tried his hand once again on songs; but not one of the six pieces that he began ever got beyond the first sketch. Then he decided to publish the chamber-music fragment as his eighty-third Quartet; it is dedicated to Count Moritz von Fries. The agent to the publisher, Griesinger, described it as the "Swan Song." ("Swan Songs" were becoming fashionable.) To explain and excuse the fragmentary quality of the work, Haydn added to it the musical visiting card of his old age, the little song (many call it a canon) on the text: "Hin ist alle meine Kraft—Alt und schwach bin ich" ("All my strength is gone—old and weak am I").

But the two movements show no signs of weakness, and the only signs of age are those of mastery. There is demonstrated for the last time the trait of character which is one of the signal features of Haydn's greatness, namely discipline of the mind, self-criticism. He only writes that which he still *can* write: the two middle movements of the Quartet. Since the Minuet is in D minor, the work must be considered as in this key, not as a Quartet in B-flat major. And these two movements still have Haydn's full originality; they point towards nothing in the future, they stay within the frame of Haydn's style, but they completely round it out. They are only parts of a whole, but these parts are valid.

## MOZART

There is certainly no more famous last work than Mozart's *Requiem*. The creator must lay it aside unfinished, the pupil must piously complete it. This composition, with its Mozart-Süssmayer relationship, has become the prototype for several cases in more recent times: for Busoni's *Doctor Faust*, finished by Jarnach; for Puccini's *Turandot*, which Franco Alfano brought to a straightforward and simple end.

The popularity of the *Requiem* is rooted partly in the mystery that surrounds it. To this day all are not agreed upon the degree of its authenticity, nor on the "romance" of its origin. The many Mozart novels we possess undoubtedly gave the impetus to this symbolic romance. A secret messenger, a tall, thin, gray-clothed figure, comes to Mozart in the year of his death, 1791, and commissions, at the order of an unnamed person, a *Mass for the Dead*. He then, according to Mozart, disappears, then returns bringing with him the stipulated fifty ducats—

handsel from the nether world. It is understandable that these strange and, even in the eighteenth century, unusual circumstances must have thoroughly disturbed Mozart, and still more the imagination of the romantic early nineteenth century. It is possible that Mozart may have said he would compose the *Requiem* for himself; he certainly never wrote the Italian letter (dated September 7, 1791) in which the unknown man is spoken of. "I cannot dismiss his image from my mind." This letter is the pious fraud of a romancing person, such as Rochlitz or E. T. A. Hoffmann.

The actual history of the inception of the *Requiem* is rather trivial. Since it is well known, I only need to outline it. A musical dilettante, Count Franz von Walsegg zu Stuppach of Lower Austria, wanted to have a Mass for the Dead performed in memory of his wife who had died in February, 1791, and he needed an unknown work because he intended to announce it as his own. He sent his steward Leutgeb to Mozart. The Count's little deceit, prompted by vanity, was parried by Constanze Mozart with a little deceit, prompted by necessity. Since the patron probably would have demanded the return of the honorarium at the sight of an unfinished manuscript, she asked Joseph Eybler to complete the fragment. Eybler began to fill in the instrumentation in the manuscript and added two measures to the "Lacrimosa." Then he saw the impossibility of his task and retired in favor of Süssmayer, Mozart's pupil, who thereupon undertook to complete the venture. The Count received the "Requiem" and "Kyrie" in Mozart's autograph and the rest in the writing of Süssmayer, which is remarkably like Mozart's. In 1796, the widow assured the interested Friedrich Rochlitz, contrary to better information, that Mozart had been able to complete the *Requiem* before his death.

She could, however, not prevent the truth from finally trickling out. In 1799, she made a half-confession to Breitkopf & Härtel; in 1800, Süssmayer himself gave out an honest account of the facts. He declared that he had done the instrumentation for the first movements, finished the "Lacrimosa," and composed the last three movements himself; for the ending he had repeated the "Kyrie-Fugue" with suitably changed text.

But the real mystery was only beginning. The world would not let itself be robbed of the belief that it possessed a *Requiem* completely from Mozart's hand. The controversy over the genuine and false parts of the *Requiem* has lasted until today and would fill two bulky volumes. Its history would be a history of human fallibility, a memorable warning to be wary. In the second edition of *Köchel* is expressed the belief that "the 'Requiem' is in all its parts Mozart's very own Swan Song, Süssmayer only had to fill out the mechanical part." In the third decade of the nineteenth century, musicians like Gottfried Weber and exceptionally clever men like Adolf Bernhard Marx had the misfortune to declare notoriously genuine parts to be false and *vice versa*. In *Köchel*, a volume that should show familiarity with Mozart's ways of working, there are mentioned the "Brouillons" of Mozart which Süssmayer is said to have worked out. But there exists in Mozart's hand only complete scores and others complete as far as they go, together with preparatory drafts for certain difficult contrapuntal places, such as could have been of help only to the composer and to no one else. The only assumption that remains is that Süssmayer found sketches and beginnings for the "Hosanna" and "Benedictus" as he did for the "Lacrimosa." This theory would agree with the newest critical research into problems of style and the psychological investigation of melody made by

Edward Sievers. But it is impossible for us to find a solution to the problems of whether a good talent like Süssmayer's could suddenly become genius, for the "Benedictus" is the work of a genius, or whether an honorable character had decorated himself with plumage not his own, or how much the mechanical work of Süssmayer harmed Mozart's creation. The "last word" about the *Requiem* will probably never be spoken.

One of Mozart's biographers believes that the *Requiem*, with its own particular combination of a strong religious character and highest art, shows us a picture of the church music which Mozart "thanks to his position at St. Stephen's might have given the world had he lived longer." It seems to us that this is merely the application to church music of a method that Mozart had long applied and realized: the combining of music of gallantry and music of learning, producing a coalescence which Haydn had attempted in a completely different way, and which would furnish sufficient substance for a whole article in itself; a coalescence which Beethoven, at another level of development, was to attempt again. Mozart's solution is the completest, the purest, the most wonderful, by which I do not refer to the finale of the "Jupiter Symphony" nor to the music of the "Armed Men" in the *Zauberflöte*, but rather to other, small wonders in his last instrumental works. Who, after beholding such perfection, wishes to maintain that the death of Mozart really robbed us? This creative work is completed, greater does not exist. But also, who can imagine where it might have led? The report of the autopsy states briefly that on December 5, 1791, the "Well-born Mr. Wolfgang Amadeus Mozart" died of acute military fever in Rauchsteingasse at the age of 36. The *Requiem* is the last Opus, if there is one at all. No sketches hint of anything further, nor were Mozart's plans known. The *Requiem* is dated 1792, a year which he did not live to see.

### BEETHOVEN

At first glance, the question of Beethoven's last work is an involved and obscure one. There exists even a so-called "last thought" that is little known, a fragment of a string quartet in C major which (together with a piano sonata for four hands) Beethoven had promised the publisher and composer Anton Diabelli and had really begun. Diabelli bought the manuscript from the estate—it came up as number 173 in the auction catalogue—and published it as *Beethoven's letzter musicalischer Gedanke* ("Beethoven's Last Musical Thought") in a collection tastefully entitled *Wiener Lieblingsstücke* ("Favorite Viennese Pieces").

The fragment, an Andante maestoso in $\frac{3}{4}$ time, *à la Polonaise*, was written in November, 1826, in Gneisendorf at the house of the composer's brother Johann. Beethoven returned to Vienna a dying man; and then the horrible suffering began which, after four operations and unspeakable torments, ended on March 26, 1827. He died needlessly early, a victim of lifelong neglect. He died full of plans and projects. He had in mind a Tenth Symphony for the London Philharmonic Society; the introduction was to be in E-flat major, the first Allegro—of which the opening theme is preserved—in C minor. He had promised the Gesellschaft der Musikfreunde an oratorio, Bernard's "Sieg des Kreuzes" ("Victory of the Cross"), a theme and text with which, to be sure, he was not greatly in sympathy. He was more seriously considering a "Saul," text by Kuffner, with choruses in the old modes; he had already finished the first part "in his head." He had told this to Grillparzer more than once, and had said very often about Grillparzer's own *Melusine* libretto: "Your opera is finished." He was also contemplating a Requiem in the manner of the first *Requiem* of Cherubini, which he preferred to Mozart's. He wanted to write an overture on the notes B-A-C-H. All of this is proof that he was not "finished," or dried up, that he did not believe he had completed his task.

Beethoven's last Opus comprises the five great string-quartets of which—in the order of composition—the first three are those in E-flat major (Op. 127), A minor (Op. 132), and B-flat major (Op. 130), all commissioned by Prince Galizin, and the last two those in C-sharp minor (Op. 131), and F major (Op. 135) which were added of his own accord. It is obvious from the opus numbers that they were chosen at random: they give no information about the dates of origin. Beethoven did not end his work with the F major Quartet. The last piece he finished was the Rondo in the B-flat major Quartet which replaces the *Grosse Fuge*, so that the *Grosse Fuge* now stands alone with a separate opus number. It lies beyond the reaches of this article to discuss the strange question of whether to play the B-flat major Quartet with the Rondo, according to Beethoven's "last wish" (which in reality was prompted by the publisher Artaria's insistence), or with the *Grosse Fuge*, as the composer originally intended. And so the last work of Beethoven remains the F major Quartet which, as has often been emphasized, cannot, in spite of the indescribably beautiful slow movement in D-flat major, compare in substance and power with the other four. This last quartet closes with an almost playful movement, the Finale with the title *Der schwer gefasste Entschluss* ("The Difficult Decision"). But is this in jest or in earnest? Cannot gayety be sublime? Does not the second theme of the movement, with all its softness, suggest a lost victory? It seems to me that, in spite of the "accidental" nature of this "last opus" by the greatest sufferer among composers, it forms a logical and fitting conclusion.

## SCHUBERT

While Mozart lived to the age of almost thirty-six, Schubert had to be content with thirty-one years of life. Five years less, five years in which it was granted to Mozart to write *Figaro*, *Don Giovanni*, *The Magic Flute*, the three great Symphonies and the last four Quintets. Truly, we cannot blame Grillparzer for his tombstone inscription.

Schubert had no immediate premonition of death; at least he did not write more feverishly in the first ten months of the year of his death than in previous years. Nevertheless, these ten months brought forth, besides some of the most beautiful songs, the great C major Symphony (March); *Mirjam's Siegesgesang;* the E-flat major Mass; the 92nd Psalm; the three Piano Sonatas in C minor, A major and B-flat major (September); the C major String Quartet, Op. 163; the Rondo for piano, four hands, Op. 107; and twenty other works which in themselves would have made the reputation of a lesser composer. He died on the 19th of November. From August to October, his last month of good health, he had written the fourteen songs in the collection, *Schwanengesang;* the scene for voice, piano and clarinet, *Der Hirt auf dem Felsen*, (Op.

129); and a "Benedictus" for an earlier *Mass in C major*. The order of these pieces, or a more exact dating of them is not known.[1] The song, on words by Seidl, "Die Taubenpost," which is inferior to most of the songs in the *Schwanengesang*, is generally considered to be Schubert's last work. It is in any case a relatively insignificant ending.

One thing is certain: with the year 1828 an epoch in Schubert's life would have come to a close. The last work that Schubert listened to was the C-sharp minor Quartet of Beethoven, which Beethoven himself had not lived to hear performed. Schubert's friends have testified to the state of deep emotion and excitement that the hearing of this work created in him. He would not have imitated it, he was already too great for that; but the aftereffect, the fermentation of the impression, would have lifted all his subsequent work to a higher plane. There was precedent in Schubert's life for such mental reaching out and assimilation. Perhaps I should remark here that Schubert is one of the least known, least investigated of all our great masters, and that for him no Wyzewa or Saint-Foix has yet arisen. For example, one unknown chapter in Schubert's development is that of his indebtedness to Rossini.[2] Another influence that Schubert felt most strongly was that of Handel, just as had Beethoven.

Schubert, the greatest harmonic inventor of all time, wanted to master polyphony and counterpoint. Shortly before his death, he arranged for lessons with Simon Sechter. Still, it was not he who took counterpoint lessons, but, later on, Anton

[1] More exact chronology is now available in Otto E. Deutsch's *The Schubert Reader*, New York, W. W. Norton, 1947.]

[2] A modest, yet searching investigation was contributed a few years after this was written by Einstein himself: *Schubert: A Musical Portrait*, New York, Oxford, 1951.]

Bruckner. And we can only imagine what new fields, new wonders, new miracles would have been bestowed upon German music if Schubert had lived and worked five more years.

.

### MENDELSSOHN, SCHUMANN, CHOPIN, BRAHMS

I should like to skip over a number of masters because their "last works" were not characterized by any distinctive quality, as were those of the men we have thus far discussed. I refer to Mendelssohn, who in *Elijah* spoke his last word, and to Chopin. Both died at about the same age and almost in the same year. Only a few people know that Chopin's last work was the Sonata for violoncello and piano, Op. 65, which was published in October, 1847. It is surely a composition that occupies no very conspicuous place in Chopin's musical output.

But when it comes to Schumann, it is a sorrowful task to discuss the last work, the one that was written before his complete collapse, the final contribution to a series that shows evidence only of an ever increasing failing of his mental power and imagination. Schumann had neither the perception nor the gift of self-criticism that Haydn demonstrated when he refused to command his unwilling Muse. It is on the early works of Mendelssohn and Schumann—and even of Chopin— that the spotlight of fame rests. Mendelssohn's Overture to *A Midsummer Night's Dream*, and Chopin's C minor Sonata would be enough to guarantee the composers their places among the masters. And Schumann could have stopped with the C major Fantasy, Op. 17, without losing his share of immortality.

It is a different question with Brahms. Brahms is one of the great composers who reached fulfillment, and, however doleful his last year, he had at least the good fortune to finish his task. I should like to point out that his last work is not clearly defined; it is divided among three opus numbers. It seems proved that he worked last, that is to say, in May and June, 1896, on the eleven chorale settings which are related to the earliest exercises of his youth, perhaps to the A-flat minor Organ Fugue of 1856; and, strangely enough, of these settings, half impersonal, half personal, the last uses the melody, *O Welt, ich muss Dich lassen*. Preceding these are the *Vier Ernste Gesänge*, containing a confession of pessimism (*Denn es gehet dem Menschen wie dem Vieh*), and a glance, veiled with tears, into a great brightness: "And now abideth Faith, Hope, Charity, these three; but the greatest of these is Charity."

Here speaks Brahms, bringing an offering for the dead— some say for Clara Schumann, others for Elisabeth von Herzogenberg; but, without knowing it, it was for himself that he was singing a song of departure. The antepenultimate "work" are the two Clarinet Sonatas in F minor and E major, Op. 120. They are the artistic legacy of Brahms: the proof that mastery was still possible in the nineteenth century— that the whole burden of the musical past could rest on the shoulders of a contemporary German musician, and that this inheritance could become a true possession.

### WAGNER

Wagner left no "last theme." Beethoven's, Schubert's, Bruckner's last themes could be expressed only in notes.

Wagner's musical gifts were never absolute in their greatness, for, in spite of their greatness, they were always subordinated to some unrelated purpose, such as the drama, or a so-called *Weltanschauung*. His "last work," characteristically, was a cultural-political newspaper article.

It was over an article, "Über das Weibliche im Menschlichen" ("On the Feminine in Humanity"), for the *Bayreuther Blätter*, that Wagner was brooding on the 12th and 13th of February, 1883. He died without finishing it; the last words he wrote were "Love-Tragedy." Apparently Wagner did not write another note of music after the completion of *Parsifal* on December 25, 1881. We know of projects that were not carried out: he had planned a Buddha drama, *Die Sieger* ("The Victors"), of which the underlying thought was so completely expressed in *Parsifal* that the sketch could scarcely have had much importance in Wagner's eyes. We hear of four dramas and a comedy that Wagner is said to have had "fully drafted" in his head as early as 1872. They are: *Luther, Hans Sachsens zweite Ehe, Herzog Bernhard von Weimar* and *Friederich der Grosse und Lessing*. But it is doubtful whether any such schoolmaster subjects ever haunted Wagner's brain. With *Parsifal*, the musician Wagner had pronounced his last word, and after it nothing more could come.

Really, could nothing more come? A writer about Wagner —not a German—recently remarked, and rightly, that on the 13th of February, 1883, not Wagner's imagination or brain, but his heart ceased to function; that an almost lifelong battle in Dresden, Zürich, Paris, Munich, Bayreuth, had prematurely worn away the strength of Wagner's heart muscles. Actually, *Parsifal* shows no slackening of mental power. Perhaps a slackening of creative power, if one wants to split hairs; it does not have the full-blooded vitality of *Tristan*. But the lessened sensuousness was perhaps in keeping with the more spiritual story. Even the "glow" of the music in the second act of *Parsifal* shines as if through a veil. And if we know that this second act cost Wagner endless trouble—he had to stop composing in the Love Scene—we must remember also that exactly the same exhaustion overcame him when writing the third act of *Tristan* and the first act of the *Meistersinger*. Had Wagner's heart held out a little longer, his victorious, heroic life and work as a composer would not have ended, his tireless brain would have gone on producing music dramas, not merely critical, cultural, and political essays. Only seemingly was this lifework brought to a harmonious end.

## VERDI

When Verdi last set pen to paper, the result was neither an article nor letters but, quite appropriately, music—real music. Verdi's last work is the *Quattro pezzi sacri* consisting of the *Ave Maria* (*scala enigmatica*) for *a cappella* chorus; the *Laudi alla Vergine Maria*, after Dante's *terze rime*, for women's voices; and the *Stabat Mater* and *Te Deum* for double chorus and orchestra. The *Ave Maria* was planned in 1889, but the four pieces were written down for the first time in 1895 and 1896 by an eighty-three year old man. Verdi himself characterized the *Ave Maria* as a childhood work, and it is little more than a curiosity, an artistic *tour de force*. But the *Laudi* and especially the two larger choral pieces are products of the greatest and most mature mastery and of unexceptionable creative power. What do they mean? They are an epilogue and a legacy. The last message that Verdi wrote holds such a key to these remarkable pieces as one could scarcely have expected of him. When the Countess Negroni-Prati suggested that he set to music the prayer that Queen Margherita wrote after the murder of her husband, he answered that modern music was too swollen and *ricercato* to do justice to such words, one would have to go back three hundred years to find the right medium. He sought, in his passionate love for truth, a new simplicity in music. He did not want a return to the past, but rather a bond with it and with the masters whom he honored—shall we say, Palestrina and Benedetto Marcello? The *Stabat Mater* and the *Te Deum* are examples of such a new-old art, an art of tradition and of personal creation as well. The almost ninety year old man made a few sketches for the prayer of the Queen in July, 1900. They were his last notes. He died exactly half a year later, on January 27, 1901.

The four pieces are, as I said, an epilogue. Verdi's really "last work" is *Falstaff*, performed for the first time on February 9, 1893, the most astounding creation of old age that exists. The question that confronts us is this: Was *Falstaff* necessary, inevitable, in the whole line of Verdi's work? How would we have judged his work if, to express it very tritely, Verdi had died at seventy or seventy-five, and ended his operas with *Otello*? If, as with Wagner, the heart had left the unweakened brain in the lurch? We would then say: Verdi is a master of tragic passion; not the smallest gleam of humor ever brightened the prodigious realm of his dark melodic power. The *opera buffa* called *Il finto Stanislao*, the work of a twenty-year old boy, does not count; it was a failure into the bargain. And the comic scenes in *La Forza del Destino* are not really funny; the preaching monk does not excite any comfortable cheerfulness in us, his scene is there merely for the sake of contrast. As for the rough porter, Fra Melitone, he is not for one moment a *buffo* character, but rather an insolent man possessing the same kind of operatic "reality" as does the grave and worthy prior. In no other of Verdi's operas does one find even the slightest inclination towards humor. And now the old master writes a work that gives his whole past the lie, so to speak, an *opera buffa* raised to the *n*th power, the sublime example of its kind. *Falstaff* throws a light back over all of Verdi's previous work. It changes the aspect of this work; there must be more to it than we believed; the master who could create such an opera did not write *Trovatore* as mere hand organ music. And, indeed, the brighter ones among us have already come to the conclusion that Verdi's secret (I am not now speaking of the so-called secrets of form) lies as deep as Wagner's, and is much less obvious than is that of the calculating Wagner—rationalizing sometimes to the point of excess.

If any conclusion can be drawn, it must take into consideration the question of *history*, the history of the creativeness of a great man, which we call biography, and of the interrelation between artistic happenings, which we call history of art. History has been called "putting sense into the senseless." In other words, we must, as we trace it, read a sense of higher mental and moral necessity into a sequence of happenings that may appear to have only a physical consequentiality, and whose occurrence in itself would seem foolish and futile. It is we who put order into these events, separate the apparently essential from the apparently unessential, and make "History" of them. And if we want to investigate the history of art and music at all, we must collect all the facts and bring them into proper connection in order to interpret them correctly. Beethoven did not merely follow after Haydn and Mozart and Cherubini; he came *out* of them. He was their product *plus* the ever unknown quantity—eternally unpredictable—which is called personality, individuality, and which, of course, determined the real Beethoven. But, granted this unknown quantity, the history of art shows a development much more logical, much more comprehensible than does that of political history, precisely because in art there exists a clear "descent" of schools and methods which is so often absent in political ideas and creeds.

The history of the individual artist is much more problematical. Can we properly say: "The work of this man was cut off short, the development of that man was complete"? In the history of musicians, that which we call Fate seems in too many cases to have raged blindly and cruelly and so to have robbed us of the finest and ripest fruit. There comes to mind that remarkable chapter with which Goethe ended his biography or appreciation of Winckelmann. There could not have been a more senseless or violent end than Winckelmann's; he was murdered out of mere covetousness by his servant, while on the way back from Italy to Germany. And now hear what Goethe wrote:

> He was at the summit of the greatest happiness he could have wished for, withdrawn from the world. . . . And . . . we should consider him fortunate in that he stepped up to the dwelling of the Blessed from the peak of human existence, in that a short fright, a quick pain took him away from the living. He never felt the infirmities of old age, nor the decline

of his mental power. He lived as a man, and went from here a complete man. Now he enjoys the advantage of living on in the memory of posterity as an eternally vigorous and strong personality; for, in whatever form a man leaves the earth, he wanders among the shadows; and so Achilles remains ever present for us as the eternally striving youth. That Winckelmann died early benefits us too. From his tomb radiates the breath of his power and strengthens us, and arouses in us the urge always to carry on and forward with zeal and love what he began.

If this is not meant to be rhetorical, and it is not, then it is superhuman, that is to say, godlike, heroic. And so we will admit that in the history of music, in the life of a musician, there rules a demon; that things come to pass according to a higher plan; and that each "last work" is, even if not obviously so, not only the ultimate but the consummate, not only an end but a completion.

# VI

## Words and Music

THE combination of the word—the articulated, meaningful word—with tone, i.e. musically fixed pitch, results in a problematic union or unity. While the starkest expression of pure emotion is found in the wails of mourning of primitive peoples, the meaningful word weakens rather than strengthens such pure expression, since convention tends to attenuate it. On the other hand, the most abstract speech is unthinkable without the concrete utterance, the tone of voice, the various inflections—in short, without a rhythmic and melodic flow. Speech itself "has a dual nature: it is both logical and magical." [1] How much more complex, composed of how many more chemical ingredients, is the combination of speech and music!

This compound seems to be an impure species of art, an indeterminate area between two specific spheres in the realm of esthetics. No pure mode of expression is apparently quite

[1] Friedrich Gundolf, *Goethe*, Berlin, 1930, p. 64.

proper to it. In the domain of fine arts, the sculptural relief is comparable to it, althought this comparison admittedly limps as much as any. For the relief doubtless is a subspecies of sculpture; it molds stone, even if it does so on a plane surface rather than in the round. However, there are many degrees between the high-relief of the Pergamene frieze and the doors of the Florentine Baptistry (whose surface treatment still does not exclude perspective), in other words, between full-fledged sculpture and painting in stone. Similarly, the combination of word and tone inclines now to one side, now to the other.

It is one of the paradoxes inherent in the development of art that this combination was already in an "impure" state when it came into existence as a species of art, even though as a composite it is not a primal manifestation. (But since we are here concerned with art, we need not regress to the origins of more primitive phenomena.) From the very beginning the combination was indissoluble; only later was there any separation. Lyric poetry derives its name from the lyre, as if to indicate that music is an integral part of this genre. Epic poetry was declaimed or chanted, rather than spoken; and the elevated tone of the drama developed into full-fledged "composition" in the choruses. It is evident that even in such early art as that of the Greeks, all specimens of intrinsic junction of word and tone show an ever-varying balance of these elements, that, in fact, there is a continuous search for a different equilibrium, depending on the emotional or rational weight of a word. To trace through the ages the various solutions of this eternal problem is a worthy task.

Even in pure "unaccompanied monody" the relationship of word and tone is not a fixed one. Gregorian Chant contains a minimum of music. It is elevated speech. It is the official chant of the Catholic Church, and, since it is a universal language, it must have no national traits; hence, Rome has always looked askance at any dialects, such as those practiced in Milan or Spain, even though they are mere dialects. In order to avoid any national or regional deviation, the chant utilizes a universal language, which has been dead for a considerable time. In the pastoral letter on the chant of the Catholic Church written by the future Pius X when he was still Patriarch of Venice, it is the universality of Gregorian Chant that, in addition to its sanctity and artistic merit, receives special emphasis. It is said to be "above all private and national tastes." Further, it is strictly diatonic, for diatonicism is a bulwark against the intrusion of affective elements. The nature of the chant must be neutral, since it serves a strictly ordered rite, i.e. the liturgy of the Church, which does not permit anyone to turn to God in a spirit affected by subjective or personal impulses.

But however much the word preponderates in Gregorian Chant, from the very beginning there has been inherent in it an internal contradiction, a danger that language, once it is intensified by music, may turn into subjective utterance. The elemental power of things sensuous is an innate quality of music. The word is thus imperiled by music, even in this strict, official, neutral language. St. Augustine, in a famous chapter of his *Confessions* [1] is already fully aware of the danger to which the elemental nature of sound exposes the holy word. He confesses and laments the fact that earlier in his life he had been greatly tempted to indulge in what delights the ear; he mistrusts the religious ecstasy induced by the singing of sacred texts; he divines something uncanny

[1] X, 33.

behind song; he feels that it is safer to follow the instructions of Athanasius, Bishop of Alexandria, and to perform the psalms only "with few tones in order that the performance be closer to speech than to singing." These thoughts of the Bishop of Hippo had, of course, considerable effect throughout subsequent centuries, and emphasis on them recurred whenever musical adornment threatened to overwhelm the holy word. They formed the background of the "anti-musical" deliberations of the Council of Trent; likewise, their influence is evident in the strict precepts of Calvin, who, in the preface to the Geneva Psalter of 1542, distinguishes between spoken and sung prayer, attributing to music the greater power, but at the same time warning that it must not be granted an excessive role in the liturgy. There can be no doubt that humanism was a factor in both cases, in Trent as well as in Geneva; Calvin cites, in the enlarged version of his Psalter of 1543, not only St. Augustine, but Plato as well. Nonetheless, the principle that the word has supremacy over music remains intact.[1]

All of them were right, St. Augustine as well as those who transmitted and perpetuated his ideas, because even the wondrously "plain" chant of the Catholic Church is capable of modulation in performance. They were right, because this chant had to defend itself against anything "subjective," against intrusion of affective features, against "Orientalism." One of the bulwarks against such intrusion was the system of church modes with its strict diatonicism. In the early centuries of Christianity, prior to the codification of Gregorian Chant, a struggle must have been carried out against the Oriental

---

[1] Charles Garside, Jr., "Calvin's Preface to the Psalter: A Re-Appraisal," in *The Musical Quarterly*, XXXVII (1951), 566–77.

elements; the result was a purification that eliminated everything overly affective or subjective. This kind of self-purifica-
tion is symbolized in the strict diatonicism of the chant. That
strictness shows most clearly in the structure of the Phrygian
mode with its careful avoidance of the *subsemitonium.* Gregorian Chant is archaic and may well have been so from the
beginning, in contradistinction to secular song; archaicism is
symbolic of dignity, immutability, asceticism. The Middle
Ages used a characteristic method to achieve this asceticism
and to make sure that all personal elements were excluded.
For it is possible that, in line with the tradition of Pythagorean
and neo-Pythagorean ideas, the number symbolism of the
early Middle Ages played a part in the invention and shaping
of Gregorian melodies. At least, Zdzislaw Jachimecki has attempted to explain the peculiar melodic structure of the earliest Gregorian Credo by pointing out that certain intervals
may have had certain symbolic theological meanings.[1]

Gregorian Chant is musically elevated speech or declamation, in which the sensuous element of music is reduced to a
minimum. Nonetheless, it is capable of a more intense expression without necessarily changing into personal or subjective utterance. During the Easter season it was permissible
to perform the liturgical melodies at a higher pitch level in
order to express joy. For chants of mourning or laments the
singer unwittingly uses narrower intervals than for chants
expressing jubilation. The most expressive element of Gregorian Chant, however, is the melisma, which contrasts with

[1] "Symbolismus in der Motivik des ersten gregorianischen Credo," in
*Studien zur Musikgeschichte, Festschrift für Guido Adler,* Vienna, 1930,
pp. 43 ff.

neutral and plain declamation. In a largely declamatory chant a melismatic episode or climax may be employed to emphasize a word or a name; this is an instance of emphasis, the first and foremost category in the development of musical rhetoric. Conversely, solemn declamation can have an emphatic effect in a largely melismatic chant.

On the whole, the melismas in liturgical chants were reserved for the soloists, the chorus generally performing the declamatory passages. Thus it may well be that, in the spirit of St. Augustine, the fear of anything sensuous and elemental, of virtuosity and subjectivity, as embodied in the melismatic style, played a part in the invention of the sequence. There are other explanations for this custom of providing a syllable for each note of a melisma: the process is said to have been designed as a mnemonic device, or to mitigate the difficulties encountered by Germanic or Nordic singers in St. Gall and elsewhere when trying to sing jubilations created for Italian vocal cords. But Peter Wagner is certainly correct in saying that "the sequences with their syllabic treatment of the text are nothing but a negation of the melismas, a protest against too great a dominion of the musical element in the melody; in this respect it is a highly important stage in the development of medieval music." [1] This last statement, however, is true only with regard to the rise of polyphony. The sequence is, above all, an attempt to curb the danger of overly subjective expression and to return to an anonymous and neutral type of performance.

The "anonymity" of the musician that is characteristic of

[1] Peter Wagner, *Einführung in die gregorianischen Melodien*, Freiburg i.d. Schweiz, 1895, p. 80.

Gregorian Chant begins to lift, and his participation becomes more prominent in the secular music of the Middle Ages, the chansons of the troubadours and trouvères, and the songs of the Minnesinger. It is true that the musician is entirely in the service of the poet, that he is socially beneath him in this purely social art. The poetry comes first, the music second, at least in the process of creation. In many instances the aristocratic poet created the melody, too. However, even in those cases where the creative artist is not a poet-musician, but where the poet entrusts his poem to another to equip it with suitable music, the musician, his dependence on tradition notwithstanding, takes over a little less from the fund of ready-made music, of the formulas and traditional rules, than he does in sacred chant.

But just as he, as a commoner, is subject to the aristocratic poet, so his melodic invention is always subject at least to the strophic structure of the poem. Even if he is a real musician and thus feels and unconsciously expresses the emotional content of the poem—and as a commoner he is closer to nature that his patron—he must stay within definite formal limits; he cannot create otherwise. He is bound by the rule to observe the length of the lines and the rhyme scheme of the stanza, and his melody consists of members that correspond exactly to the structure of the stanza. Thus, if only a single rhyme is used for a *rondeau*, a single melodic line will suffice; likewise, two melodic lines of the same length suffice for a stanza utilizing only two rhymes for any number of lines of equal length. I give an example which, while containing text lines of unequal length, still has only two rhymes:

**Ex. 1.** *Rondel Williamme d'Amiens paignour.* (From Friedrich Gennrich, *Rondeaux, Virelais, und Balladen aus dem Ende des XII., dem XIII, und dem ersten Drittel des XIV. Jahrhunderts mit den überlieferten Melodien*, Dresden, 1921, I, 31.)

Love dwells in my heart; it causes me to languish if it will not leave me; otherwise, such pain is no cure for me; Love dwells in my heart; Thus it makes me cast away the wise desire which should save me; Love dwells in my heart; it causes me to languish if it will not leave me.

Thus, the musical material is confined to one melodic pattern consisting of three formulas, the pattern as a whole of course being repeated at the end to go with the repeat of the first three text lines. The intervening five text lines are set as follows: first there are two statements of the first melodic line and then the whole pattern is restated, as if to prepare the recapitulation.

However, the musician can show more freedom and independence when the poet furnishes him with only one rhyme ending or, rather, *because* the poet furnishes him with only one. Such a case differs from the most primitive specimens; it already signifies the beginning of a freer treatment of the poetic model by the musician. An example is the famous *estampida* or *ballade*, *Kalenda maya*, of Raimbault de Vaqueiras, *c.* 1200. The musician disregards the rhyme of the third of the short lines (*auzelh*), and first groups four lines into one unit, then two lines, finally again four, repeats each group—the last one being somewhat elaborated—and thus creates an organism of infinite charm. I choose Friedrich Ludwig's version: [1]

**Ex. 2.** From Guido Adler, ed., *Handbuch der Musikgeschichte*, Vol. I, Berlin, 1930, p. 190.

Ka-len-da maya Ni fuelhs de faya Ni chanz d'auzelh Ni flors de glaya
Non es que'm playa, Pros domna guaya, Tro qu'un ysnelh Mesatgier aya

Del vostre belh Cors que'm retraya  E jaya E'm traya Vas vos
Pla-zer no-velh Qu'a mors m'e - traya, E chaya De · playa 'Lge los

Dom-na veraya
ans          que'm n'estra - ya.

Neither the first day of May nor the budding foliage of the beech trees, neither the singing of the birds nor the blooming lily can gladden my heart, noble, sweet lady, ere I receive a swift message that your fair heart will let me again offer you my love, and unless I can see my jealous rival felled by your scorn before I leave you.

Still freer, though no less logical, is the structure of a dance song (*entrada*) in the MS Saint-Germain-des-Prés, which alternates between chorus and solo:

[1] Another version, in even meter, is in Hugo Riemann's *Handbuch der Musikgeschichte*, Vol. I, Part 2, Leipzig, 1905, p. 234.

**Ex. 3.** From Pierre Aubry, *Trouvères and Troubadours*, New York, 1914, p. 47.

When the fine weather returns, Eya! To resume her pleasure, Eya! And to annoy the jealous, Eya! The queen wishes to show that she is so in love. Go away, go away, you jealous people, leave us, leave us, so that we may dance by ourselves.

In those times there is as yet no evidence of any literary lyrical forms, like, for instance, the Italian sonnet, which originated late in the thirteenth century and was no longer composed, but at best sung to melodic formulas. But there can be no doubt that the musician begins to emancipate himself from the poet, that is to say, from the rigid formalism of poetry, not from poetry itself. The loveliest examples are probably found in the early Italian *laude*, in which religious enthusiasm lifts the singer above all rules and impels him to conclude the two-line refrain not in a tried-and-true fashion, but in a musically convincing manner. The first example I choose is a very simple one:

Ex. 4. From Fernando Liuzzi, *La Lauda e i primordi della melodia italiana*, 1935, I, 386.

Spirito sancto da servire, dann' al co-re de te senti-re.

Spiritu de ve-ri-ta-de, è fon-ta-na da bonita-de,

per la tu-a benignita-de la tu-a vi-a ne fa seguire.

Give that we may serve the Holy Ghost,
And that we may perceive Thee in our hearts.
Spirit of truth and fountain of goodness,
Make us follow Thy way through Thy benignity.

Inevitably, the second line of the refrain and the last one of the stanza correspond; but the penultimate line of the stanza should not repeat the music of the first line of the refrain, if the rhyme scheme had been strictly observed. The musician has spurned the rule in favor of a beautiful musical ending. And, as Liuzzi has pointed out, the return to the beginning is accomplished by a daring melodic leap, a seventh. (We need not consider a later version of the same *lauda* text in Cod. Magl.[1] in which the obviously clumsy composer now disregards the verse structure entirely.) Freer still is the *lauda*, *Ave, donna santissima*, whose textual structure is identical with that of the preceding example; here every line receives a different setting, and even the conclusion of the refrain by no means corresponds exactly with that of the stanza.

[1] Liuzzi, *op. cit.*, II, 14.

Ex. 5. From Liuzzi, *op. cit.*, I, 264.

A-ve donna san-tissima, re - gi - na po-ten-tis - si-ma.

La ver-tu ce - le - sti-a-le, colla gra-ti-a su - pernale,

en te, virgo vir-gi-na-le, disce - se be-ni - gnis-si-ma.

The same features prevail in that loveliest of all Christmas *laude*,[1] in which some sort of correspondence is evident only in the last two lines of the *ripresa*, exactly there where such musical similarity is not required. The white heat of emotion has carried the composer so far that he concludes the stanza on the fifth, thereby, according to Liuzzi, necessitating repetition of the refrain "per avere il senso di conclusione sulla tonica."

These and similar melodies come to mind when one recalls the precept from the troubadour era (late twelfth century) that "an inner urge must produce the melody" or when, two hundred years later, we encounter the same thought expressed by Guillaume de Machault: "Qui de sentement ne fait, son dit et son chant contrefait." Certainly, he who coined this phrase could not have been thinking of polyphonic works.

It is fair to say that, despite all deviations from the rules and from rigid formalism, the monody of the Middle Ages is characterized by a very close interdependence of word and tone, of poetry and music. In Gregorian Chant, which is an official liturgical language, the word predominates overwhelmingly;

---

[1] Reprinted by Liuzzi in *op. cit.*, I, 336, and by Ludwig in Adler, *op. cit.*, p. 211.

in secular song it does so as an amicable and less powerful leader; but the union is indissoluble in either case.

With the rise of polyphony the word is forced to lose its supremacy. A looser union of music and text is a patent result of the emancipation of music. For with the growth of polyphony the constructive element gained such an ascendancy that the word as such could no longer be respected and, in fact, had to be violated in many cases. This statement is not inconsistent with the following quotation from one of the earliest of Friedrich Ludwig's pioneering essays on the origin of polyphony: "The greatest event and the weightiest in consequences in the entire history of music is the discovery of polyphony, of the ability of music to intensify, by means of the simultaneous sounding of two or more lines of music, the expression of feelings, which are realized in the art of music because of humanity's natural musical bent." [1] Surely, Ludwig is here thinking of a much later development of this art, not of its beginnings. What are these feelings and in which way are they supposed to be intensified? Possibly there is intensification of the factor of elemental sensuousness, which is inherent in the nature of consonance; even that is questionable. But certainly such a claim cannot be made unqualifiedly with reference to a closer union of word and tone. On the contrary, music is no longer fitted so snugly to the word as before; it is now draped more loosely around the text, which, in fact, usually disappears under the smothering new garb. It seems like an atavistic defense that the polyphonic structure of a secular song still retains the over-all form of the text with repeats and refrain, or that in a sacred work the *cantus firmus*,

---

[1] Friedrich Ludwig, "Die mehrstimmige Musik des 14. Jahrhunderts," in *SIMG*, IV (1902–3), 16.

no matter how much it was changed or transformed, still shows some relationship with the Gregorian model. Even where the Middle Ages seem in a state of revolt, tradition or a semblance of tradition is preserved.

Jean-Jacques Rousseau knew nothing of the polyphonic art of the Middle Ages; but what he said about polyphony in general in the article *Mélodie* in his *Dictionnaire de Musique* (1768) is precisely applicable to medieval polyphony, too:

> If music is descriptive only because of its melody and derives from it all its power, it follows that all music that does not sing, no matter how harmonious, is not imitative music [i.e. it does not follow nature]; since it can neither represent anything nor rouse our feelings with its beautiful chords, it soon tires the ear and always leaves the heart cold. It follows further that, despite the diversity of parts introduced by harmony—a much-abused practice these days—as soon as two melodies are heard simultaneously, they cancel each other, and are devoid of effect, be they ever so beautiful separately: . . . it is as though someone had decided to recite two speeches at the same time in order to impart more power to their eloquence.

It is difficult to guess what Rousseau would have said if he had lived to hear the *Allegretto* of Beethoven's Seventh Symphony, which seems as if composed to refute him. But for the beginnings of polyphony his comments hold true; what if he had known that two or three such "speeches" were even delivered in different languages!

The use of parody proves the secondary role of language in this art. Of course, parody exists in monody, too, mostly in the guise of a new, devotional, sacred text for the melody of an originally secular, profane song; but in those cases strophic and metric identity, and, usually, the spirit of the model remain untouched. However, in the parodies of sacred motets—

parodies were also made for profane purposes—the French version only rarely is a faithful transformation of the Latin original and is mostly a new, heterogeneous text. And in the much more frequent process of changing French motets into Latin ones or, generally, of transforming profane pieces into sacred or devotional works, the substance of the poetic concept often is lost, and the only remaining connection with the original is a formal one. Friedrich Ludwig has pointed out a drastic example: the drinking song *Bone compaignie, quant ele est bien privee* over the tenor *Manere* becomes, in 1265, a song in praise of the Holy Virgin: *Virgne glorieuse et mere diu clamee;*[1] it must be admitted, though, that the parodist, a canon, was a very meticulous craftsman.

Already in so early a century we therefore encounter the problem of parody, of the *contrafactum*, a problem that will be a frequent and variegated object of our investigations. The parody procedure, i.e. the transmutation of a sacred composition into a secular one—Perotin seems to have initiated this process—and vice versa, is no great esthetic problem for the medieval artist. There is no difference between sacred and secular in the medieval polyphonic style; both thrive in the same creative climate, and hence there is nothing unnatural or strange about the combination of Latin, French, etc.

Since we are not attempting to write a history of polyphony, it is not our task to trace its experimental beginnings step by step. We can confine ourselves to a consideration of the two chief forms of polyphonic music of the *trecento* and *quattrocento*, the motet and the *ballade*, the latter here representing the other musico-poetic forms as well. As regards the motet,

[1] Friedrich Ludwig, "Studien über die Geschichte der mehrstimmigen Musik im Mittelalter," in *SIMG*, VII (1905–6), 524.

we may restrict ourselves to the typical or "ideal" form, which sets—or, rather, ties together—two voices over a tenor, both frequently having texts in different languages, or in one language but with different words. The *cantus prius factus* of the tenor is the part that was "conceived" first. We intentionally put quotation marks around the word "conceived," since a real artistic conception, i.e. a free creative process, was not involved; this was purely a matter of adaptation, of utilization of traditional material. The adapted tune, usually of Gregorian origin, was hammered into appropriate shape, cut up into melodic formulas, and in actual fact torn completely from its textual context. Only the first words of the text appear under the beginning of the tenor, which doubtless served merely as instrumental support. Even where it is still possible to provide such a "hammered" tenor with the liturgical text, this text simply does not exist for the listener; the performer himself would have had to be one of the learned few, if he was still to be aware of the relationship to the original melody. The composer's utterly arbitrary rhythmical treatment of a perfectly good tune reduced to fragments what had once been a sensible whole (Friedrich Ludwig). To combine tradition with arbitrariness, to use the former to justify the latter, is a typically medieval procedure. Moreover, even if in the two upper voices "the melismatic passages of the old melody retained their original oratorical rhythm," [1] these upper voices taken as organic entities also often had to become caricatures of themselves. (Elsewhere Ludwig speaks, much more correctly and simply, of the "total neglect of both the prosody and the speech-accents of the texts.") Guillaume de Machault, the

---

[1] Friedrich Ludwig, "Die mehrstimmige Musik des 14. Jahrhunderts," in *SIMG*, IV (1902–3), 29.

great French master of the fourteenth century, loosens the tie between word and tone more and more: he progresses to four-part writing by adding a *contratenor* and thus doubling the fundament for the two sung parts, and generally complicates the form still further. From the very beginning, though always in varying degree, this music is based on the principle of musical construction, on a principle that forces together more or less heterogeneous ingredients. Its unity is spiritual; it is a matter of the conceptual substance, as demonstrated by the choice of texts, and not of any immediate relationship of word and tone.

Any polyphonic piece from that time can serve as an example. Our first is one of Machault's motets, in which a motetus *Fine Amour . . . la mort en lieu de guerredon* and a triplum *Hé! Mors, com tu es haie* are coupled with a tenor *Quare non sum mortuus.*[1] Musical unity is achieved only through the device of repeating the tenor in diminution, which may have been intended as a symbol of the ebbing of life in old age. It is not at all unlikely that as subtle a master as Machault might have had such an idea in mind—it certainly would be an eminently medieval idea. But any really tangible unity derives solely from the poetic and topical affinity of the texts, which, regardless of such "thematic" affinity, become incomprehensible when sung simultaneously. In that sense Rousseau's complaints are certainly borne out, since in this type of performance the texts cancel each other's effectiveness, even if their declamation were less forced.

To call such music expressive in the modern sense just because of some mistaken notions about its artfulness would

[1] Johannes Wolf, *Geschichte der Mensural-Notation . . .* , Vols. II & III, No. 14; Machaut, *Musikalische Werke* (ed. Ludwig), Leipzig, 1929, Vol. III, No. 3; *Oxford History of Music*, II, 28.

amount to a gross lack of insight. Machault provided music for conventional poetry—impersonal love poems, as it were; thus, being restricted to poetic structure, the musician served an aristocratic ideal. Basically, there has been no change in the relationship of musician and poet, of minstrel and troubadour, except that the composer's task has grown in artistry and complexity, that his *scientia* is greater. Subjective expression not only remains forbidden, it is not possible at all.

A still older example of this type of intellectual art is a three-part motet by Petrus de Cruce (before 1300), a well known piece, since it was first published by Coussemaker [1] and was subsequently reprinted by Johannes Wolf.[2] In the motetus the poet tells of his creative urge reviving after a long silence (*Lonc tans me sui tenu de chanter*), and the triplum varies that theme (*Aucun ont trouvé chant par usage*). The tenor complements the two texted parts with the cue word *Annunciavit*. This makes exquisite sense and bespeaks exquisite sensitivity, but neither can be appreciated without a knowledge of the specific thought processes involved.

When the number of voices is raised to four, this textual or ideational "heterophony" becomes even more pronounced; negatively speaking, this means that the texts are even less intelligible and that what we call spontaneous expression is impossible. This is exemplified in a motet from the late thirteenth century (No. 49 in the Codex Montpellier). The tenor is the liturgical *Veritatem*, a familiar motet-tenor, which here, however, is perhaps used in the spirit of parody (*in vino veritas?*), since its text is

[1] E. de Coussemaker, *L'Art harmonique aux XIIᵉ et XIIIᵉ siècles*, Paris, 1865, Ex. 11.

[2] Johannes Wolf, *Geschichte der Mensural-Notation von 1250–1460*, Leipzig, 1904, Vols. II & III, No. 1.

a French song beginning *Par verite vueil esprover*—a reference to the original tenor text—and continuing with a comparison of several French wines. The spirit of parody is obvious. With the tenor text goes an eating and drinking song in the motetus, which is the liveliest voice of all (a strange phenomenon, since usually the triplum is the liveliest part). Triplum and quadruplum present love songs, which combine, after a fashion, with the other two voices. The whole is reminiscent of the later quodlibets, and there is a superabundance of voices, which produce confusion rather than fusion, as they compete in singing their different texts.[1]

But the comparison with the quodlibet is lopsided, because there the trick is to fuse heterogeneous material, i.e. to combine popular tunes or fragments of such tunes. In the motet, however, unity is a result of combining more or less homogeneous texts, i.e. ideas; in this particular case it seems fairly certain that the composer must have bethought himself of the old proverb, *Sine Cerere et Baccho friget Venus*, and that he therefore joined a gorge-and-guzzle song to the love songs. The education necessary to appreciate such intellectual games was an anachronism even then; it reflects monastic humanism, and not the living sensuousness of real life.

Our last example of this type is the motet *Nuper rosarum flores* written by the greatest master of the *quattrocento*, Guillaume Dufay, then in his youth, on the occasion of the consecration of the cathedral in Florence (March 24, 1436). Any motet composed for such a purpose must have a liturgical fundament; therefore, Dufay takes his tenor from the beginning of the Introit "*In Anniversario Dedicationis Ecclesiae*" (*Terribilis est locus iste*), but this substructure is reinforced

---

[1] Friedrich Ludwig, "Studien über die Geschichte der mehrstimmigen Musik im Mittelalter," in *SIMG*, V (1903–4), 196.

with a second tenor which, in a quasi-canonic manner, presents the same melody four times in the lower fifth in diminution. The melodic lines of the motetus and triplum, which are likewise not freely invented, but derived from the same chant, are arranged in a no less carefully woven pattern. The text of the motetus describes the participation of the populace of Florence; the triplum relates the presence of Pope Eugene IV, "*vicarius Jesu Christi et Petri successor*," who officiated. Everything in this piece rests on sheer structural organization and in this way everything assumes symbolic connotations. But the symbolism is in the construction itself and no more accessible to personal feeling than is the stonework of a Gothic cathedral. Dufay here uses a new device for purposes of emphasis. Earlier composers, e.g. Machault, used homophony or block-chord style, involving long note values with fermatas, to make certain text portions stand out (*cf.* the setting of the words *ex Maria Virgine* etc. in the Credo of Machault's Mass). In this motet the name of Pope Eugene (measures 47–48) or mention of the city of Florence (measures 87–91) is given special stress by means of the so-called double notes, i.e. by adding a third or some other consonance to a voice. However, this procedure, rare even with Dufay, was apparently short-lived.[1]

The musical forms of the early polyphonic era never carried the *cantus prius factus* in the top voice. In the conductus the text was in the lowest voice; one, two, or even three essentially syllabic parts were added above it. And in the motet, which in the thirteenth century gradually replaced the conductus altogether, it was again the tenor that was the *cantus prius factus*, even though the upper voice or voices had become

[1] *Cf.* Heinrich Besseler, *Bourdon und Fauxbourdon*, Leipzig, 1950, pp. 171 ff.

much more prominent, especially when their text was in the vernacular, the latter being a much more stimulating language than the neutral Latin.

A new period in the development of polyphony began with the renewed stirring of the subjective creative urge. The corollary of this turn of events was a different relationship of text and music. In the fourteenth century new forms, based on the art of the troubadours and trouvères, begin to share the stage with the motet. The composer first invents the top voice, while the other voices are reduced to a more lowly function; they are accompaniment, mere support for the melody. In France these new forms are the *ballade* (with three stanzas), the *rondeau*, the *chanson*, and the *virelai* (or *chanson balladée*), Guillaume de Machault being the most important composer; in Italy, where Florence stands out as the center of creative activity, they are the madrigal and the *ballata*.

One would think that here there should have been a possibility of returning to or continuing the ideal union of word and tone, as it exists in folksong or in the troubadour literature. And we shall see later that there actually are examples of such a style, such as those polyphonic compositions that are really nothing but *laude* for more than one voice, and certain parts of the Mass which, because of the length of the text, forced the composer to write in a pseudo-homophonic, declamatory style. But in general the polyphonic style had by then reached such complexity as to make this development impossible. Thus, the vocal part in the new French *ballade* and in the new Italian madrigal develops into a complex and highly melismatic organism, which, though conforming to the over-all poetic structure, seems nonetheless dominated by the musical component. This simply means that precise text adaptation usually causes great difficulties, in the case of an entire piece as well as in its details. (We say "usually" for here, too, we find significant exceptions.) If the situation were any different, it would not have been necessary to invent theories such as that these organisms are nothing but unrestrained coloration of simple melodies, which can be uncovered by means of "decoloration," i.e. by denuding them of their melismatic adornment, or else that they are conglomerations of vocal and instrumental parts, which can and should be distinguished as such.

The simple fact is that composers and singers attach no importance to text adaptation, in contrast to their respect for the form of the poem. (We repeat that there are exceptions.) Is it not significant that there are (three-voiced) *ballades* by Machault in which the text-bearing melody, lying *under* a textless and hence instrumental triplum, is thus obscured by it? Is it not significant that whenever an Italian madrigal has two upper parts, the second also has a text? This is generally true of the *ballata*, too. In the three-voiced *ballate* the *cantus* and tenor have texts, while a textless middle voice has a more instrumental character; an ideal example is Francesco Landini's *Gran piant' agli ochi*.

As a rule, such pieces present the following external appearance: they start with an extended melisma over the first syllable of the text, then continue with more lively declamation, and conclude with another more or less lengthy melisma over the penultimate syllable. It is hard to escape the impression that this is a reminiscence of Oriental practices or a reflection of them extending over and past the later development of Gregorian Chant; but this Orientalism is now purified so that its appearance is Western, artistic, European. The men of the time themselves probably were aware of the exuberant excesses of the melismatic style; Franco Sacchetti, for instance, ridicules Ser Bartolomeo Giraldi in these words: "Cotanto che diceva, lo diceva con molte note, come se dicesse uno madriale." ("Whatever he said, he said with many notes, as if he were rendering a madrigal.")

The syllabic declamation in the middle part of a *ballata* or of many a French *ballade* is almost raised to an artistic principle in a fourteenth century genre that, with its wealth of text, was too formless to fit into the ordinary scheme. We mean the Florentine *caccia*, which, of course, also goes back to French "pastoral" or "realistic" models from the second half of the thirteenth century. Their performance presents no problem; two voices, in canon at a considerable distance, are supported by a free instrumental bass. The texts are full of vivid realism: hunting (hence the name of the genre), fishing, going to a fair—these are their subjects.

The most vivid and poetic scene of this kind depicts women picking flowers and after a while being interrupted by a thundershower; introduction and epilogue contain the comments of the charmed spectator, Franco Sacchetti. The music for this idyl is by Nicolo Preposito da Perugia.[1] Even though his fairly rapid declamation shows some care, the setting cannot be called realistic or programmatic. He begins with the customary long melisma, disregards correct prosody, and cannot forgo the hocket device, which is certainly the most flagrant instance of "*laceramento della poesia*"; what is more important is that canonic form is again merely the product of intellectual endeavor and not spontaneous expression or living symbol. Here we confront the problem of the canon

---

[1] The composition is readily available in Johannes Wolf, *Sing- und Spielmusik aus älterer Zeit*, Leipzig, 1931, No. 7.

for the first time. A composer may have decided to write canonically for any number of reasons, which range from purely musical intentions to highly symbolic considerations, and each case requires an investigation of this problem. At an early stage one of the many meanings of the canon was already used with humorous intent. There is a three-voiced canon by Matheus de Perusio with the following text:

> Andray soulet au mielz que je pouray
> Jusque a le tamps primier Delasolre.
> Lors tu prendras desus Alamire:
> S'ainsi fera le tiers canterons gay.

> I'll walk alone as best I can
> Until the first Delasolre
> Then you'll start with Alamire above
> And, if the third part is made thus,
>     we'll sing gaily.

This stanza is patently invented for music; and, indeed, it is not just set to music, but the setting is, in the true sense of the word, the embodiment of the meaning and thought content of the stanza. Each voice "walks alone" and follows the other. The union of text and music has here been regained in a new manner. (Ex. 6.)

There is a three-voiced composition by Machault which, though no canon, is a similarly witty trick, as far as the text setting is concerned. The tenor of this piece—it is the famous *rondeau, Ma fin est mon commencement*—has the following text:

Ma fin est mon commencement et mon commencement ma fin
    et teneure vraiement
Ma fin est mon commencement
Mes tiers chans trois fois seulement

Ex. 6. From Willi Apel, ed., *French Secular Music of the Late Fourteenth Century*, Cambridge, Mass., 1950, No. 22.

Se retrograde et einsi fin
Ma fin est mon commencement et mon commencement ma fin.

My end is my beginning and my beginning my end, and this
　　holds truly.
My end is my beginning,
My third song only reverses itself three times and thus ends.
My end is my beginning and my beginning my end.

Machault takes the meaning literally and reverses the direction of the treble in the tenor, while the third part, the contratenor, reverses itself. This is purely abstract "eye music,"
comprehensible only to the cognoscenti, not to the ordinary
listener.

The application of the canon technique itself in the *caccia*,
however, remains an intellectual, inexpressive device without
a special topical meaning. Take, for example, the hunting
scene in Messer Piero's *Con bracchi assai*,[1] with its affectionate
depiction of details:

1. Con bracchi assai e con molti sparveri
   Uccellavam su per la riva d'Adda,
   E qual dicea: "da da"
   E qual: "va qua, varin; torna, picciolo"
   E qual prendea le quaglie a volo a volo;
   Quando con gran tempesta un' acqua giunse.

2. Nè corser mai per campagna levrieri
   Come facea ciascun per fuggir l'acqua;
   E qual dicea: "dà qua,
   Dammi'l mantello" e tal: "dammi'l cappello";
   Quand'io ricoverai co'l mio uccello
   Dove una pastorella il cor mi punse.

3. Perch'era sola, in fra me dico e rido:
   Ecco la pioggia, il bosco, Enea e Dido.

[1] Johannes Wolf, *Geschichte der Mensural-Notation* . . . , Vols. II & III,
No. 56.

1. With plenty of setters and many bird hawks
   We went bird-hunting on the banks of the Adda,
   And this one said, "Give me this and that,"
   And that one, "Come here, bend, little stalk,"
   And a third one caught the quails in flight,
   When, with great fury, a rainstorm arrived.

2. No longer did the hounds run through the countryside,
   While everyone was busy fleeing the rain;
   And this one said, "Let's get away from here,
   Give me my cloak," and that one, "Give me my cap,"
   As I, with my bird, was finding refuge in a spot
   Where a shepherdess—like Cupid—pierced my heart.

3. She was alone, and so I now laugh and say to myself:
   "You see, first the rain, then the woods, and then
   Aeneas and Dido!"

But even if "realism" had been Messer Piero's intention, he was thwarted by writing the same music for both the first and the second stanza.

Such purely intellectual use of the canon was bound to change its erstwhile meaning as a form; the canonic Gloria and Credo movements from the beginning of the fifteenth century contained in various manuscripts, especially in the Old Hall MS, demonstrate how quickly the canon had become a purely musical device without any extraneous intellectual connotations. Here the imitating voices no longer share the same text. While one starts with *Et in terra*, the other answers with the words *bonae voluntatis;* or, to give another example, *Qui tollis* is immediately followed by *Miserere*.[1]

---

[1] *Cf.* Oliver Strunk's examples in Manfred F. Bukofzer, *Studies in Medieval & Renaissance Music*, New York, 1950, pp. 82 ff.

In order to find stronger realism in the *caccia* we must move on to the beginning of the fifteenth century. In the market scene *Cacciando per gustar di quel tesoro*,[1] the composer, Nicolas Zacharias, member of the Papal Chapel after 1420, achieves this stronger realism by letting the supporting third voice inject its street cries into the music of the canonic upper voices. And these seem to be genuine street cries, echoes of real life; there are only few melismas. It seems to me that this stronger realism, this closer union of word and tone, was encouraged by compositions from the school of papal musicians in Avignon; many of these works, which, to be sure, are not *caccia* types, but *virelai* types, were brought together by Willi Apel in a recent publication.[2] The three-voiced *Ma trédol rosignol* (by Borlet) [3] is polytextual, and its effect derives essentially from the imitation of birds twittering ("*oci, oci, oci*," "*liry, liry, liry*," "*tantiny, tantiny*"). In Vallant's *Par maintes foys* [4] only the top voice carries a text, but the jubilant song of the nightingale is imitated—one is tempted to say, onomatopoetically—in the instrumental tenor. (The subsequent anonymous *Or sus vous dormez trop* has similar features.) There is a naive and somewhat clumsy imitation or *contrafactum* of Vaillant's *virelai* by Oswald von Wolkenstein, entitled *Der May*.[5]

The *caccia* has a free poetic form; in fact, it could be said to have no poetic form at all. Like other poetic types, for

[1] Johannes Wolf, "Florenz in der Musikgeschichte des 14. Jahrhunderts," in *SIMG*, II (1901–2), 618 ff.

[2] See p. 114.

[3] No. 68 in Apel.

[4] No. 69 in Apel.

[5] *DTO*, IX. *Jahrgang, Erster Theil*, Vienna, 1902, p. 179; Archibald T. Davison and Willi Apel, *Historical Anthology of Music*, Cambridge, Mass., 1946, I, No. 60; facsimile and transcription in Wolf, *Geschichte der Mensural-Notation* . . . , Vols. II & III, No. 76.

⇛ ⇛ ⥲ ⥲

# VII

# Some Musical Representations of the Temperaments

## I. DEMOCRITUS AND HERACLITUS:
## A DUET IN MAJOR AND MINOR

IN THE seventh book of his *Musurgia* (Rome, 1650) whose
complete title is *De musurgia Antiquo-Moderna in qua de
varia utriusque Musicae ratione disputatur*, the learned
Jesuit Athanasius Kircher devotes the ninth chapter to a discussion: "De Mutatione Modi, sive Toni, sive stylo Metabolico,"
by which he means the change of mode as well as the change of
key, in terms of modern usage. His arguments on the expressive powers of major and minor are of special interest. They
state clearly, perhaps for the first time in history, the equa-
tion of the major key with the gay mood and of the minor
key with the gloomy. The passage deserves to be quoted in
full both because of its intrinsic importance and because of
the example to which it refers:

Furthermore, each modulation has great force and produces extraordinary changes in its hearers; it can be infinitely varied, and for any affection you may wish to express it is most appropriate. This secret, which we call not unsuitably the metabolical style, is known only to the more experienced judges. It would be worth while if I were to insert here some examples of this metabolical style so that the reader can more easily grasp what I mean.

Giacomo Carissimi, the celebrated director of the choir at the German College, employs a style of this sort most judiciously when he beautifully and ingeniously represents Heraclitus and Democritus, the one laughing, the other crying, in the following metabolical melisma. In this the flats are neither chromatic nor enharmonic, as the ignorant are persuaded, but merely change the mode. The dialogue, in which these concluding phrases of laughter or lament are represented with truly incredible variety, is composed with notable skill. Since this composition is too long, we decided that it should be omitted, content with only one concluding phrase, so that in this example judgment may be clearly exposed to an instance of the so-called metabolical style:

In this example you see the second voice, when it delivers the Italian words *è pur da ridere*, suitably express laughter in its notes; and now you see the first voice, when it delivers the words *è pur da piangere* express lament and tears in an altered style, one contrary to the preceding:

Surely this contrast, as it progresses from one change of mode to another and falls on the ear unexpectedly, will excite the feelings extraordinarily, provided that the singers are those who know how to express it beautifully.

Kircher expresses his admiration for Giacomo Carissimi in yet another passage of the *Musurgia* (I, 603):

Leading all others in natural capacity and felicity of composition, he has the power to move the minds of his listeners to any affections whatsoever, for his compositions are filled with vigor and liveliness of spirit.

The praise is just. Giacomo Carissimi (1605–74), a native of Marino in the Alban mountains, began as an organist at Tivoli; from 1628 until his death he was conductor at Sant' Apollinare, the church of the Collegium Germanicum at Rome. He was not only the greatest Italian musician of his day, but also the first great modern composer in the classical sense: unlike the older Claudio Monteverdi, he stands on this side of the boundary which separates baroque music from modern.

The piece Kircher quotes from is a duet for two sopranos and basso continuo, which is extant in two manuscripts: one is a copy of vocal parts, dated 1662, in the Bibl. Estense at Modena (G. 31); the other a score in the Liceo Musicale at Bologna (K. 234). In the Modena manuscript the composer's name originally was recorded as Mario Savioni, who was one of the most prominent contemporaries of Carissimi. The title is *I filosofi*, and the poet's name is also mentioned: Benigni. According to Mazzuchelli, Domenico Benigni was *Cameriere Segreto* to Pope Innocent X and a member of several academies: the poem actually appears in the collection of his *Poesie* (Macerata, 1667). As the composition is quoted by

Athanasius Kircher, its date must be some time before 1650; but probably it was considerably earlier. We may assume that Benigni's poem was written at the command of the musician, who required a vivid poetical subject on which to build his contrast of major and minor. This presupposes that the new form invented by Carissimi, the humorous rondo-cantata, had already been fully developed; and this can scarcely have been the case before 1640.[1]

We need not reprint Carissimi's composition, as Ludwig Landshoff has published it in an excellent edition.[2] But the text must be given:

> A piè d'un verde alloro assisi un dì
> Eraclito e Democrito sui fiori,
> Vider per l'aria andar schiere d'Amori
> E tra lor favellarono così:
> È pur da ridere
> È pur da piangere,
> Sentir ognor gli amanti stridere,
> Ch'un duro cor non si può frangere.

> O miseria, ⎱
> O follia! ⎰ Se l'impietà
> Di ria beltà
> Piegar non lice,
> Fuggi, ⎱
> Mori, ⎰ infelice!

---

[1] Friedrich Chrysander suggested (*G. F. Händel*, III, 134) that at any rate the poem might be dated some time before John Milton's Italian tour (1637–38), because this would conveniently explain the origin of *L'Allegro* and *Il Penseroso*. However, it is generally assumed that Milton's poems were written before he set out on his journey; according to Masson, even as early as the autumn of 1632, at Horton, his father's country seat. Moreover, Benigni's text is not the first of its kind. Antoniotto Fregoso wrote a long allegorical poem on the laughter of Democritus and the complaints of Heraclitus which was first printed in 1506 under the title *Doi filosofi*, and frequently reprinted.

[2] *Alte Meister des Bel Canto*, II, 28. Leipzig; Peters, 1927.

Che d'un penoso amor il lungo tedio
Altro rimedio
Alfin non ha, no no,
Che fuggir, }
Che morir, } come si può

H.: E come puote un moribondo amante
Alla fuga fidar l'inferme piante,
Come scampar d'una beltà severa,
Se, dovunque egli fugga, Amore impera?
  à 2: È pur da ridere, *etc.*

Se al pregar un cor s'indura,
Taci; }
Prega; } che, s'avrà

Da cangiar giammai ventura
Tuo desir, tua ferita { al pregar }
{ al tacer } si cangerà.
Non conviene
Tra catene
A chi certo è di morte
Gettar i prieghi, non tentar la sorte.
E in dono avete e coi sospir mercate.
Sono le gioe d'Amor sempre più grate.

D.: Ma che, mentre il rigor d'alta bellezza
Suol nudrirsi di lagrime, a che vale,
Alimentar col pianto il proprio male?

H.: Han le lagrime ancor qualche dolcezza,
Poichè, piangendo un core,
Spesso annega nel pianto il suo dolore.
  à 2: È pur da ridere, *etc.*

D.: Quanti, quanti, perchè si lagnano,
Mai non trovan mercè;

H.: Quanti, quanti, muoiono, perchè
   Dentro ai lor petti i pianti stagnano.
{ Deh scopri,
{ Deh cela,
{ Ricopri,
{ Rivela,
      Amante, il duolo atroce,
      Poichè in amor per prova
      Quel che nuoce una volta, un'altra giova.

The new feature of Carissimi's piece was the humorous juxtaposition of the two ancient philosophers. But Benigni's poem had its antecedents as *poesia musicale*. On July 8th, 1483, Niccolò di Correggio sent Isabella of Mantua a chapter in dialogue: "il capitulo è una egloga pastorale, dove Mopso et Dafni pastori parlano insieme. *Mopso si duole di la fortuna, Dafni se ne gloria.* El senso alegoricho lo dirò a bocha alla Ex. V. como li parlo." [1] This is a theme very similar to Carissimi's, the chief difference being that music written about 1500 was not yet able to express these contrasts, even though the poem was undoubtedly meant to be put to music by one of the two favourite composers of the Mantuan circle, Tromboncino or Cara. It is interesting that Niccolò should explicitly point out the allegorical meaning of his eclogue. Perhaps the so-called secret of Giorgione, of his Venetian contemporaries and pupils, may also be found in the eclogues of this period.

To express the contrast of passions remains a pre-eminent aim of musicians throughout the sixteenth century. It would take us too far afield to discuss the extent to which they employed the strange conventional symbolism of the medieval church modes in which an allusion to the gay or gloomy

[1] S. Davari, *La musica a Mantova, Riv. stor. mantovana,* Vol. I, 1885, p. 53.

mood could only be expressed by illustrating single words by means of "lines" or "chords," high or low notes, or by the timbre of the voice. Vincenzo Galilei, in his *Dialogo . . . della musica antica e della moderna* (1581), ridiculed the alleged incapacity of polyphonic music to express unambiguously a sad or happy emotion. A person who laments, he says, never leaves the high pitch; one who is sad seldom deviates from the low one; modern musicians, however, confuse everything. Galilei rejected not only polyphonic composition but also the whole aesthetics of imitation propounded by the musicians of his time. He refers them to the example of the ancients:

> When the ancient musician sang any poem whatever, he first considered very diligently the character of the person speaking—his age, his sex, with whom he was speaking, and the effect he sought to produce; and after these conceptions had been clothed by the poet in words chosen to suit such a need, the musician then expressed in the tone, and with accents and gestures, the quantity and quality of sound, and the rhythm appropriate to that action and to such a person. . . . And rightly; for if the musician . . . has not the power to direct the minds of his listeners to their benefit, his science and knowledge are to be considered null and vain. . . .

Rousseau, in the article on Scene in his *Dictionnaire de Musique*, repeats almost word for word this passage of Galilei's.

It is evident that Carissimi tried to fulfil an ideal of sixteenth-century musicians—a dream which could come true only after the "invention" of the homophonic style and the modern definition of modes. There may have been several imitations of his duet; I am able, however, to mention only one, the "Heraclite et Democrite" in M. Batistin's third book of his *Cantates françoises* (1711). The real name of this Batistin was Batistin Stuck; he was born, apparently of German extraction, in Florence about 1680, came to Paris as a virtuoso on the violoncello, and composed several French and Italian operas. This "Deuxième Cantate à deux Voix, & Symphonie," i.e., two violins and basso continuo, gives the role of Heraclite to a soprano and that of Democrite to a basso; Heraclite uses for his arias the keys of B minor and E minor, Democrite G major and F sharp minor. It is an ambitious and stiff little composition; Italian in the *da capo* arias, French in the *recitativos*.

After this, Democritus and Heraclitus survive chiefly on the operatic stage. Democritus appeared alone at Torino in an opera by Carlo Francesco Gasparini (1718), and in an *opera buffa* by Karl Dittersdorf, *Democrito corretto*, in Vienna, 1787. Both philosophers together figure in a rather inferior musical comedy, *Eraclito e Democrito*, by Antonio Salieri, Vienna, 1795. The libretto, by Giovanni de Gamerra, who once supplied young Mozart with an equally miserable text, is one of coarse buffoonery. An old fool, Filemone, infatuated by philosophy, but also father of a beautiful daughter, Pulcheria, invites Eraclito and Democrito to his house so as to profit by their wisdom. He is the only one to admire the dismal expectorations of Eraclito. Pulcheria's lover appears under the mask of Democrito and easily prevails upon the old dotard to give him his daughter in marriage. In the end, of course, the real Democritus arrives, but everything is resolved happily. The powerful figures of the two ancient sages have not been treated by musicians with much respect.

The only one really to solve the problem—to combine Democritus and Heraclitus in a contrapuntal duet—is Johann Sebastian Bach; of course not in an opera or secular cantata, but in his earliest church cantata "Denn du wirst meine Seele nicht in der Hölle lassen" (Nr. 15), most probably written in 1704. He was nineteen or twenty years old. It is not impossible that he knew about Carissimi's duet, for he had met Johann Jacob Loewe in Lüneburg, who, as a pupil of Heinrich Schütz, had a vivid interest in Italian art. In Bach's duet the soprano enjoys the victory of the soul over the powers of Hell, while the alto describes their miserable lot. Bach surpassed Carissimi by far. Not by the contrast between major and minor, but by a contrapuntal combination, which is one of the triumphs of Bach's polyphony.

## 2. THE *Melancholicus* IN INSTRUMENTAL MUSIC

In the seventeenth century, almost contemporary with Carissimi's duet, there arose a problem which has not since lost its hold over the musical imagination: the expression of an emotion or passion by purely instrumental means. Seventeenth-century musicians were satisfied with representing such a mood in a single movement, and juxtaposing the contrasts; the sequence of movements in the so-called *sonata da chiesa* —Largo-Allegro and Adagio-Vivace—may be regarded as the typical alterations of the elegiac and the cheerful moods. In one strange instance, however, the melancholic person appears in the flesh, in the second sonata of a work entitled *Musicalische Vorstellung einiger biblischen Historien* (Leipzig, 1700), written by Johann Kuhnau, Bach's predecessor as *Kantor* at St. Thomas' School in Leipzig. The title of the sonata is: "Saul malinconico e trastullato per mezzo della Musica." The first movement introduces the melancholic and distracted king by means of a sombre minor key, chromatic developments, violent changes of time, and a fugue with unusual intervals in the theme.

Heraclitus and Democritus appear again, though not under their proper names, in a much discussed and famous sonata by Carl Philipp Emanuel Bach, second son of Johann Sebastian. The question of programme music greatly occupied the North German circle of eighteenth-century wits. They connected it with Galenus's theory of the temperaments, which at that time had begun to be discussed again by aestheticians. C. Ph. E. Bach appeared to be the right man to give effect to such ideas, for his instrumental music was observed to be directed towards and capable of producing "sounds of sadness, of affliction, of pain, or of tenderness, or of pleasure and merriment in monologues; or of maintaining by mere passionate sounds a sentimental conversation between similar or opposed characters." [1] Under the influence of these ideas Bach wrote in 1749 a descriptive sonata for two violins and bass, which is meant to represent "a conversation of a sanguine with a melancholy person." He published it in 1751 as the first of *Two Trios* at Nuremberg, and added to it a detailed programme. It is among the most witty and brilliant pieces ever written. Bach goes far beyond Carissimi, for he includes in his contrasts not only the major and the minor keys, but also tempi and phrases.[2] Bach himself was sceptical about the value of his experiment. In a conversation with the poet Matthias Claudius (1768), who had asked him why he did not compose any more of those "Piecen, darin Charaktere

[1] J. G. Sulzer, *Allgemeine Theorie der schönen Künste*, 1774, II, 1094.
[2] For particulars see Hans Mersmann, *Ein Programmtrio C. Ph. E. Bachs*, Bach-Jahrbuch, 1917; and E. Fr. Schmid, *C. Ph. E. Bach und seine Kammermusik*, pp. 113 ff. Kassel, 1931.

ausgedrückt sind," which the poet praised for their attractive originality, Bach replied that "words would be the shorter way."

There is a tradition that Joseph Haydn who, according to his own confession, owes so much to C. Ph. E. Bach, represented "characters" in his symphonies—but Haydn was too musical and tactful to reveal his secret intentions. Beethoven also, in the finale of his string quartet Op. 18, No. 6, tried to represent the changing moods of a person afflicted with melancholia ("La Malinconia"): it was not one of his most inspired inventions.

# VIII

## The Elizabethan Madrigal and Musica Transalpina

To ATTEMPT an investigation of the textual relationships between the Elizabethan and the Italian madrigal is to follow a path that has long been trodden by Dr. Edmund H. Fellowes. It is to him that I dedicate this little study, which would have been impossible without his preliminary work, without his edition of *The English Madrigal School* and without the publication of his *English Madrigal Verse, 1588–1632* (1920 and 1929). My aim is nothing more than to furnish a few facts supplementary to his conclusions. My justification is, perhaps, that I have possibly been occupied longer than anyone else with the Italian madrigal in all its forms and all its elements, both cultural and poetical.

The result of my observations will not by any means be a notion of the English madrigal as being more thoroughly indebted to its southern model than has been recognized so

far. That would be true only in a quite superficial sense. On the contrary: the inherent independence of the Elizabethan madrigalists, and particularly of the greatest among them, William Byrd, will show itself all the more plainly, even if it should be found—as indeed it will—that several of his texts are based on Italian words.

Byrd's first publication, which includes "secular" music, the *Psalmes, Sonets, & songs of sadnes and pietie*, appeared in 1588, a few months before Yonge's *Musica Transalpina*. It contains a piece (No. XXIV) set to Italian words, the stanza "La verginella è simile alla rosa," to which Yonge added the next stanza in Byrd's composition (though only in the English translation, not in the Italian original) and conspicuously mentioned it even on the title-page. The two stanzas are from Ariosto's *Orlando furioso* (I, 42 and 43). What of them? Byrd is not the first or only composer to have set these two *ottave rime* to music; rather is he one of the last. They were composed dozens of times by Italian and Italianate musicians, often together with the stanza next following (I, 44), always as festival music for a betrothal, very much as Ariosto's description of the fair Alcina's charms (*Orlando furioso*, VII, 11–15) was always used as table-music during a wedding. Byrd's composition too presumably served for such an occasion, perhaps in the household of Lord Talbot, to whom Yonge dedicated his collection.

These stanzas from Ariosto have, however, a specially musical significance. The people and its improvisers had their own locally differentiated tunes for *Orlando furioso*, as well as later on for Torquato Tasso's *Gerusalemme liberata*, pairs of melodic lines which, continually repeated and varied a hundredfold, served for the performance of *ottave rime*. Fragments of these tunes or allusions to them may be found in many compositions for several voices of *ottave rime* from these two epics, not excluding Byrd. Travelers—and Byrd's employer may have been such a traveler—must have brought home tunes of that kind, much like Montaigne, who is known to have become acquainted with the Tuscan version of such melodies in the neighborhood of Empoli.

However, we shall have to confine ourselves to textual and literary questions. If there are relationships between the *forms* of English and Italian poetry, they must certainly apply to the sonnet, little as the English sonnet may resemble its Petrarchan model. Thus I suspect Byrd's "Ambitious Love" (1588, No. XVIII) of Italian descent, as also the lament within a narrative framework, "As I beheld I saw a herdman wild" (No. XX), which is a so-called "pre-existing cantata." More obvious still are the relationships as seen in the *Songs of sundrie natures* of 1589. The sonnet No. XVII–XVIII

> Wounded I am, and dare not seek relief
>> For this new stroke, unseen but not unfelt;
>> No blood nor bruise is witness of my grief,
>> But sighs and tears wherewith I mourn and melt.
> If I complain, my witness is suspect;
>> If I contain, with cares I am undone;
>> Sit still and die, tell truth and be reject;
>> O hateful choice, that sorrow cannot shun.
> Yet of us twain, whose loss shall be the less?
>> Mine of my life, or you of your good name?
>> Light is my death, regarding my distress,
>> But your offence cries out to your defame.
> A virgin fair hath slain for lack of grace
> The man that made an idol of her face.

may be referred back to the words of one of Palestrina's most famous madrigals (*Works*, ed. by Haberl, Vol. XXVIII, p. 179), first published in 1561:

> Io son ferito, ahì lasso, e chi mi diede
>> Accusar pur vorrei, ma non ho prova,
>> E senz' indizio al mal non si da fede:
>> Ne getta sangue la mia piaga nuova.
>> Io spasm' e moro; il colpo non si vede,
>> La mia nemica armata si ritrova.
>> Che fia tornar a lei crudel partito,
>> Che sol m'abbia a sanar chi m'ha ferito.

An *ottava* has become a sonnet, and the imitator departed more and more from his model; yet his dependence is nevertheless plain to the eye.

A similar resemblance occurs between Byrd's (No. XXXVI–XXXVII):

> Of gold all burnished and brighter than sunbeams,
>> Were those curled locks upon her noble head . . .

and one of Petrarch's most famous sonnets:

>> Erano i capei d'oro all' aure sparse . . .
>> Che 'n mille dolci nodi gli avvolgea; . . .

which must have been composed a dozen times before Byrd—by G. Guami, G. M. Nanino, Feliciani, Sabino, Luyton, Vinci, Mel, Vecoli and others. It is a free imitation, metrically so free that Dr. Fellowes was forced to try to give it a more correct form. One is at first inclined to think that Byrd must originally have set Petrarch's text and only fitted the English words to the music later; but this is not the case, and the ill-fitting version remains as inexplicable as ever.

Byrd's last semi-secular publication, the *Psalmes, Songs, and*

*Sonnets: some solemne, others joyfull* of 1611, is separated
from the two earlier ones by more than a couple of decades,
and "solemn" words predominate in that valedictory work.
But "This sweet and merry month of May" (No. IX), twice
"composed after the Italian veine" by Byrd, also appears to
go back to the words of a "transalpine" *canzonetta* verse.
That is quite certain in the case of Geoffrey Witney's

> In crystal towers and turrets richly set
>> With glittering gems that shine against the sun,
> In regal rooms of jasper and of jet
>> Content of mind not always likes to woon.
> But often times it pleaseth her to stay
> In simple cotes enclosed with walls of clay.

This is an imitation of one of those stanzas, full of fancy and
worldly wisdom, with which Ariosto loves to open his songs:

> Spesso in poveri alberghi e in picciol tetti,
>> Ne le calamitadi e nei disagi,
>> Meglio s'aggiungon d'amicizia i petti,
>> Che fra ricchezze invidiose et agi
>> De le piene d'insidia e di sospetti
>> Corti regali e splendidi palagi,
> Ove la caritade è in tutto estinta,
>> Ne si vede amicizia, se non finta.
>
> (*Orlando furioso*, XLIV, 1)

It was often composed, generally as a dedicatory piece; most
whimsically by Lassus, who apostrophized the wealthy Fugger
family of Augsburg with this stanza. In Byrd's edition another text (No. II), "Of flattering speech with sugared words
beware," had precisely the same form and the same character
of worldly wisdom. It is an imitation of another stanza by
Ariosto (*Orlando*, VIII, 1):

O quante son incantatrici, oh quanti
Incantator tra noi . . .

and may likewise be due to Geoffrey Witney. A third text
(No. V), "Who looks may leap and save his shins from
knocks," has a similar construction and character; but there
no model is to be found in Ariosto.

On passing from Byrd to Thomas Morley, the enthusiastic
apostle of the *canzonetta* and the *balletto*, we may from the
first expect a closer connection with Italian models, even in
textual matters. And, sure enough, it is so, even though more
or less literal translations of Italian words occur rarely in his
case. Sometimes only the subject has been taken over, as in the
*Canzonets or Little Short Songs to Three Voyces* of 1593,
No. XI, "O fly not! O take some pity! I faint, O stay her,"
which goes back to a sonnet by Benedetto Varchi (frequently
composed, *e.g.* by Regolo Vecoli, 1577), "Filli, deh non fuggir! deh, Filli, aspetta!" In Varchi the poem ends as a little
cantata-like narrative; with Morley it is a pure monologue. A
closer relationship is found in No. XVI:

Do you not know how Love first lost his seeing?
　　Because with me once gazing
On those fair eyes, where all powers have their being,
　　She with her beauty blazing,
Which death might have revived,
Him of his sight, and me of heart deprived . . .

which resembles a *sestina* by Valerio Marcellini often set to
music (by Marenzio, among others, in 1584):

Sapete amanti perche ignudo sia,
Perche fanciullo, e perche cieco Amore?
Perche mentre l'angelica armonia

> Della mia bella Donna intento udia,
> Per gran dolcezza uscito di se fuore
> Perdè la veste, il senno, gl'occh' e 'l core.

It is true, that both versions go back to Propertius, so that there was not necessarily any immediate connection.

Again, in Morley's *Madrigalls to Foure Voyces . . . the First Booke* of 1594 the spirit of the words is Italian in the majority of the numbers, although a direct affinity may be conclusively proved in only a single case. Dr. Fellowes had already pointed out the source of No. IV:

> Since my tears and lamenting,
> False love, breed thy contenting,
> Still thus to weep for ever
> These fountains shall persever,
> Till my heart grief brim-filled
> Out alas, be destilled.

> Poi ch'il mio largo pianto,
> Amor, ti piace tanto,
> Asciutti mai quest' occhi non vedrai,
> Fin che non mandi fuore
> Ohimè, per gli occhi il cuore.

That is a madrigal text—by a poet unknown to me—which, thanks to its brevity and its epigrammatic point, was probably composed dozens of times in the course of the century, for the last time (in 1619) by the Sicilian Antonio il Verso, it would seem. To my mind, however, it was the setting by Lassus (first printed in 1583) which Morley took for his immediate model, a piece the existence of which, curiously enough, Dr. Fellowes denies.

In the other numbers of this book of Morley's the subjects at least are thoroughly Italian. No. VII, "In dew of roses sleeping," is particularly characteristic of those love plaints in pastoral surroundings of which hundreds of specimens may be found in Guarini and his followers. In No. IX–X:

> Now is the gentle season freshly flowering,
>  To sing and play and dance, while May endureth,
>  And woo and wed, that sweet delight procureth.
> The fields abroad with spangled flowers are gilded,
>  The meads are mantled, and closes,
>  In may each bush arrayed and sweet wild roses.
>  The nightingale her bower hath gaily builded,
> And full of kindly lust and love's inspiring,
> "I love, I love," she sings, her mate desiring. . . .

it is difficult not to think of two of the "Maggi" by Giovan Battista Strozzi (1504–1571), published by his sons Lorenzo and Filippo in 1593, the year before that of Morley's book:

> Ecco Maggio seren, chi l'ha vestito
>  Di sì bel verde, e giallo?
>  Ninfe, e Pastori, al ballo;
>  Al ballo Ninfe, e Dij per ogni lito;
>  Ecco Maggio fiorito:
>  Lice al ballo, e tu Clori,
>  Grazie al ballo, al ball' Aure, al ballo Amori.

> Ecco Maggio, inchinatevi Arboscelli
>  Di fior carchi, e di fronde;
>  Ecco Maggio aure, ombre, onde
>  Scherzate; fugge, riede, e scherza anch' elli:
>  Ecco Maggio, oh bel dì, cantate augelli;
>  E voi tacete o venti,
>  Agli amorosi accenti rispondete
>  Deh piagge, e valli più che mai pur liete.

The somewhat lascivious dialogue, No. XIV, "Beside a fountain of sweet briar and roses," is a free variant of Guarini's "Tirsi morir volea"; and No. XVIII, "Ho! who comes here along with bagpiping and drumming?" is a *caccia*, the suggestion for which was given by Marenzio in his composition of a *caccia* by Franco Sacchetti. It is worthy of notice that this *caccia* by the old Florentine novelist and *ballata* poet ("Passando con pensier") was composed by an Englishman as well as by Marenzio: Peter Philips, 1598. But Morley—for he was presumably his own poet—wholly anglicized the subject by transforming its pastoral character into blunt rusticity.

For the majority of Morley's canzonets the Italian model is textually quite easy to recognize. Dr. Fellowes has proved this in the case of seven numbers of the two-part songs (1595) by reference to the *Canzonette* by Felice Anerio (1586) and in that of ten of the five-part *Ballets* (1595) to the *Balletti* by G. G. Gastoldi.

Rather looser in that respect is No. XXI, the dialogue

> AMYNTAS: Phyllis, I fain would die now.
> PHYLLIS: O to die what should move thee? . . .

Yet the relationship is unmistakable: it points to the "Dialogo" in Orazio Vecchi's *Secondo libro delle Canzonette* (1580), No. 19:

> Lucilla io vò morire.
> "Deh non morir cor mio!"
> Perchè viver debb' io?
> "Per aspettar il ben che ha da venire."
> Ah misero mio core!
> Ha certo il duol, dubbia la gioia Amore.

But Morley made of Vecchi's modest four-part *canzonetta* a spacious, seven-part *scena* for double choir and for that purpose destroyed the strophic form of his model. However, an observation such as this belongs rather to the difficult subject of the *musical* relationships between Elizabethan and Italian art—a theme that is not to be approached here.

As regards the *Madrigals to Fiue Voyces* arranged by Morley in 1598, the very first piece, "Such pleasant boughs the world yet never vewed," is nothing else than the second stanza from Petrarch's *sestina*, "Alla dolce ombra de le belle frondi," which Alfonso Ferrabosco had set at the head of his *Secondo Libro de Madrigali* in 1587. The Italian original begins: "Non vide il mondo sì leggiadri rami." The translation is horrible and bristles with false accentuation.

It was to be expected that some immediate textual affinities would be found in John Farmer's madrigals (1599), since he was a confessed admirer of the Italians, or at least an advocate of the most intimate fusion of words and music: "a virtue so singular to the Italians, as under that ensign only they hazard their honour." To start with, No. IV–V:

Lady, my flame still burning and my consuming anguish
  Doth grow so great that life I feel to languish.
O let your heart be moved
  To end your grief and mine, so long time proved;
  And quench the heat that my chief part so fireth,
  Yielding the fruit that faithful love requireth.

Sweet lord, your flame still burning and your continual anguish
  Cannot be more than mine in which I languish.
  Nor more your heart is moved
  To end my grief and yours, so long time proved;
But if I yield, and so your flame decreaseth,
I lose my love, and so our love then ceaseth.

is nothing else than a fairly literal translation of the frequently composed *proposta* and *risposta*, a remnant of the old "*jeu-*

parti" (*e.g.* by the Italianized Greek Francesco Londarit, Venice, 1566; by Filippo di Monte, 1567; by G. G. Gastoldi, 1588):

"Donna, l'ardente fiamma,
    E la pena e 'l tormento
    Crescie in me tanto che morir mi sento.
  Deh vengavi desire
    Di por un giorno fin' al mio martire,
    E di smorzar questo mio grave ardore,
    Dandomi il frutto che ricerca amore."

"Signor, la vostra fiamma,
    E la pena e 'l tormento
    Non è punto maggior dì quel ch' io sento.
  Ne più grand' il desire
    Di terminar il vostro è mio martire.
    Ma s'egli avvien ch' io smorzo il nostro ardore,
    Io mi privo d'amant' e voi d'amore."

How characteristic the small discrepancies are, though! The Italian signora is courteous and a psychologist, and talks as though she had read Stendhal in advance; the English lady is seriously in love and mindful of the worst consequences.

Dr. Fellowes had already observed that the same words were set also by the younger Ferrabosco in 1587 and that it was taken up, translated, into the second set of *Musica Transalpina*.

In the case of Wilbye's *First Set of English Madrigals*, too, Dr. Fellowes has drawn attention to the Italian models for some of the texts, as for example to Livio Celiano's "Quand' io miro le rose" (Wilbye's No. X, "Lady, when I behold the roses sprouting"). He has also shown that No. XI, "Thus saith

my Cloris bright," goes back to "Dice la mia bellissima Licori";
No. XIX, "Alas, what a wretched life is this," to "Ahì dispietata morte"; and No. XX, "Unkind, O stay thy flying," to
"Crudel perchè mi fuggi." It need only be added that "Dice
la mia bellissima Licori" is one of Guarini's most famous madrigal texts and "Ahì dispietata morte" the stanza of one of the
most celebrated *ballate* by Petrarch, *i.e.* the one beginning:

> Amor, quando fioria
>   Mia spene, e 'l guiderdon d'ogni mia fede,
>   Tolta m'è quella ond' attendea mercede.
> Ahì, dispietata morte, ahì crudel vita! &c.

Wilbye, of course, took the words from Watson's collection
of 1590, where it is to be found as the translation of a madrigal
by Marenzio, for it is here alone that the text occurs in this
mutilated form.

No. XXI in Wilbye's Book I opens thus:

> I sung sometimes my thoughts and fancy's pleasure
> Where then I list or time served best and leisure; . . .

an opening that is nothing else than the reminiscence of a
sonnet by Pietro Bembo which had often been set to music
(*e.g.* by Filippo di Monte *Secondo libro a 6*):

> Cantai un tempo, e se fu dolce il canto,
> Questo mi tacerò, ch' altri il sentiva . . .

It is true that the continuation no longer tallies: Bembo remains in the vein of Petrarchan imitation, while Wilbye's poet
points the words anecdotally and dramatically. But the practice of borrowing the opening of a madrigal poem from
some famous model and then continuing independently is
thoroughly "Italian."

A few more of the texts in this first book of Wilbye's bear the hallmark of an Italian origin, though I am unable to cite their sources, such as No. IV, "Weep, O mine eyes," or No. XXVI–XXVII, the sonnet "Of joys and pleasing pains." On the other hand No. XXIX:

> Thou art but young, thou say'st,
>     And Love's delight thou weigh'st not.
> O take time while thou may'st,
> Lest when thou would'st, thou may'st not.
>
> If Love shall then assail thee,
>     A double double anguish will torment thee;
> And thou wilt wish—but wishes all will fail thee—
> O me, that I were young again! and so repent thee.

is clearly enough related to Torquato Tasso's

> La bella pargoletta
>     Ch' ancor non sente amore,
>     Neppur not' ha per fama il suo valore,
>     Col bel guardo saetta,
>     Et col soave riso
>     Ne s'accorge che l'arme ha nel bel viso.
> Qual colp' ha nel morire
>     Della misera gente
>     Se non sa di ferire?
>     O bellezza omicida ed innocente!
>     Tempo è ch' Amor ti mostri
>     Homai nelle tue piaghe i dolor nostri.

The connection is unmistakable, although this is certainly no literal translation and something very personal, something very aggressive has been made of Tasso's epigrammatic pointedness.

In Wilbye's *Second Set* (1609) we meet, in No. IV, with

one of the many imitations of the most celebrated fashionable poem of the time, Guarini's *Pastor fido*, printed in 1590 but current among musicians in manuscript copies before that date. The only difference is that the purveyor of Wilbye's words reverses the subject (his lady takes pleasure in the shepherd's plaints, whereas Guarini's is offended by them) and avoids the verbal wealth of the original. Let the reader make his own comparison:

> Ah, cruel Amaryllis, since thou tak'st delight
> > To hear the accents of a doleful ditty,
> > To triumph still without remorse or pity,
> I loathe this life; Death must my sorrows right.
> And, lest vain Hope my miseries renew,
> > Come quickly, Death,
> > Reave me of breath.
> Ah cruel Amaryllis, adieu, adieu.

> Cruda Amarilli, che col nome ancora
> > D'amar, ahi lasso! amaramente insegni
> Poiche col dir t'offendo,
> I' mi morrò tacendo . . .
> E se fia muta ogni altra cosa, alfine
> Parlerà il mio morire,
> E ti dirà la morte il mio morire. ('Pastor fido' 1, 2.)

The effect, it will be seen, is the same, in spite of the inversion. The affinity of No. X in this book, "Happy streams, whose trembling fall," to Luca Marenzio's "Questi vaghi concenti" (*Libro settimo a 5*, 1595) has already been pointed out by H. Heurich (*John Wilbye in seinen Madrigalen*, Augsburg, 1932, p. 59). The subject is the same, but freely treated: the elegiac and epigrammatic manner of the Italian model is turned into that of a simple and natural lover's complaint.

Knowledge of Italian originals entitles us to claim that Nos. XXII and XXV in Michael Cavendish's *Ayres and Madrigalles* of 1598, "Zephyrus brings the time" and "To former joy now turns," belong together, for they are nothing else than a translation of a sonnet by Petrarch that was set to music by, among others, Filippo di Monte (1554), Pietro Taglia (1555), Horatio Faa (1569), G. Conversi (1584), Marenzio (1585), Alfonso Ferrabosco (1587) and Monteverdi (1614). Conversi's piece is to be found in *Musica Transalpina* and Ferrabosco's in Yonge's collection of 1597, from which Cavendish took the first eight lines. Here are the words for comparison:

Zephyrus brings the time that sweetly scenteth
    With flowers and herbs, and winter's frosts exileth;
    Progne now chirpeth and Philomel lamenteth,
    Flora the garlands white and red compileth.
Fields do rejoice, the frowning sky relenteth;
    Jove, to behold his dearest daughter, smileth.
    The air, the water, the earth to joy consenteth,
    Each creature now to love him reconcileth.
To former joy now turns the grove, the fountain,
    The jolly fresh April now loden with flowers;
    The seas are calm, hoar-frost falls from the mountain,
    Shepherds and nymphs walk to their wanton bowers.
But I, all night in tears my pillow steeping,
Soon as the sun appears renew my weeping.

Zefiro torna, e 'l bel tempo rimena,
    E i fiori, e l'erbe, sua dolce famiglia;
    E garrir Progne, e pianger Filomena,
    E Primavera candida e vermiglia.
Ridono i prati, e 'l ciel si rasserena;
    Giove s'allegra di mirar sua figlia;
    L'aria e l'acqua e la terra è d'amor piena;
    Ogni animal d'amor si riconsiglia.

Ma per me, lasso! tornano i più gravi
  Sospiri che del cor profondo tragge
  Quella ch'al ciel se ne portò le chiavi;
E cantar augelletti, e fiorir piagge,
  E 'n belle donne oneste atti soavi,
  Sono un deserto, e fere aspre e selvagge.

In the Italian original the contrast between the octave and the sestet is sharply accentuated, and that is the reason why this sonnet tempted musicians to composition. Monteverdi especially cannot do enough to underline this contrast. In the translation, however, it becomes blurred. All the same, the exactitude of the translation so far as the octave goes proves how well Nicholas Yonge understood the character of the Italian madrigal, for there is an intimate relationship between words and music and a striking perception of each detail.

Thus, through Yonge and Watson, some of the most famous of Italy's lyrics penetrated into English literature:

### Musica Transalpina, Part I.

Sonnets and *ballate* by Petrarch:
  "In qual parte dal ciel,"
  "Amor quando fioriva"
*Ottave rime* by Ariosto:
  "Questo ch' indizio fan"
  "Chi salirà per me"
Madrigals:
  Pietro Bembo's "Gioia m'abbonda al cor"
  Torquato Tasso's "Già fù mia dolce speme"
  Guarini's "Tirsi morir volea"
Ippolito Capilupi's famous sonnet:
  *Vestiva i colli.*

### Part II

Guidiccioni's "Il bianco e dolce cigno"

Tansillo's "Dolorosi martir"
Torquato Tasso's "Bruna sei tu"
Guarini's "Dice la mia bellissima Licori"

Thanks to Watson's enthusiasm for Marenzio the list grows even longer and richer:

PETRARCH: "Ahì dispietata morte"
"Non vide mai"
SANNAZARO: "I lieti amanti"
"Madonna sua mercè"
"Venuta era Madonna"
ARIOSTO: "Non rumor di tamburi"
BERNARDO TASSO: "Ohimè, dov' è 'l mio ben"
G. B. STROZZI: "Questa ordì il laccio"
TORQUATO TASSO: "Di nettare amoroso"
"Vezzosi augelli"

The translation of Bernardo Tasso's stanza was afterwards, as Dr. Fellowes had already observed, used by Thomas Bateson as text for a madrigal of his own (I, No. XVIII).

The *Madrigals to Five Voyces, Celected out of the best approved Italian Authors* (1598) yields less material for the present subject, owing to the preference shown for the species of the *canzonetta* by its editor, Thomas Morley. For a whole series of pieces in this collection, by Giovanni Ferretti, Ruggiero Giovanelli and Orazio Vecchi, consists, not of madrigals at all, but of vocal music of that lighter and shorter kind. And the degrees of accuracy in the translations are very unequal. Only in one instance did the translator take a fair amount of care: in the piece Morley borrowed from Marenzio (*Terzo libro*, No. 2):

Caro dolce mio ben chi mi vi toglie!
   Come potrà giammai questo mio core
   Viver senza di voi?
   Haime che l'aspre doglie
   E 'l mio acerbo dolore
   Mi fa miser e puoi
   Versar da gli occhi lassi
   Lagrime ch'a pietà movono i sassi.

O my loving sweet hart, leave of thy madnesse,
   How can my wounded hart to live be able,
   That without your fervent love,
   Alas, what griefe and sadnesse,
   In my torments doe make mee miserable,
   Which from mine eies doe wring such tears and grones,
   That unto pittie move the hard rocks and stones.

On the other hand, No. XII in this collection is one of the most curious, because one of the freest, adaptations of an Italian original—by Alessandro Orologio—that could possibly be imagined. The words are:

Soden passions, with strange and rare tormenting,
   Increaseth griefe, and more, it breeds my sorrow,
   The cause increast, doth bleare mine eyes with weeping.
   And daunts my thoughts from even untill the morrow,
   In this unrestful paine long must I languish,
   Till death draw neere to rid my hart from anguish.

In Orologio (*Primo libro a 5*, 1586, No. IV) this is not an independent piece at all, but the second part of a sonnet:

Deh perche non poss' io di quel bel viso,
   Di quelle pure guancie, ed amorose
   Coglier' i gigli, e le purpuree rose,
   Con lo spirto da me tutto diviso?

Venga pur Ganimede, Ati, e Narciso,
  Che qui dove 'l suo seggio Amor ripose,
  Scorgerà il vel delle bellezze ascose,
  E quant' ha in se di vago il paradiso.
Ma se pietà del grave incendio mio
  Strignerà mai quel delicato petto,
  Si che di par si mostri, e bello, e poi
Non mi curo di fiamm' esser oggetto,
  Ne continuo versar da gli occhi un rio,
  Si degna è la cagion, dolce l'effetto.

As will be seen, the text fitted by Morley not only has nothing to do with the original: it even flagrantly contradicts it. It is related rather to an *ottava rima* by Tansillo, to be found in Yonge's *Musica Transalpina* with music by Marenzio (No. IX): "Dolorous morneful cares, ruthless tormenting." For all that, Morley's collection does contain one piece of great Italian poetry in Peter Philips's setting of Petrarch's sonnet, *Quel rosignuol che sì soave piagne*. The translation follows the original word for word:

The Nightingale that sweetly doth complayne
  His yong once lost, or for his loving mate,
  To fill the heavens and fields himself doth frame
  With sweet and dolfull tunes, to shew his state:
So all the night, to doe I am full fayne,
  Remembring my hard hap, and cruell payne,
  For I alone, am cause of all my payne,
  That Gods might dye, I learned to know to late.
O false deceit, who can himself assure,
  Those two faire lights aye clearer than the Sun,
  Who ever thought to see made so obscuer,
Well now I see, fortune doth mee procure
  To learne by proofe in this case that I runne,
  That nothing long doth please, ne can indure.

Philips, with this piece, entered into competition with no lesser masters than Nasco, Monte, Donato, Lassus and Wert, and he came out of it very honorably in the spirit of Maren-zio. Nor does it seem to me as though he had set the original Italian words, which in some parts could not be fitted to the music without difficulty, but that he dealt direct with the English translation.

In order to offer a closer survey of the relationships of each piece with the Italian originals (in so far as I am able to determine them), I append a list. The originals are easily traceable in Vogel's *Bibliothek* according to the dates. Nos. 17 and 18 are somewhat uncertain, although highly probable; it would seem that the former, given without a composer's name by Morley, is likewise by Ferrabosco.

1. Such pleasant boughes (Alfonso Ferrabosco) = Non vide il mondo, 1587 (Petrarch)
2. Sweetly pleasing (Battista Mosto)
3. I thinck that if the hills (Ferrabosco) = Sì ch' io mi crede, 1587 (Petrarch)
4. Come lovers foorth (Giovanni Ferretti)
5. Loe Ladies were my love (Giovanelli)
6. As I walked (Giovanelli)
7. Delay breeds daunger (Giovanelli)
8. My Ladie still abhors me (Ferretti)
9. Do not tremble (Orazio Vecchi) = Tremolavan le fronde, 1589

10. Harke and give eare (Giulio Belli) = Udite amanti, 1592

11. Life tell mee (Orazio Vecchi) = Deh dimmi vita mia, 1589

12. Soden passions (Alessandro Orologio) = Ma se pietà, 1586

13. If silent (Ferrabosco) = Se taccio, il duol, 1587 (T. Tasso)

14. O my loving sweet hart (Marenzio) = Caro dolce mio ben, 1582

15. I languish to complaine mee (Ferrabosco) = Vorrei lagnarmi appieno, 1587 (T. Tasso)

16. Loe how my colour rangeth (Ippolito Sabino) = Ecco i' mi discoloro, 1589

17. Thirsis on his faire Phillis (? Ferrabosco) = Godea Tirsi, ? 1587

18. For verie griefe I dye (Giovanelli) = Morirò di dolor, ? 1593

19. The Nightingale (Peter Philips) = Quel rossignuol (Petrarch)

20. O false deceit (2nd part) (Peter Philips) = O che lieve è ingannar (Petrarch)

21. As Mopsus went (Stefano Venturi)

22. Flora faire Nimphe (Ferretti)

23. My sweet Layis (Giovanni di Macque)

24. Say sweet Phillis (Ferrabosco)

This study has confined itself mainly to an attempt at investigating the direct relations of Elizabethan madrigal texts to Italian models. Examples could no doubt be multiplied by an examination based on a more intimate knowledge of Italian literature than I happen to possess.

The dependence of the Elizabethan texts appears to be even greater if one considers the indirect influences, the similarities and the resemblances of subjects found in the common literary bases: the poetry of antiquity and the fashionable literary complaint of the time—the pastoral. Neither Tasso's nor Shakespeare's compatriots could in the long run manage without Venus and Cupid, Thyrsis and Mopsa, or Mirtillo and Amarillis.

Yet—and this brings us back to the beginning of this essay —the Elizabethan madrigal composers were no mere imitators, even when they set to music naked and unashamed translations. They are national musicians; with the possible exception of Morley as a composer of balletts, they are by no means wholly Italianized, in the sense that in the eighteenth century Handel and Hasse and Mysliweček were, for instance. They only took up into their style what suited them. Quite apart from Byrd, who had an ideal of secular music entirely different from the Italian in his mind and in his blood—a more "constructive" one, to put it briefly, and one less excited and less concerned with intimate connections between words and music—Wilbye and Weelkes and Farmer too borrowed only a few traits from their influential models: grace, melancholy, pastoral mirth. There is nothing in their work of Marenzio's subtle chiaroscuro, nothing of his daring counterpoint and harmony, nothing of his artistic playfulness and extravagance that could be understood only in the "academies" of Roman, Mantuan or Ferrarese aristocratic circles. It is characteristic that the English madrigal has remained without those large, cyclic compositions of whole *canzoni* and *sestine*, in which the Italian madrigal art culminates; characteristic, too, that Gesualdo, a personality of European interest after the sensational affair of his wife-murder, did not, in my opinion, make the least impression on English musicians with his art after 1594. They are far too healthy for that, even when they are very sensitive. Their art is nearer to nature, even when they toy with pastoral motives. They do not think only of their aristocratic patrons, and therefore do not cultivate the exclusiveness of so many Italian exemplars. They renounce all species with a "literary" flavoring, such as that type of *canzonetta* which from the beginning in Italy, and still at the end of the century, lived on its relationship with the madrigal, which, that is to say, partook of parody. Such a thing was incomprehensible in England, where there was no *canzon villanesca alla napoletana*, no *greghesca*, no *giustiniana*, no *vocale moresca*. Even the pastoral does not mean in England what it means in Italy. It is not a poetic category or formula. Shakespeare was doubtless no admirer of *Il pastor fido* and its classic-pastoral masquerade. He did write the enchanting dramatic arabesque of *As You Like It;* but human beings wear shepherd's dress, not costumed and perfumed puppets. Unfortunately there was no Shakespeare among the purveyors of words for the Elizabethan madrigal; yet in their poems there lives something, all the same, of that unfettered relationship to Italian models which we admire in Shakespeare's comedy.

# IX

# Abbot Angelo Grillo's Letters as Source Material for Music History

ADRE Abbate Don Angelo Grillo's letters, excerpts from several of which are presented in this article, have up to now been neglected by musicologists. Except for Winterfeld,[1] to my knowledge, only Ambros has ever mentioned them, although, to be sure, he does quote a section from one of the most important of them. This neglect is somewhat surprising. Grillo's name appears frequently in sixteenth century sacred and secular madrigal publications, and scholars must have been aware of his letters, since they were published in several editions and so have always been readily accessible. The letters contain, among other things, very valuable information about Grillo's relationship as a poet with some of the greatest musicians of a period of music history which is of the highest importance, and in which the question of the

[1] *Musikgeschichte*, IV, 174.

relationship of music and poetry was a cardinal point of interest.

Angelo Grillo, born about 1550, was a descendant of one of the most aristocratic families in Genoa. His father, Nicolo, was a gentleman from Montescagioso in the Kingdom of Naples; his mother was a Spinola. In 1572 he took orders as a Benedictine monk at Montecassino; he held various positions in his order, but steadfastly refused whenever higher honors of the Church were offered him. He traveled a great deal throughout all Italy in the service of his order, and we know that he spent some time before 1600 in San Giuliano at Canoa and at San Benedetto in Mantua. At the turn of the century he was abbot of the monastery of San Paolo in Rome; then for a time he remained on the lonely heights of Subiaco. About 1607 he was chosen to head the chapter of the monastery of Sancta Maria di Praglia su'l Padovano, after which he was appointed Superior of San Benedetto di Mantova and President General of the Congregatione Cassinense. About 1613 he withdrew into the modest monastery of San Nicolo del Lido "at the last dike and on the outermost rim of Venice." What happened to him after that we do not know from his own letters; according to another source [1] he died while he was Superior of the Abbey of San Giovanni di Parma, in September, 1629.

As a poet, Grillo won the highest praise from his contemporaries. His reputation was based especially on his *Pietosi affetti*, which was very well suited to the taste of the times. His writing brought him into contact with the aristocratic centers of poetry, the academies—he was, for instance, a member of the *Addormentati* in Genoa and the *Giustiniani*

[1] Belloni, *Il Seicento*, pp. 62, 475.

in Padua, and director of the *Umoristi* in Rome—and with most of the other poets of his time, among them Guarini, Chiabrera, and Marino. He is best known to us, however, as a loyal and solicitous friend of Torquato Tasso, whom he helped as much as possible in spite of Tasso's many capricious moods.[1] As far as Grillo's poetry is concerned, it developed along the path from Tasso to Marino, and to us it seems more worthwhile the farther it moves away from *Secentism.*

To the musician, the figure of Grillo is attractive because of the true love which he held for music and for its disciples; to his particular glory it must be said that Grillo devoted his enthusiasm to musical progress and its champions. An extraordinarily large proportion of his poetry is dedicated to music and musicians. He greatly enjoyed writing madrigals to be set to music, and he was among the first group of poets of the new *canzonetta*—which he, quite naturally, "spiritualized." One poem of his is dedicated "*al Sig. Gian Battista della Gostena, musico Eccellentissimo, e maestro di Cappella del Domo di Genova; havendo egli composto alcuni bellissimi libri di canto.*" Another is inscribed "*loda le corde del Sig. Marco Conradi, Musico, e suonatore eccellentissimo di varij instrumenti; ma mirabile nel liuto.*" A madrigal is dedicated to Laura Peperara, "*cantatrice, e sonatrice eccellentissima*"; she was one of the three famous ladies of the court of Ferrara, to whom reference is made in one of the letters to be discussed below. A sonnet (1589) is inscribed to Padre D. Hippolito Veneroso, "*ottimo Musico*"; in the *Rime* of 1599 there is a sonnet in praise of a "*libro d'intavolatura del Signor Tomaso,*" another to "*D. Adriano Datti musico,*" still another in praise of "*sonar di liuto del Sig. Cesare de Franchi,*" and so on.

[1] A. Solerti, *Vita di Torquato Tasso,* I, 385 ff. Turin, 1895.

The musicians rewarded Grillo's sympathy by buying his poems and setting them to music. The copy of Grillo's *Rime* of 1599 owned by the Münchener Staatsbibliothek was first owned by Gregor Aichinger; his bookplate is still pasted inside the book, which shows traces of industrious reading.

A great many musicians set to music the verse of the Benedictine monk. In Leone Leoni's book of five-part sacred madrigals, 1596, there is a ten line canzon written on a poem of Grillo's; Angelo Borsaro, in 1597, and Marc' Antonio Tornioli, in 1607, each filled a whole book of canzonettas with his verses. In one collection, dated 1598, there are twenty-one compositions based on verses from the *Pietosi affetti;* in another, dated 1604, there are twenty-three. In 1600 Giovanni Maria Nanino composed music to some of Grillo's secular madrigals, and in 1603 Cornelius Verdonck did the same. Among monodic compositions based on texts written by Grillo are those in the extensive collection of 1613 called *Canoro pianto di Maria Vergine.* The motets and madrigals of Serafino Patta (1614), and some compositions of Enrico Radesca di Foggia belong to this list, and Grillo's letters indicate that many other important musicians also wrote music for his poems.

Of these letters, to which we now finally turn, there are four editions, all different in size and arrangement. Two editions, published in Venice by Ciotti and edited by Ottavio Menini, are dated 1603 and 1604; the other two, dated 1612 and 1616, were published in Venice by Giunti-Ciotti, and edited by P. Petracci.

Anyone who is at all familiar with the history of epistolography knows very well that the publications of Grillo's letters, like many other sixteenth and seventeenth century collections of letters, was not due to any interest in autobiography. Nothing indicates more clearly this lack of interest in autobiography than the letter of introduction which is part of one of the oldest collections of model letters—the book of rhetoric (*literarum scholasticarum*) of the Boncompagno fiorentino (Bon Campagno da Signa) for musicians, entitled *De violatore et liratore*. The grammarian who published the models chose for himself no less a name than Bernart de Ventadorn's to sign to the letter of recommendation; however, when the letter was published, about 1215, Ventadorn had been dead for quite some time, and without doubt the letter is a fabrication from beginning to end. The character of the classical letter was described in the book as follows: "Confidential information is never included; for one writes a letter with the knowledge that it will be sent, copied, criticized, and carefully preserved by friends as a work of art. One either keeps the original draft, or has it copied before it is sent out, so that one's letters may more easily be collected and published. Thus, although the letter is addressed to a specific person, it is actually written for the literary public, for posterity, and for the people of all nations who use the ancient Latin tongue." [1]

The renaissance letter continued the classical tradition, which Bembo's authority had introduced into literature; and consequently, Grillo's letters were published deliberately. The fact that the letters are classified indicates intent; for—at least in both the later editions—they are separated into letters of condolence, consolation, recommendation, thanks, and good wishes; furthermore, very few of the letters are dated.

In this last respect, Grillo's collection differs regrettably

[1] Voigt, *Wiederbelebung*, II, p. 417. See also Burckhardt, *Culture of the Renaissance*.

from many others of the time; and any attempt to date a letter is made difficult by the fact that Grillo moved around so much. The 1604 edition of the letters separates them according to order and time ("*per ordine de' tempi*") into four groups dated 1578–1594; 1594–1598; 1598–1601; and 1601–1604, which at least places some of the letters within wide time limits. The letters cited in the following pages are all from the most complete, three-volume edition of 1616.

Two letters to Giaches de Wert in Mantua, both written in San Benedetto Mantovano, and assuredly addressed to Ferrara, ought very probably to be put first. The Choirmaster of Gonzaga had asked Grillo for madrigal texts; the poet, however, feared a comparison of his creations with Guarini's madrigals:

> I beg of you to renounce mine in favor of the madrigals of Cavaliere Guarini, so that you will have no sense of an inferior flavor, and for me there will be no reproach of boundless presumption. (I, 732)

The other letter begs indulgence of the musician:

> I have not yet finished the lines which you requested in praise of the Mesola and of the Duke of Ferrara. Please ascribe this delay wholly to the high opinion which I have of your music, for since it is divine, it cannot be brought in complete accord with earthly words. To compose verses worthy of your art is no easy matter; especially as in madrigals it is a question of conjuring up certain little spirits which are nothing else than a reflection of the soul when it is at its merriest and lightest. And I am generally a murky and muddy spring. I remain, yours most respectfully. (I, 732)

However, Grillo never seems to have written a poem in praise of the Mesola, the amusement place of Este. It is not unlikely that Wert, renouncing Grillo's muse, turned to Torquato Tasso with a plea for help, and that Tasso complied with his madrigal:

> Mesola, il Po da lati, e 'l mar a fronte.
> Ha ninfe adorne, e belle. . . .

At least Wert had Tasso's poem set to music, and published it in 1588.[1]

As Grillo grew older, he felt an increasing reluctance to employ his muse in the service of secular poetry; he refers the numerous applicants for poems to his already published works. He is much more receptive to the honors which musicians rendered his *Pietosi affetti*. From Genoa he wrote to Felice Anerio in Rome:

> In the last few months I have received three madrigals from my *Pietosi affetti* which you have honored through your music, and have made your own. Padre Don Serafino Spina, who took the trouble to send them to me, wrote me that you intend to continue so far as to make a whole madrigal book from it. Now, after thanking you for what you have already done, I feel the desire to find out what your further intentions are, so that my poetry, which is, so to speak, blessed by your highly esteemed music, may have not only a praiseworthy, but an edifying influence on the leisure hours of the lover of the noble art of music; and in the alliance of our two sister muses, the unity of our spirits may be represented in an affiliation of art and friendship. (I, 280)

In spite of this invitation, nothing seems to have come of the planned book of madrigals. Nor can I point to one madrigal which is definitely Grillo's among the extant works of Felice Anerio.

---

[1] In 1563 Wert had dedicated a madrigal to the Duke of Ferrara, but in his whole eighth madrigal book (1586), there is no composition with a dedication.

In some cases Grillo had no trouble in finding the music for his poems. The Venetian printer and publisher Giacomo Vincenti had dedicated the above-mentioned collection of 1598 to the poet and sent it to him; Grillo thanks him from Genoa in about the middle of the year with the following:

> Your words shine with good will toward me, since you have seen fit to include a part of my *Pietosi affetti* with the compositions of so many noble minds. For although the collection owes its existence to the order of the illustrious Leonardo Sanudo, it is you alone who have put it into execution. (I, 155)

The madrigal collection of 1604 was preceded by a more extensive correspondence. Grillo had long had artistic connections with one of the composers represented in the collection, Padre Don Serafino Cantone, as a letter to Cantone from San Donato proves:

> Finally one sister has awakened the other. Lately your music has stimulated my poetry to vigor and sprightliness after a long sleep of two years; even when I was still drunk with sleep, your music caused my madrigal to bubble forth in praise of Saint Hyacinth. I will endeavor to produce others, if possible, to the honor of our father, Saint Benedict, so that your harmonious spirit will have an edifying goal. (I, 698)

Later Grillo sent a letter from Prague to Cantone, who was then in Milan, which was first published in the 1612 edition of the letters:

> I send your Reverence the dedication for your sacred music which you requested of me. I have put it together very willingly, as the custom of dedicating works which fall really into the province of God and His Saints has all too often been violated by false and godless borrowing of worldly and heathenish flattery. (I, 712)

The dedication which follows in the letter, however—*"all' omnipotente Imperator della gloria, et Immortal Creatore del Cielo, et della Terra Dio Ottimo Massimo"*—shows a signal lack of taste, since in it Grillo is himself guilty of applying expressions *"di secolaresca et pagana adulatione,"* about which he had just complained, to the Highest Being. The work of Cantone for which the dedication was written was either not printed, or has not been preserved.

Padre Don Massimiano Gabbiano of Ravenna was one of the musicians included in the madrigal collection of 1598, and himself published that of 1604. Gabbione, like Grillo, was a Benedictine monk; and he asked Grillo to write texts for compositions he wished to include in the 1604 collection. In answer to this request, Grillo sent some poems from Subiaco. But shortly after sending them, his artistic conscience began to prick him for having let his madrigals go before making them perfect, and he wrote a letter to Gabbiano which makes obvious the amount of rewriting necessary for madrigal poetry—even though it was maintained that the musician himself could easily shake a madrigal text from his sleeve. The letter also indicates the respect that the poet demanded from the musician, and what a cult was made of form.

Grillo wrote chiefly in his *rime morali* much that he felt deeply and worded simply; but his *Pietosi affetti* is guilty of an abuse of the secular element by its use of the humanistic and pastoral motive of spiritual dominion, as the characteristic dedication to *"Dio Ottimo Massimo,"* quoted above, shows. This is the kind of sacred poetry which humanizes and embellishes the lofty and sublime, and thus eliminates all distances before the great and holy. In order to see God completely, therefore, it must move around Him in painful proximity. The excuse offered for this poetry was usually that it was not written in Latin, but in the vernacular, and was meant only for domestic edification.

The letter from Subiaco contains a few examples of Grillo's poetry:

. . . *male cuncta ministrat impetus.* There's no denying it: The speedy and the good do not agree quickly and well. The arrival of Don Innocentio, the receipt of the letters from your Reverence, and my answer came all at once . . . so that the little madrigal, which satisfied me at first, later, when I examined it and thought about it again, did not exactly displease me—for the theme is certainly agreeable; however, it caused two thoughts to rise in me, which seem to me very worthy of attention even in a little thing of five lines. Firstly, I wonder whether it is a good expression, when one speaks of Him on the cross, to say:

> Queste piaghe vermiglie, & questi chiodi,
> Che tieni, ò mio Giesù ne' santi nodi.

For it seems to me, that one nailed to the cross does not bear the nails, but the nails bear him. And although the expression "you bear" (*tieni*) is used here in the sense of "you have" (*hai*), that does not destroy my doubt. For "the nails bear" or "have" seems to me not to express the full meaning with the necessary strength, and thus I might alter it in the following way:

> Queste piaghe vermiglie, & questi chiodi,
> Che ti passan, Signor, frà nodi, & nodi.

The other thought is based on history and tradition and relates to the last lines:

> Ma la piaga del core
> Spira soave, et amoroso ardore.

The side wound of Christ was not in his heart, but on the right side . . . also, the opinion of the greatest scholars is that water flowed out of the wound as well as blood. Only when one interprets *piaga del cuore* as "wounded heart," *cuor piagato* —wounded by love or grief, as Christ's heart was wounded for the sins of mankind—can one allow the expression to pass as appropriate. So I would rather say:

> Ma la piaga del petto
> Spira soave, et amoroso affetto.

Therefore, if your Reverence desires to publish this madrigal under my name, I would like—if it is to be recognized as mine— to have it appear as follows:

> Son ben segni d'amore
> Quelle profonde piaghe, & que' rei chiodi,
> Che ti passan, Signor, frà nodi, & nodi,
> Ma la piaga del lato
> E nel piagato Amante Amor piagato.

This ending seems to me to have a liveliness which is fitting for a madrigal, to maintain a certain effectiveness, and to deviate a little from the ordinary. However, should the madrigal not be printed under my name, then will your Reverence please do me the favor of not making these changes: for although I am wont to have misgivings about the works of other people, I do not wish to correct them, when I might do more harm than good.

As far as my dedication-madrigal is concerned, neither *Ascendi Alto Monte,* nor *Sali sù l' Alto Monte* [1]—as I found it in my notes—has my approval. For when one sends out the spirit of harmony as the ambassador or conveyer of the work, "mount" seems to indicate a step-by-step movement. And if it is to be used metaphorically—of which there are many examples in good authors—provided that your Reverence does not

[1] The madrigal book is dedicated to Cardinal Montalto.

change too much in the music . . . and then think that the expression *ascendo* be not suitable, I should like to know that the version *Poggia sù l' Alto Monte* has been chosen. I should gain with this more universal expression a more particular one. . . . Accordingly, then, the whole madrigal will run as follows:

> Se tornar brami a' tuoi superni giri
> Musico Spirto, ed anima Canora,
> Che in queste note dolcemente spiri;
> Poggia sù l' Alto Monte,
> Dove nel sacro Ero l'ostro s'honora.
> Divoto ivi l'inchina; et dì, perdono,
> Che basso è id donator, s'humile è il dono.

(I, 491)

The first of these two madrigals is extant in the version Grillo arrived at in the course of this letter, in the 1608 edition of the *Pietosi affetti*. Gabbiani really did set both poems to music, and publish them in his collected works. Two other letters [1] of Grillo's from Subiaco deal with a third madrigal composed for Gabbiani's work:

The steel which pierced San Placido has, as I read last night of his martyrdom, also penetrated my heart. Soon afterwards from my eyes, and soon also from my pen, fell this little teardrop:

> O mio Placido santo,
> Qualhora il tuo martiro
> Odo, ò leggo, i sospiro;
> Et verso il sangue tuo per gli occhi in pianto.
> Oh, s'io l'accolgo in canto
> Già mai, com' io disio,
> Fia lingua del tuo sangue il pianto mio.

[1] Still another letter from Subiaco deals with a not otherwise mentioned madrigal that Grillo had written at Gabbiani's request: *Ecco il Madrigale, ecco la lettera, et ecco il pagamento del mio debito. . . . Hò dato nel nuovo, s'io non m'inganno; non sò, se haverò colpito nell' humore.* (I, 697, C)

This little tear belongs in my *Pietosi affetti*. . . . May your Reverence receive it as a pledge of my piety, if not as the text for a composition. . . . (I, 700)

. . . I sent your Reverence a few months ago a little madrigal about the martyrdom of San Placidus, so that you might honor it with your music, but I fear that it was lost, for you have written me nothing about it. I am sending it to you once again. Signor Lelio Bertanti [1] used to say to me that a capable musician who composed to a foolish text was like a brave knight riding a sorry jade. Though your Reverence in this case is not exactly riding Bucephalus, nonetheless I think you are not altogether badly mounted. . . . The other day the last works of Luca Marenzio of honored memory came to me by chance—madrigals which were almost all composed to poems of mine. To be sure, it was juvenile poetry set to mature music, for they were written at a time when not only the poetry but also the poet was very immature. So much the more then do I stand in debt to that immortal swan, who chose to intone his deathsong, so to speak, to the lines of a cricket [Grillo], lines which he made sweet and immortal through his melody. Such men should not die. . . . In repayment for his honoring so highly the work of an unknown person—for I never met him face to face—I have read a special Mass for him. May God receive it from me for the blessing of that harmonious soul. (I, 893)

Grillo cannot mean by *ultime fatiche* Marenzio's last printed work—his ninth book of five-voiced madrigals. For that book contains not even a single poem of Grillo's; and in the whole remaining madrigal work of Marenzio, I can find only *one* text of Grillo's, in the eighth book. Grillo must be referring to compositions in manuscript from Marenzio's papers which have since been lost. For the rest, the picture of the Bene-

---

[1] Maestro della Musica del Domo di Brescia. In his *Madrigali Spirituali a 3*, 1585, the third song is on a poem of Grillo's.

dictine abbot on the lonely heights of Sagro Speco, that magnificent setting for San Fogazzaro, praying for the soul of the great musician, is one of the most captivating and moving of all music history.

Grillo's relation to some of the most significant members of the Florentine camerata began in the sixteenth century. There are two letters which Grillo wrote between 1594 and 1598 from Genoa to Ottavio Rinuccini. In the first [1] (I, 266) he thanks Rinuccini for sending a speech on Torquato Tasso made by Lorenzo Giacomini to the Florentine Academy, which Giulio Caccini had delivered to Grillo by request of Rinuccini, together with a poem by Alessandro Rinuccini, brother of Ottavio. The second letter (I, 270), in which Grillo thanks Rinuccini for a "Libretto of Sig. Devanzati," and sends greetings to Giovanni Battista Strozzi, comes some months later. A letter written in Parma between 1598 and 1601 (I, 288) is addressed to Strozzi himself; Grillo thanks him for some poems, and remarks that in a few days he will again come through Florence. During just such a transitory stay in Florence, Grillo must have seen a rehearsal of *Euridice*, for in a letter from Subiaco undoubtedly written in the fall of 1600 at the time of the Florentine festival, he encourages Rinuccini:

Write me about your health, your work, and especially about the result of your graceful pastoral drama, which lifted us to heaven on the wings of angelic voices. I do not ask for news of the princely pageantry, of the royal plays, nor even of the king. I want only news of you yourself, and wish to see

[1] Published by Solerti, *op. cit.*, II, 413.

and hear you speak of yourself and your own affairs. Give me also news of your brother, . . . whose Latin muse and un- affected courtesy have charmed me. Greetings also . . . to Gia- como Corso, to whom I beg you to give the enclosed. (I, 128)

Trips to Florence gave Grillo an opportunity for philo- sophical talks about the art of poetry with Strozzi and Ri- nuccini, and also allowed him to make the acquaintance of Caccini, whom he had not met when he had been in Genoa, as a letter to Caccini proves (I, 360). Grillo testified to his regard for Caccini, who was the musical manager of the Florentine camerata, by having some madrigals delivered to him by the poet Lelio Paolino [Paolucci?] and sending his greetings to him and to Rinuccini (I, 375; from San Bene- detto).

A dispatch of madrigal texts accompanies another letter, an excerpt from which has been quoted by Ambros. This letter, it must be understood, was written as a piece of publicity for Caccini, the kind of thing which today appears either as a newspaper article or an advertising brochure. How much artists esteemed such public letters may be seen in the auto- biography of Vasari, in which the versatile Aretiner, full of pride, at one point refers to a letter "which is to be printed," which he had received from Annibale Caro. Caccini certainly could not complain that Grillo's letter did not find enough circulation; besides appearing in the four editions of Grillo's letters, it was included also in Bartolomeo Zucchi's much read *Idea de Segretario* (1614; II, 216), and was undoubtedly of great benefit to Caccini's reputation. It says:

My dear Giulio. I remember having read that the kings of Parthia were accustomed never to greet each other without presenting each other with gifts.[1] But, with your permission, I consider you more than a ruler of Parthians. You are a governor of hearts, which by means of your rare art you force under your gentle yoke and lead where you will. . . . Possessing as you do in addition to divine harmony, a royal and brightly shining intellect which is reflected in your countenance and your manner, I dare not appear before you without offering some of my poems to you, especially since you have often requested them of me. And the gift is the less, because to give to you is more valuable than to receive from others, as you crown one's gift with the glory of your music, and make the giver famous. I know very well how my *Pietosi affetti* earned honor in the sight of the Holy Father; for His Holiness, after having found enjoyment in fragments of my work by hearing your songs, became interested in reading it. . . . Also I know how far that successful madrigal of mine has flown and is still flying on the wings of song with which you provided it, and what sweet power it has when it is sung with the right expression [*senza fargli torto*]. I repeat, "with the right expression"; for you are the father of a new kind of music, of a singing without song, or, better, an exalted and not commonplace recitative singing which does not hamper, exhaust, and destroy the sense and the emotional content of a poem, but, rather, intensifies it, doubling its spirit and its inner force. This splendid manner of delivery is your invention; you are the rediscoverer of that antique genre which has been lost for so long in the changing customs of endless generations, buried in deep darkness for so many centuries. I was convinced of this after hearing the lovely shepherd poem of Ottavio Rinuccini performed after your style. After hearing this pastoral drama, people who

---

[1] A classic beginning, which has a counterpart in the *Poesia musicale*. G. L. Primavera begins a dedication sonnet with words and music written by himself (1566; *IIIrd Book of Madrigals for 5 or 6 voices*), with the lines:

> *Jl Re de' Parti visitar con dono*
> *Ciascun solea di gemme d'or' e d'ostro*
> *Et io sol con quest' opra d'inchiostro*
> *L' animo chiaro e'l proprio cor vi dono. . . .*

regard the chorus in dramatized poetry as a vain thing may understand (as Ottavio himself explained to me) how and why the ancients used it and how important it is in such poems. In short, this new music is universally recognized today by the refined ear as the true music, and it has spread from the courts of the Italian princes to those of Spain and France and the other parts of Europe, as I know from reliable sources. . . . (I, 384)

The compositions which Caccini wrote to Grillo's verses have not been found; that they did exist is shown by a later letter from Grillo at Rome (I, 402), in which the poet thanks Caccini for sending the songs. A letter from Grillo to Gabbriello Chiabrera, written from Venice, reminds us of Caccini's stay at the papal court:

Venice pleases me as much on account of its situation as on account of its society. It is a seat of the muses and the graces, and will thrive and blossom still more under the present breath of universal peace. . . . Ottavio Rinuccini visited me in Ferrara. . . . We spoke of you; and Giulio Romano was present, too. You can imagine whose mouth overflowed, since you know whose heart was full. Giulio Caccini is [now] at the court of His Holiness, who values him highly. . . . (I, 862)

Grillo also esteemed the work of Caccini's daughters. A letter from Venice to Francesca Caccini in Florence accompanies the sending of one madrigal:

A few days ago I sent you three madrigals about the ascension of the famous queen of the angels; the poems compensated by their number for their light weight. Today I am sending to you, along with this, another,[1] which is perhaps more delicate and submits more easily to declamation and expression; it will certainly guide many hearts and many souls if it is

[1] It begins: "T'amo si, ma si poco"; the title is, *Peccator poco amoroso à Christo sviscerato Amante*. In Francesca's published works, 1618, neither this nor any other poem of Grillo's appears.

adapted to the sweet power and the gentle force of your heavenly harmony. . . . May God bless you together with your father, mother, and husband, to whom I send very affectionate greetings. (III, 213)

A letter from Grillo in Venice to Giulio Caccini in Florence speaks of a visit of Settimia Caccini in Mantua. In the letter Grillo makes the excuse that illness and his duties robbed him of the pleasure of hearing Settimia sing at the court during his stay in Mantua; he expresses the hope that he will soon take up residence in the Badia in Florence, and then will be able to enjoy seeing Caccini.

Grillo's most noteworthy artistic connection was undoubtedly with Claudio Monteverdi the greatest musician of his time. This connection had already been formed during Monteverdi's activities at Mantua, when the musician had either sent to the poet a sacred madrigal composed in monodic style on Grillo's words, or Grillo had heard it performed during a visit to Mantua. That Grillo did visit Mantua in 1610 is proved by a letter dated the 28th of March. He writes to Monteverdi from Venice:

How well your divine music corresponds to the divine subject of my sacred madrigal, and how completely heavenly it has become through your heavenly harmony! And what harmonious collaboration! I wish I had the tongue to praise it according to its merits, as I have the ear to appreciate it as it deserves, especially when it is sung by [Francesco] Campagnola, or a comparable singer. For only a perfect singer with a heavenly voice, such as the Signora Adriana [Basile], should dare to approach such a composition. When Signora Adriana unites her voice with the instrument, and gives the strings life and speech with her direction, she wins our hearts with her sweet enchantment; we are carried to Heaven although our bodies remain on earth.[1] And this rose of mine, blossoming from the bloody tears of Christ's body will, because of the gentle emphasis [of your music] . . . bring from the eyes of the listeners real tears of compassion, from their mouths a thousand blessings for you, who do not merely add notes to the text in your creations, but form magic wands directing the heart and intellect through your art, to say nothing of darts which inflict wounds of joy and astonishment. (II, 137)

I do not know to which of his poems Grillo refers here, for he used the motive *sovra gli occhi* of the dead Redeemer many times; but no composition can be found based on one of these poems in Monteverdi's printed works.

Monteverdi and Grillo became better friends while Monteverdi was Choirmaster for San Marco. Grillo was then living near Venice in San Nicolo del Lido and taking an active part in the musical life of Venice. In a letter from San Nicolo to Giovanni Matteo Bembo (III, 289), Grillo tells the reason why he could not come to the city to enjoy the music which was heard regularly in Bembo's palace. In another letter to an otherwise unknown Venetian musician, Bartolomeo Conte (III, 170), Grillo praises this artist [*virtuoso*] who had set a poem of Grillo's to music, for his singing and playing.

A second letter from Grillo to Monteverdi can be dated quite accurately. The contents make it clear that it was written in 1614, and the address—Capo d'Istria—means it was written between the 2nd and 23rd of August, for Grillo has left us an exact, attractive report of this trip of his from Venice to the Istrian coast.

---

[1] In an earlier letter than the one dated from Padua to Perazzo Perazzi in Venice (I, 417), Grillo praises "*la celeste voce della Sua vertuosa Angioletta, che à giorni passati m'entrò per gli orecchi sotto le dolci misure della musica.*" He also encloses two sonnets in which he exhorts the young singer to dedicate her art to heaven alone.

It is quite right and proper that the sixth book of your recently published madrigals should come to me from your hand
and no other's; for no one exceeds me in estimation and admiration of your high talents and your rare courtesy. I can
assure you of the eminent worth of your harmonious gift;
it seems to me not so much to belong to the earth on which
I accept it, as to the heaven in which I listen to it. My monks
here first studied it in the most careful manner—for the work
requires a thorough preparation—and then sang a part of it
to me. My heart was as much carried away by the loveliness
of the harmony as my mind was refreshed by the newness
of the devices. This is not music for the ears or minds of the
common people; for it is not vulgar in its nature any more
than is its creator, who is a sublime disdainer of the ordinary,
and an aristocrat among the plebes of musicians. . . . I must
praise the same thing in the compositions in manuscript in
which you prove yourself such a great master, though you
are given less support by the text; but even a mule looks like
Bucephalus under a heroic rider. You have bestowed too much
honor on my poems, by your praise and by your music. Where
my lines sound worst, there is the sweetest harmony in your
composition. (III, 127)

These compositions by Monteverdi to poems of Grillo's
cannot be identified either. Grillo may mean pieces from the
*Pietosi affetti*, which a Pater C. Gio. Battista Magnavacca de'
Chierici Regolari in Venice had been commissioned to give to
Monteverdi at San Marco. Three of Grillo's letters to the
monk explain the transaction. In the first one, which is un-
dated, he speaks of Magnavacca's plans:

You may of course give our Claudio, the true emperor
[*imperatore*] of music, permission to erect a harmonious tower
on his green hill, so high that it reaches to heaven; and if he
wishes to use my edifying and poetic stones, he may well make

me into the person you, in your exceeding politeness, make me seem. . . . (III, 322)

In the second, from Venice, Grillo thanks Magnavacca:

My rough stones have become, through the art of your eloquence . . . valuable jewels, indeed; for they have received their finest setting in their union with the music of Monteverdi. (III, 124)

The third, from San Nicolo d'Oltra (1614), runs more positively:

All the creations of the truly harmonious and sublime spirit of Monteverdi are to my ears a portion of human, and a presentiment of heavenly, bliss. Witness his sixth book of madrigals, which has just been published, as well as the two sacred poems and some others of mine which he has so honored with his angelic harmony that his green hill will always be for my poetry a capitol of everlasting glory despite time and death. I only regret that I am no longer young enough and no longer familiar enough with the muses to supply worthy material for the heavenly patterns of his glorious tunes. The works of this unique mind miraculously arouse a state of sympathy whenever they aspire to awaken it. He has, in my opinion, reached the ultimate perfection. . . . In these last madrigals especially his melancholy and forceful eloquence appeals to the most jaded ears. To be sure, the music has so much new in it, that trained voices and assurance are essential to perform it. (III, 128)

With this, the musical correspondence of Grillo is, with a few insignificant exceptions, exhausted. It is to be regretted that no later edition of the letters was published to allow us to follow his career further into the seventeenth century.

# X

# *Agostino Steffani*

O N FEBRUARY 12, 1728, there died in Frankfort-on-Main one of the most gifted and remarkable men of his time—Agostino Steffani. Composer, diplomat, occupant of high ecclesiastical office, he held a dozen positions and honors, ranging from court composer and organist to bishop. Today he is known to us only through his relation to Handel, a relation that was for him, though not for Handel, merely an episode. The essay or novel that focuses on a significant figure from the past is currently in vogue; if our authors were capable of handling any more difficult or remote chapters of music history than those represented by Beethoven, Weber, or Schubert, Agostino Steffani would not lack for biographers.

He was born on July 25, 1654, at Castelfranco in the Veneto, a town near Treviso. The town is still surrounded by its original ivy-covered walls; against them is built the church whose greatest treasure is Giorgione's noble and serene Madonna. Steffani's forebears came from Padua and Venice, and at the age of thirteen young Agostino was at school in Padua. There the Elector Ferdinand Maria, who was on a pilgrimage to the "Santo," heard him sing, and decided to take him back to Munich. Steffani was at first placed in the care of the Elector's chief equerry; then afterward he was entrusted to the Hofkapellmeister Johann Kaspar Kerll for three years. Under Kerll he learned to play the piano and the organ, and he also probably sang a soprano part in Kerll's *Le pretensioni del Sole*, a musical introduction to a contest. For all this he repaid Kerll only with ingratitude, mercilessly exacting payments of debts that Kerll had contracted with him.

In 1671 he went to board and lodge with the Elector's bursar, a personal servant of long standing; there he caused great expense, which was grumblingly borne by the high treasury. All this time the court showed the greatest forbearance toward the youth, who must have radiated an extraordinary personal charm. At the age of eighteen Steffani went to Rome and spent two years under the instruction of Ercole Bernabei, learning the vocal chamber style and the grandiloquent churchly style. At twenty he was a finished artist and a mature personality; so much so that news of Kerll's departure from Munich was kept from him for fear that he would attempt to succeed to Kerll's position himself.

And then followed fourteen decisive years in Munich. He rose in the hierarchy of musical offices as high as was possible during the lifetime of Ercole Bernabei, whom he had brought back with him as successor to Kerll. He also brought his whole family to Munich: father, mother, sister, and his brother Ventura (Terzago), who was to provide him with the librettos for his first operas. At the age of twenty-six Steffani became a priest; after 1682 he styled himself Abbot

of Lepsing, as incumbent of a living in the county of Oet-
tingen-Wallerstein. He intrigued ceaselessly in the attempt to
become a high ecclesiastic, but the papal curia remained un-
moved. Steffani did not get along with Ercole Bernabei's son,
Giuseppe, with whom he was on equal footing.

Steffani made several trips to Italy; and in 1678–79 he made
perhaps the most important professional tour of his life. He
went to Paris, where he probably met his compatriot Lully
(whom he excelled in intelligence, adaptability, and talent)
and became acquainted with his *Bellerophon* (January 31,
1679). He was permitted to play for Louis XIV, and on his
homeward journey he passed through Turin, where his "delicate playing" was much admired at the court.

Steffani also made other trips with darker purposes, which
are not discussed in the public records. He had become a
diplomat or agent, and was sent on special missions for Max
Emanuel, who had been the Elector since 1679. In the official
annals of Bavaria, Max Emanuel is called "Conqueror of the
Turks"; in the clear glass of history he appears as one of the
most unprincipled and unscrupulous individuals who ever
burdened a throne. Steffani's primary concern was with the
possible candidates for Max Emanuel's hand. He made the
princesses of Neuburg appear ridiculous (they undoubtedly
were quite countrified); he intrigued against the Viennese
court and its candidate, Archduchess Maria Antonia; and he
ardently supported Sophie Charlotte, the daughter of Duchess
Sophie of Hanover. When Max Emanuel finally married the
Hapsburg Archduchess and Sophie Charlotte married the
Elector of Brandenburg, thereby becoming the first Queen of
Prussia, Steffani took care that relations with the Hanoverian
court did not grow cold. In the summer of 1688, after sam-

pling the operas being given in Venice, he journeyed to Hanover.

Here he advanced in all three of his careers. First of all, he was an opera composer, and the new opera house in Hanover opened brilliantly with the performance of one of his works, *Enrico Leone*. His succeeding operas, which were as a whole most influential in the development of German opera, were all imitated in Hamburg; and composers like Kusser and Keiser, with their blending of French and Italian *goût*, must be considered in the light of Steffani's work. But soon Steffani's diplomatic assignments became more important. It was his task to break down the opposition in various German courts to the conferring of electoral privileges on Braunschweig-Hanover, and he visited all the electoral courts, staying the longest time with Max Emanuel in Brussels. Between court visits he went again to Venice (1690), and to Padua (1692). As a reward for his diplomatic services he was made an apostolic prothonotary.

After the death of Ernst August in 1698, Hanover became less attractive to him, and he spent more time than ever in travel. He sought to attach himself again to a Catholic court. In 1701–02 he endeavored to prevent Max Emanuel from going over to the French, making this attempt at the commission of Elector Johann Wilhelm of the Palatinate, a member of the very same Neuburg family, the Wittelsbachs, of whom Steffani had once made such fun. In the year 1703 he entered into the service of Johann Wilhelm. This prince, married to a Medici, was, despite some limitations, a lover of art and splendor. Steffani became a privy councilor and district administrator. During this period he also composed some of his most brilliant operas, although not under his own name.

At this point he began an undertaking of the grandest scale

—the reconversion of the German princely courts to Catholicism. In 1704, for example, he was in Dresden; in 1711 he was seeking to win the Landsgraf of Hesse-Darmstadt to the true faith. His subversive efforts appeared so promising that in 1706 the Pope named him Bishop of Spiga—*in partibus infidelium* to be sure, but nevertheless Bishop. He was at the height of his career when he traveled to Rome in the winter of 1708–09 and celebrated Mass at St. Peter's. He returned to Germany with most ambitious plans, and I am convinced that a cardinal's hat was then not too much for him to hope for. He even tried, with the help of petticoats, to convert the King of Prussia, the "Soldier King"! Had he succeeded, he might have made a bid for the tiara; but far from succeeding, he found himself obliged to leave Berlin amid thunder and lightning.

The first step toward Steffani's goal was his taking charge of Catholic northern Germany. In 1709 he had himself named apostolic vicar of northern Germany, and took up residence again in Hanover. But his star began to fade at the very moment when he aspired to his greatest achievement. He dissipated his energies in the concerns of church building and in the daily routine of mission work. Moreover, he was in continual need of money. In so short a space it is impossible to give an account of these years of suffering and growing old. Let it suffice to say that by 1722 it was all over for him, and he fled, first to Venice and the next year to Padua. There he remained until 1725 in the quiet provincial city that Padua had become. ("It was a wonder if two people could be found talking in the street.") Then he returned to Hanover in the vain hope that he would be granted the revenues from his abbacy of Selz in Alsace, for which he had fought during most of his life. He had debts amounting to 6000 scudi; for 550 thaler he sold his magnificent collection of paintings. He was on his way to seek shelter with one of his greatest patrons, the Elector of Mainz, when death came to him. The battle still rages over his legacy. In opposition to his heirs, the papal see maintained its own claims to Steffani's papers: three vast coffers. Two of these, which contained documents, found their way to Rome; while the third, containing musical compositions, went to Castel-franco. The contents of the first two have been kept in the Archives of Propaganda in Rome. They consist of 86 sizable volumes, every page the record of an incredibly lively mind. All trace of the third casket, however, has been lost.

In fact, we possess only fragments of Steffani's lifework. What we have is a series of operas, two sacred works that were published, one powerful Stabat Mater, a few cantatas, with or without instrumental accompaniment, and 85 chamber duets. But even judging by this mere torso of his work, he is obviously the greatest Italian composer between Carissimi and Scarlatti; for Germany, at all events, he was the most influential master of his day. He owed a certain debt to his travels in France, chiefly for the style of his overtures and for his arias based on a dance form. Despite this, he is not at all an eclectic, but an Italian through and through. Insofar as the concept of genius is reconcilable with matchless proportion and perfect formal balance, he was certainly a genius. He lived in a period when "form" was not yet frozen but still fluid and a living thing. This may be most clearly seen if one compares his profound, individual, plastic, and richly wrought Stabat Mater with that of Pergolesi, or his duets with those of Handel. The chamber duets of Handel, certainly modeled after Steffani's, are more monumental than his, but not greater. We must look to Mozart for such a blending of

❧❧ ❧❧ ❧❧ ❧❧

# XI

# *On Certain Manuscripts of Mozart*

THE HARVEST is small and unprepossessing. For it is scarcely to be expected that mere chance should bring to light again the autographs of those larger works of Mozart's whose loss is so distressing, among them those of the *Kleine Nachtmusik* with its missing minuet,[1] the *Musikalischer Spass*, the String Trio K. 563, the Fantasia K. 475, and the last sonatas for the piano. The upheavals of the past thirty-odd years have done much to scatter, to bury, and to destroy such treasures; they have brought little to the surface. Yet, even though the harvest is small, every page in Mozart's hand is worth a mention and an identification, no matter how unprepossessing, and for me, as the editor of the third edition of Köchel's thematic catalogue, the recording of such fragments has become an obligation.

To begin with, it is a question of two sketches, both dating from about the same time, namely from the years 1782 and

[1 While the original manuscript of this work has been rediscovered and published in facsimile by Bärenreiter Verlag, Kassel, the second minuet, torn from the manuscript, is still missing.]

1783, the years when Mozart was endeavoring to come to terms with the music of J. S. Bach and was at work on his C Minor Mass.

The first of these sketches, which at the time of writing was in the possession of Dr. Hermann Vollmer in New York, is a single leaf in oblong folio with twelve staves to the page, written on one side only; on staves 2 to 9 Mozart has begun a fugato which leads—in its ninth, penultimate measure—to a tutti. He has at first intended a double chorus, as is evident from the crossed-out alto and tenor clefs below the first soprano, but his final decision is for two sopranos, two altos, two tenors, and two basses. Nissen has identified the sketch as "The beginning of an eight-voiced fugue" (*Anfang einer 8-stimmigen Fuge*). But this will scarcely do as a description of a sketch that gives only the entrances for the first representatives of each of the four pairs. In my opinion, it must originally have been preceded by the sketch of a Qui tollis in the a cappella style whose last chord (in C major) actually appears on the leaf we have; Mozart has then begun a Quoniam:

Profoundly stirred, just at this time, by the "crisis" of his acquaintance with Bach and older music, Mozart may have toyed with the idea of giving certain parts of his C Minor

Mass an archaistic dress: the explanation is by no means improbable.

A year or two later he used the top staff of the page to set down the subject of the Rondo (8 measures) from his B-flat Major Piano Concerto (K. 450), but whether this is the first draft of the idea or was done for some other purpose, I cannot say. After the double bar there follow two additional measures in the 6/8 rhythm, sketched in pencil; above them are the letters "Ob C," which I should interpret as "Oboi Clarinetti" if only the concerto were scored for clarinets.

A more precise date can be assigned to the second sketch, a single oblong leaf with ten staves to the page, written on both sides, which at the time of writing was in the possession of Mr. R. F. Kallir in New York. On the two top staves of the recto is written the beginning of a fugue, similar to those dating from the early months of 1782, when—under the influence of the *Well-Tempered Clavier* and his wife's expressed fondness for contrapuntal things of this sort—Mozart wrote a whole series of them. In the upper margin Nissen has written: "Intended for his wife" (*Bestimmt für seine Frau*), and after this: "By W. A. Mozart, Sr., and in his hand" (*Von W. A. Mozart, Vater, und seine Handschrift*). That Mozart is here called "Senior" (*Vater*) would seem to imply that Constanze and Nissen were presenting or selling the sketch to some admirer of Mozart's music who knew of the younger Mozart [1] and insisted upon being assured that he had become the owner of a page in the handwriting of the *famous* Mozart. The heading "Fuga," written in pencil above the first two

[1 The younger Mozart, also a composer and pianist, was born in the year of his father's death and died in 1844.]

measures, may have been added by Mozart himself. The fragment runs as follows:

As usual with compositions intended for Constanze, this beginning remained a beginning. Later on, Mozart made use of the page in teaching counterpoint, although not until he had bracketed the remaining eight staves together, four and four, as though for the beginning of a string quartet, and had sketched two measures of a sonata for piano and violin. For the rest, the page is covered with exercises in harmony and counterpoint. A pupil—perhaps Storace or Attwood—has written a counterpoint to a bass set down by Mozart and has then worked out the whole for three voices.

On the verso is the beginning of a four-part fugue with basso continuo, by Mozart himself and undoubtedly intended for voices. At first glance the sketch looks like one of the copies made in 1773 after Eberlin and Michael Haydn; nonetheless, it can only have been written during Mozart's first years in Vienna—this follows from the handwriting and from the personal stamp of the music itself. I cannot be sure whether it is merely an "abstract" exercise of Mozart's or once again a study for the C Minor Mass. Perhaps the facsimile published herewith will enable some one of my readers to find a solution.

The most important manuscript that has come to light is the autograph of the piano version of the so-called "Prague Dances," K. 509, listed in the third edition of Köchel's catalogue on page 647. This was owned at one time by Carl

*Fragmentary Beginning of a Four-Part Fugue with Basso Continuo, in Mozart's Handwriting*

August André of Frankfort-on-Main, whose certification of its authenticity, dated January 27, 1856 (!), appears on its last page. It too is at present in private hands and in New York City. But the two oblong leaves with their closely written staves, twelve to each of the four pages, run counter to expectation in that they prove not to have been written in Prague in the early months of 1787, as heretofore assumed.

Presumably it was towards the end of 1789 or at the beginning of 1790 that Mozart prepared them for Artaria, who published them early in 1790 with the plate-number 290. Mozart needed money. One can recognize this even in the carelessness of the notation; seldom did Mozart make more frequent use of the conventional abbreviations of his day. Yet he was at the same time incapable of making a servile copy, however faithfully he may have followed the general layout of his original. In the coda he has shortened the "composed-out" fermata in measures 279 to 282, so that the piano version is actually a few measures shorter than its orchestral model. And although he has made his arrangement as simple as possible, as befits an arrangement for amateurs, he has gone beyond the trivial "pianistic" revisions that imposed themselves as a matter of course and has been unable to resist introducing the little variants that presented themselves to his always alert and active imagination. The articulation likewise departs in many respects from that of the orchestral version. And strangely enough, the "Alternativi" of the original are now all of them called "Minori," although only one is actually in minor. All of us would like to see a new complete edition of Mozart's works—it would fill a genuine need. Should such an edition ever become a reality, the volume of music for the piano will be enriched by a delightful little work.[1]

[1 Einstein's work is about to be fulfilled: a new complete edition of Mozart's works is being issued under the patronage of the International Mozart Foundation in Salzburg.]

# XII

## Mozart and Tarchi

L E NOZZE DI FIGARO was twice performed in Italy in Mozart's lifetime—in the autumn of 1787 at the theatre at Monza, and in the spring of 1788 at the Teatro di Via della Pergola in Florence. Both performances took place in the presence of members of the house of Hapsburg—at Monza before the governor of Austrian Lombardy, the Archduke Ferdinand, and his consort, Maria Ricciarda Beatrice d'Este; and at Florence before the Grand Duke of Tuscany, Peter Leopold, Archduke of Austria.

As I write I have in front of me the two librettos issued on these occasions, both now in the possession of the Istituto Musicale at Florence, and also Da Ponte's original, published in 1786, of which there seems to be only one other surviving copy, in the Library of Congress at Washington. It is quite likely that there is a definite connection among the three performances before members of the royal house. *Figaro* did not have such a decided success in Vienna that it was necessarily bound to attract attention in Milan and Florence. It is a reasonable assumption that Joseph II had recommended the work to his illustrious brothers. If he did this, it would materially improve the reputation which posterity has given him for his treatment of Mozart; as a rule he certainly made a practice of relegating Mozart to the background in favor of men of far inferior abilities.

The Florence performance I do not propose to discuss. The precious copy of the Vienna libretto preserved at the Istituto Musicale differs in several particulars from Mozart's score; it includes an aria for Cherubino in Act III, for instance, which Mozart subsequently eliminated. With its abundance of stage directions, this version of the libretto could give even a modern producer some valuable hints, for it obviously served as the source for printing the Florentine libretto. It contains directions for the guidance of the printer and indicates deletions which show that the performance at Florence was anything but complete. The most striking change is that Cherubino is deprived of his Aria "Non so più cosa son." In its place Susanna sings an arietta, "Senza speme ognor saggira," which is probably the work of Bartolomeo Cherubini, *maestro al primo cembalo* at the time, and father of Luigi Cherubini. The unusual length of the work—at both Florence and Monza ballets were interpolated in the entr'actes—caused it to be spread over two evenings.

The opera had undergone quite a different kind of alteration six months before at Monza, although there, too, there was no lack of clumsy interference. The principal change made then was that Barbarina was removed completely from the list of characters; consequently, Cherubino must forgo his delightful flirtation with her, and at the beginning of the last act the gardener Antonio has to look for the lost pin (without, of course, singing the cavatina). In the first act Count Almaviva sings Cherubino's canzonetta at his first appearance on stage, since it is essential, of course, that the Count should enter singing an aria. In the second act the whole of the corresponding scene with Cherubino, the Countess, and Susanna is naturally omitted. But these changes, eccentric as they are, are not all; there is yet more. In the dedication of the libretto to the Archduke and Duchess we read that their Royal Highnesses had taken Mozart's opera under their special protection, for they directed that the third and fourth acts should be completely reset.

The list of names at the beginning tells the same story: "The composer . . . of the first and second acts is: Sig. Maestro Volfgango Mozart; of the third and fourth: Sig. Maestro Angelo Tarchi." It is interesting to note that it was for the wedding of this same Archduke and Princess that Mozart had in 1771 written the serenata *Ascanio in Alba*; it was also for them that in 1773 he wrote *Lucio Silla*.

It is not my intention to embark on an elaborate critical study of the composer Angelo Tarchi or even to track down the remains of his half of *Figaro*; it might be possible to discover it in one of the libraries at Milan. All the reader need know is that Tarchi was born at Naples in 1760, that he wrote forty Italian and six French operas from 1781–1800, and that he died in 1814 in Paris, where he had lived since 1798. In the spring of 1787 he had achieved such success at Milan with a tragedia per musica, *Il Conte di Saldagna*, that he obviously had to be rewarded by being entrusted with the partial resetting of *Figaro*.

For us this curious story has only a historical, or perhaps I might say a psychological, interest. It is not to be supposed that their Royal Highnesses knew Mozart's *Figaro* and liked Acts I and II but not Acts III and IV. It is possible that Acts III and IV seemed too long, and that they wanted a setting which would get them to the end more quickly than Mozart's. In any case, it shows what little respect they had for Mozart, or, for that matter, for music, even when it had been written by the greatest operatic genius of all time. The most astonishing thing is that Angelo Tarchi was also guilty of this indifference to musical values. To be willing to reset the duet between the Count and Susanna, the sextet in which Susanna makes the acquaintance of her future parents-in-law (Mozart's masterpiece and his favorite ensemble), the Countess's aria in the garden, the letter duet, Figaro's "cucko la" aria, and the two finales, demonstrates a supreme ability for not recognizing genius, even taking into consideration the popularity of pasticcios and the widespread custom of setting a favorite text a hundred times over. Angelo Tarchi's achievement entitles him to take his place in glory by the side of Ferdinando Giuseppe Bertoni, who reset the text of Gluck's *Orfeo*. It must be noted, though, that Bertoni felt obliged to apologize for his audacity.

# XIII

## A "King Theodore" Opera

No GOOD Londoner should need an introduction to King Theodore of Corsica, since His Majesty was buried in St. Anne's, Soho; and his memorial tablet is there on the west wall of the tower, with Horace Walpole's epitaph for all to read.

What is not mentioned there, however, is the part the Corsican monarch was to play in the history of comic opera. Let me fill the gap.

How did it come about that this German adventurer should have won a royal title? There is little need to go into the details of his career, since the whole story has been brilliantly told by Valerie Pirie in her book *His Majesty of Corsica*. Enough to say that the Corsicans have never willingly been Italians. They were not so in 1020, when they fell under Pisan rule; and still less when, 80 years later, Pisa relinquished the indigestible island to the Republic of Genoa.

They revolted again and again, and in the course of a particularly violent insurrection at the beginning of the eighteenth century they adopted as their king a German adventurer, Baron Theodor Neuhoff, whose destiny was tragicomic. His Corsican kingdom lasted less than a year—from April till November, 1736. Repeated attempts to regain the orb of dominion failed, for the Genoese called in the aid of French troops, and the feelings of the islanders towards their monarch grew cooler as his financial resources dwindled.

Theodore fled to England. Here the exertions of the Genoese Envoy brought him into debtors' prison, whence he was freed after five years, only to die miserably. Meanwhile the Corsicans looked after themselves. A new insurrection, led, after 1755, by Pasquale Paoli, made the Genoese tire at last of their troublesome subjects; and in 1768 the island was sold to France. So it happened that a year later, when Napoleon came into the world, it was as a subject of France.

Small wonder, after all this, if King Theodore excited curiosity; but it was audacious in the eighteenth century to turn him into the hero of an opera. This was actually done by the Abbate Giovanni Battista Casti (1724–1803). Casti is one of the Italian poets whom literary historians have treated scurvily. He was no pious cleric. This, however, did not prevent the Emperor Joseph II from taking him from Florence, where he was Court Poet to Joseph's brother Leopold, off to Vienna in his train.

Vienna did not retain him for long, though he often went back there. He went to St. Petersburg, where he enjoyed experiences that were later to serve him for a satirical epic at the expense of Catharine the Great (*Il poema tartaro*); we find him at Venice, Rome, Paris. Among other things, he wrote 48 tales in verse, which are not edification for virgin minds. They are relegated by many libraries, including the British Museum, to the chamber of horrors.

At the same time, Casti was one of the best of librettists, not to say the very best, of buffo operas; and his *Il re Teodoro* is his masterpiece. True, the idea of this libretto was not his own, for it derived from Voltaire, who in *Candide* had been the first to introduce King Theodore into literature. He figures there among the six dethroned monarchs with whom Candide sups at Venice (26th chapter, "D'un souper que Candide et Martin firent avec six étrangers, et qui ils étaient"). But if the idea was borrowed, the witty execution is Casti's own.

The dethroned king, accompanied by his ever loyal major-domo, Gafforio (in history the Corsican gentleman, Don Luigi Giafferi), finds himself at a Venetian inn without a crown on his head or—what is more serious—in his pocket.

There is nothing for it but to make up to the innkeeper's pretty daughter, and to persuade the father to favor a marriage. But Lisetta is already betrothed to a young merchant of Venice, who has King Theodore's bonds assigned to himself.

Now the ex-monarch unexpectedly discovers in Venice his sister Belisa—an adventuress, too, but far more astute than her brother. She has in tow another dethroned king, one Achmet, whom she has lured to Venice with all his riches, like an enamored bear with a ring in his nose. He is the rock of hope to which, drowning in debt, King Theodore clings. But the end is tragical. Like Don Giovanni, King Theodore is torn from the festive board—not indeed by demons, but by Messer Grande, the head of the *sbirri*—to be arrested and thrown into the debtors' prison. And the opera ends with melancholy sententiousness:

Come una rota è il mondo
Chi in cima sta, chi in fondo. . .
Felice è chi fra i vortici
Tranquillo può restar.

There is no way to give the reader an idea of the vivaciousness and wit of the text, or the brilliant conduct of the action of this libretto without quoting the whole. It is farcical, but there is a sombre background to the frivolity. Debts, debts, debts! These are the furies that haunt the action and persecute their victim in his very dreams. As for Theodore's kingdom, it gives Casti his opportunity for the most comical and wittiest parodistic play at the expense of Metastasio's *opera seria*. What a misfortune that this text fell into Paisiello's hands and not Mozart's!

Paisiello's music had a huge success. *Il re Teodoro* was at once welcomed into the repertories of the German opera houses, and only two years after its composition it reached Paris, in a wretched adaptation. But Paisiello had not appreciated his exceptional opportunity, and produced nothing more than routine music, pretty and dainty enough, but tame, and never once vivid enough to match the comedy.

It was Lorenzo Da Ponte's fault that Mozart never came into contact with Casti at Vienna. Da Ponte hated, feared, and admired his rival, who had a hundred times his talent. And all the same we have, in a measure, to thank the *Il re Teodoro* for *Figaro*.

That Mozart must have been acquainted with *Teodoro* we should have known, even had the fact not been confirmed by documents which tell us that at its first performance at the Burg Theatre, on August 23, 1784, he caught a severe cold, which kept him from work until the middle of September. Certain things from Paisiello's opera, especially in the ensembles, ran in his head; one can easily put a finger on them. Still other things from Casti's libretto ran in Da Ponte's head. Lisetta's ditty, which is taken up by the chorus of girls—

> O giovanette
> Innamorate,
> Deh, mi spiegate
> Che cos' è amor.

—cannot but remind us of Zerlina's first scene and of Cherubino's canzonetta. And Messer Grande's recital of the King's debts was to be echoed by Da Ponte in Leporello's Catalogue Song:

> Venti mila gigliati ai Tunesini:
> Quattro mila e seicento ai Livornesi;
> Ghinee quindici mila e due scellini
> Per più cambiali ai negozianti inglesi;
> Quaranta mila ottantasei fiorini,
> In varj tempi e date, agli Olandesi.
> Debiti in oltre in Cadice, in Lisbona,
> In Amborgo, in Marsiglia, in Barcellona.

More considerable is the bearing that *Il re Teodoro* was to have upon *Figaro*. The former was the first *opera buffa* with a modern political subject. To appreciate Casti's courage one must be acquainted with earlier libretti. *Opera buffa* had previously drawn its matter from quite other regions of human stupidity and frailty. Saucy it had often been, but never before audacious. It may be mentioned that Casti also wrote an *opera buffa* with Catiline as its hero, which no composer was daring enough to set to music.

✦✦✦ ✦✦✦ ✦✦✦ ✦✦✦

# XIV

# Mozart and Shakespeare's The Tempest

ON THE 31st of October, 1791, a few weeks before Mozart's death, the poet Gottfried August Bürger, the author of *Lenore*, wrote to his pupil and friend August Wilhelm Schlegel:

> Gotter has written a magnificent free adaptation of Shakespeare's *Tempest* under the title *The Enchanted Isle*. The ladies cannot praise it enough. Mozart is composing the music.

The meaning of this portion of the letter, which, strange to say, has been little noted up to now by Mozart investigators, is so explicit that it admits of only one conclusion: namely, that Gotter had his own version of the *Tempest* lying on his desk (we will later find that confirmed), and was searching for a suitable composer for the libretto. The news of the success of *Die Zauberflöte*, which had had its first performance four weeks before the date of Bürger's letter—on the 30th of

September, 1791—evidently led him, then, to request Mozart to set his text to music; and Mozart must have answered favorably.[1] And so Mozart probably occupied himself in the last weeks of his life, at least in thought, with one of the later works of the greatest of all dramatists—although only in the adaptation, that is, a diluted version, of a very modest German poet.

Gotter's name was not unknown to Mozart. The Herzoglich Sachsen-Gothaische Geheime Secretarius Johann Friedrich Wilhelm Gotter (1746–97) was, among other things, the author of the text to Georg Benda's melodrama *Medea*, which Mozart in his Mannheim days (1777–78) had admired so much that he himself wanted to experiment in this form of art, and he may perhaps have tried, with the beginning of the composition *Semiramis* by his patron Otto Freiherr von Gemmingen. Gotter's dramas were very often produced in Vienna, but not always very successfully; and he once cherished the plan of making a journey to Vienna, although without carrying it out. It must have been thought remarkable in Vienna that Gotter was chosen to fulfill a wish of Kaiser Joseph II, to revive Alexandrine tragedy at the National-Theater—and his *Alzire*, written for this, a freely versified adaptation of Voltaire's play, failed so thoroughly that it was only repeated twice. Gotter's *Mutter* (1783) met no better success, and his *Veit von Solingen* (1784) was abandoned after the first repetition.

But with some other adaptations, Gotter had extraordi-

---

[1] Max Friedländer, in an essay on the *Wiegenlied*, written by Gotter and supposedly composed by Mozart—*Vierteljahrsschrift für Musikwissenschaft* (VIII), 277—assumes that Gotter only intended to send his libretto to Mozart. But then Bürger would have written: "We hear that Mozart is to compose the music."

narily good fortune, especially in Vienna. His *Falsche Vertraulichkeiten*, after Marivaux, was given forty times between 1776 and 1798 at the Burgtheater. (Along with Gotter's *Orest*, it was done also at Esterház in 1776, where Haydn must have seen it.) His revision of a French comedy which was based on Calderon's *La Dama Duende*, so loved by opera composers of all times, under the title *Der Kobold*, exactly suited Viennese taste with its "Hanswurst" episodes, and was performed forty-eight times between 1778 and 1806. Moreover, we hear of the Viennese performances of Gotter's *Jeanette* (1778 and after), *Die Ehescheue* (1783), *Der Argwöhnische* (1781 and after), *Juliane von Lindorack* (1780 and after), *Das öffentliche Geheimnis* (1781), *Der Liebhaber* (1783), *Der schwarze Mann* (1784 and after), and *Romeo und Julie*—after Shakespeare with incidental songs by Benda —(1780 and after, Kärntnerthor-Theater.) A dramatist whose works were performed that often could not possibly have remained unknown to such a lover of the theater as Mozart. If we add the fact that Gotter was the author of the *Wiegenlied*, the music of which was attributed to Mozart for so long, we have listed all the possible ways Gotter would have been known to Mozart. And if Mozart had really been the composer of *Schlafe mein Prinzchen schlaf ein*, his acquaintance with Gotter must have been very intimate: for the song, part of Gotter's Biblical travesty *Esther*, had been written well before 1789, although it was first printed publicly in 1795. Thus Mozart would have been able to get the text only from Gotter himself or from Gotter's circle of intimate friends.

It is strange that Gotter made a slighter impression on Vienna with those works which were his best—his musical comedies. The center of his reputation was Gotha, where he worked directly with the musicians Georg Benda and Anton Schweitzer. The *Dorfgala*, with Schweitzer as collaborator, and the *Jahrmarkt*, composed by Benda, were his most famous works; but his fame spread to the west and north, towards Mannheim and Berlin and Hamburg, rather than to his own country of Austria. The reason for this perhaps lies in the fact that these works are among the Middle German imitations of the French light opera, whose chief literary exponent was Christian Weise, and whose musical champion, Johann Hiller. These were refined, rather insipid, works, based on the ever happily resolved conflict between the classes—nobleman, shopkeeper, peasant—and with only a touch at most of frivolity; their music was as poor as the texts. They had long outgrown that sort of thing in Vienna, where, under the influence of *opera buffa*, the fantastic and exotic were being enjoyed even in comic opera; and the audience there demanded the right to whole handfuls from the pot of musical colors, and found Mozart's *Entführung* epoch-making.

In his *Geisterinsel*—for this, not *Zauberinsel*, was the final title—Gotter showed that he himself was influenced by Viennese taste. *Der Geisterinsel* is not a *Singspiel*, but rather a *Teutsche Oper*, an opera of magic like *Die Zauberflöte* itself. One might even assume a direct influence on *Der Geisterinsel* through *Die Zauberflöte*, if there were not authentic proof that Gotter had his text ready long before Schikaneder and Mozart had even thought of their joint work. For as early as the end of March or the beginning of April, 1791, Gotter was looking for a suitable composer for his libretto, without finding one. Acquaintance with the contents of *Die Zauberflöte*, or with the libretto itself, must have brought about in him the sudden light of recognition: Mozart—that was the

ight man! Whether a closer acquaintance with Mozart's opera
ed to later alterations in *Der Geisterinsel*, we cannot estab-
ish: perhaps a simpler version existed originally. But to as-
ume that is not at all necessary. For *The Tempest* and *Zauberflöte* have so much in common that one must only wonder
at how little these similarities have been noted before. In
*Zauberflöte*, to be sure, there are no farewells. Sarastro, unlike
Prospero, does not lay down his magic wand forever. But
Sarastro is related to Prospero; Tamino and Pamina are related
to Ferdinand and Miranda, whose "love at first sight" must
also undergo the Fire and Water test; the monster Caliban
has his parallel in the Moor, Monostatos, and his mother
Sycorax hers in the Queen of the Night; related are the three
boys to Ariel and his followers; and even Papageno has a
slight kinship with Trinculo and Stefano.

Now, Mozart could not have composed the music to Gotter's libretto; and it is questionable whether he really would
have done so if he had been able, for two reasons. First: he
never composed a duplicate in the field of opera, as he had
done occasionally as a composer of instrumental music—one
is reminded, perhaps, of the two double concerti, one for
violin and viola, the other for two pianos. If, on the other
hand, one looks at the list of his operas, from *Entführung*
to *Clemenza di Tito*, one notices that each work is sui generis.
It is as if Mozart wanted to widen the whole circle of his
creative work—he allowed his genius no repetitions. Second:
Mozart would soon have realized that Gotter's *Geisterinsel*
was a magic opera and nothing more, without the deeper
charm and meaning which had made Schikaneder's text seem
to him bearable and even attractive. He would not even have
needed any comparison with Shakespeare's original. One can

only repeat and emphasize the following criticism of Schlos-
ser's. "The piece under Gotter's hands has become a dull fairy
story of commonplace stamp . . . it is furnished with the
silliest operatic effects . . . the clowns' scenes, which, moreover, have sunk to the level of the most wretched insipidity
occupy boundless space. . . . From Caliban there has sprung
a being half opera-villain, half idiot."

Bürger's report about the libretto seems to have been based
on hearsay. The "ladies" of whom he speaks in his letter to
Schlegel were Caroline Michaelis, at that time still Mme.
Böhmer, and her Göttingen friends. The famous Caroline of
Romanticism was just ending the long series of her love affairs
as the wife of August Wilhelm Schlegel, and later of the
philosopher Schelling. She was a family friend of the Gotters.
It must have been she who sent the libretto to Goethe, and
was then able to write to the author at Gotha (October 3,
1796) that Goethe considered it a "masterpiece of poetry and
speech." Whether Goethe really was so enthusiastic, no one
knows. It is not impossible; for Goethe himself already had
made a number of more or less successful attempts in the field
of *Singspiel* librettos, and planned others, among them a sequel
to *Zauberflöte*; and he was tolerant whenever he discovered
even a spark of technical skill.

Schiller thought otherwise. In the summer of 1797, Gotter's
widow offered him the libretto for publication in the *Horen*,
and received the answer that he would "always consider it
as an excellent contribution." But to Goethe he wrote, on
August 17, 1797, much less politely: "I have received from
the works left by Gotter his opera *Geisterinsel*, which is
adapted from Shakespeare's *Tempest*. I have read the first act,
which is very weak, and poor fare." This opinion nevertheless

did not prevent him from finally printing all three acts in the *Horen* (Vol. XI, items 8 and 9), with the introductory remark that the opera, "set to music by Herr Franz Fleischmann in Meiningen, by virtue of a formal and exclusive contract with the author, and completed during the lifetime of the latter," was awaiting now its imminent production. In fact, Fleischmann did publish the Overture as Opus 7 with André in Offenbach. He was, moreover, a real Mozartean—he was a twelve-year-old schoolboy at the *Gymnasium* in Mannheim during Mozart's stay in that city, and the many arrangements of Mozart's operas for eight wind instruments discovered in European libraries originate mostly from him. He, too, set Gotter's *Wiegenlied* to music.

Fleischmann was not the only one besides Mozart to have attributed to him the text of *Der Geisterinsel*. The actor Beck, who was one of Gotter's most intimate pupils and friends, had, on April 7, 1791, expressed doubt whether Mozart would compose the music for any more *deutsche Sujets;* and on his advice the libretto was sent after Mozart's death to Dittersdorf. But when nothing was heard from Dittersdorf for two whole years, a writer and chamberlain at the court of the Duchess Amalie in Weimar, Franz von Einsiedel, who had been involved in the libretto to an undetermined extent, suggested sending it to another musician. Then, in 1795, at Einsiedel's instigation, the first act was sent both to Himmel in Berlin and to Fleischmann in Meiningen as a test of composition on approval; and the final choice seems then to have been Fleischmann. The remarkable thing about this incident is that the author appointed the musician—although usually the reverse was the case. This makes clear the great value which Gotter attached to his work.

The "exclusive contract" to write the music to Gotter's libretto gained nothing for Fleischmann. After his death, his work was simply annexed by both a northern and a southern musician: Johann Reichardt in Berlin, and Johann Zumsteeg in Stuttgart. Reichardt's opera was produced at the Berlin National-Theater on July 6, 1798, and Zumsteeg's opera four months later, on the 7th of November, at the Stuttgart Hoftheater. Piano versions of both appeared in the same year, 1799, both dedicated to crowned heads—Reichardt's to Friedrich Wilhelm III, King of Prussia, and Zumsteeg's to George III of England.

A comparison of these two works, although exceedingly instructive, would overstep the bounds of this essay. It is enough to say that a true imitation of Mozart would be more likely by the South German Zumsteeg than by the Gluck admirer Reichardt, who depicted the entrance of Sycorax in a broadly descriptive instrumental scene. Zumsteeg is much more earnest, sensitive, and imaginative than Reichardt, who paints with a coarser brush. But even Zumsteeg's composition is unpalatable today—it has only historical interest.

The historical interest of *Geisterinsel* is, to be sure, great. From Reichardt's descriptive orchestral piece come threads leading to the Wolf Glen scene of *Der Freischütz*, which was written for Berlin; and the invention of the good spirit Maja who renders the angry witch Sycorax harmless, and who scatters flowers on Miranda's grave, is the direct ancestor of the mysterious spirit woman Emma in *Euryanthe*. The downright dull scenes between the kitchen-maid and the butler in Gotter's work made a great impression on Gustav Adolf Lortzing. *Geisterinsel* was the starting point and forerunner of a very definite type, the romantic opera, which, with Lortzing's *Undine* has by no means had the last word. Any true successor of Mozart would have written very differently. To put it plainly: Mozart had no successor, either as master of the *opera buffa* or as composer of the greatest *Teutsche Oper, Die Zauberflöte.*

***

# XV

# *The First Performance of Mozart's Entführung in London*

C. F. POHL has already definitely stated the order in which Mozart's six chief operas appeared in London.[1] First, oddly enough, came *La Clemenza di Tito* (27th March 1806), not because the Londoners had a special interest in Mozart's late—one might almost say posthumous—*opera seria*, but because the famous, or notorious, Mrs. Billington (born Weichsell) was all afire to play the role of Vitellia. In sharp contrast to her, the other singers in the cast, with the exception of Braham in the title role, took part only grudgingly; and also in sharp contrast to the lady, the public received the work with icy coldness. Nevertheless it was revived several times, in 1812, in 1816, and in 1821.

Five years later followed *Così fan tutte* (9th May 1811) and *Die Zauberflöte* (6th June 1811)—or rather *Il flauto magico*, for they used the Italian text in the version by de

[1] *Mozart and Haydn in London*, I, 145 ff. Vienna, 1867.

Gamerra. *Così fan tutte* likewise owed its introduction to a singer, Signora Radicati, who chose the role of Dorabella for her benefit performance, ostensibly "to gratify the wish of the British musical public to hear an *opera buffa* by Mozart." Since Catalani refused to take part, a Madame Bertinotti sang Fiordiligi; but both the big arias were too hard for her "so she substituted something easier for them. The other singers also found ways of making things more comfortable for themselves." (Pohl, *l.c.*, 147.)

Perhaps the success of *Così fan tutte* drew the *Zauberflöte* in its wake, which in spite of zealous publicity proved to be of course a fiasco of the first order. It survived for only a single repetition (4th July) and then was laid on the table. But we must not hold the people of London too much to blame for this; even though the work was undoubtedly extensively "arranged," the public was in no way prepared to understand its meaning.

A year later came the *Nozze* (18th June 1812) or rather, as the *Times* announced it, *Le mariage de Figaro*. Mozart's first Susanna, Anna Selina Storace, was still living, though in retirement, in Herne Hill. Her role was sung by Catalani, along with Mrs. Dickons as the Contessa, L. Fischer as the Conte, and Naldi as Figaro. But the work seems to have had no real success until it was taken up again (1st February 1817) with an all Italian cast. A few weeks after this (12th April 1817) with more or less the same singers and only one English woman, Miss Hughes (Donna Elvira), *Don Giovanni* was at last performed. *Don Giovanni* was the opera that won England for Mozart. It was not only an immediate but a lasting success, the best proof of which is the popularity of many grotesque travesties of it. Pohl mentions one of the most amusing of these, a performance in a circus of "Don Giovanni or a Spectre on Horseback," in which the stone horse was represented by a real live pony and the music derived from Arne, Blow, Carter (and so on through the whole alphabet).

Presumably the lasting success of *Don Giovanni* led to the production of Mozart's first Vienna opera, the *Entführung* on 24th November, 1827, this time at Covent Garden. It was "translated by W. Dimond, with additional airs by J. B. Cramer." [1] The "additional airs" and also their alleged author, J. B. Cramer, point to a curious state of affairs. And since in general we know little about the form in which Mozart's operas were presented to the nineteenth century, this rather entertaining case of the *Entführung* gives us something to think about.

In the Forbes Library, Northampton, Massachusetts, there is a complete pianoforte score of this first London version. The title reads:

*THE SERAGLIO.* | The Celebrated Opera by *MOZART*, with additional Music, | as Performed at the | Theatre Royal Covent Garden. | Composed and Arranged for the | Piano Forte, | and Dedicated (by Gracious Permission) | with the most Profound Respect to | His Most Gracious Majesty, | *THE KING.* | By | His Majesty's most Humble and Dutiful Servant | *C. KRAMER.* Master and Conductor of His Majesty's Band. | *LONDON,* | Published (for the Author) by Clementi & Co. 26 Cheapside & S. Chappell, 135 New Bond Str.

In addition to the page numbering of the separate pieces there is a continuous numbering of the whole edition, 219

[1] Alfred Loewenberg, *Annals of Opera*, p. 196. Cambridge, 1943.

engraved plates. The overture has, as page one, its own title page:

The Overture | to the *OPERA* of | *THE SERAGLIO* . . . Adapted from | Mozart's Celebrated Opera | by | *C. KRAMER.*

No certain information about the C. Kramer named in the title is to be found in any dictionary. Pohl calls him Christopher (or Christian) Kramer, "Master of the Royal Band of Wind-Instruments." Eitner in the *Quellen-Lexikon* (Vol. 5, 427), following Burney, recognizes a Kramer from Hanover who came to London from Schwetzingen about 1772 and was still working there in 1822 "as a highly esteemed musician." That can hardly still be our Kramer. Kramer is mentioned in the *Gentleman's Magazine* of November, 1827 (Vol. 97, II, 472), as one of the chief mourners at the burial of the violinist, Christoph Gottfried Kiesewetter. Grove, in the article on the King's Band, calls him Christian Kramer, successor to William Shield as "Master of the Musick" in 1829, a date that cannot be right and is probably based on the fact that Shield died in 1829 at the age of eighty-one. For the installation of Kramer's successor, François Cramer, Grove gives two dates, 1827 and 1834. While 1827 is impossible, 1834 does not sound unlikely. But let us not grow any grey hairs over these uncertainties. Let us be content with the fact that Christian Kramer is certainly not John Baptist Cramer, and thus the composer of the famous études and sonatas is throughout eternity absolved from having to answer before Apollo for his "additional music" to Mozart's *Entführung.*

The pianoforte edition gives us the names of those who took part in the performance. Here they are:

| Constanze | Miss Hughes |
| --- | --- |
| Blonde | Madame Vestris |
| Belmonte | Mr. Sapio |
| Pedrillo | Mr. Wrench |
| Osmin | Mr. Penson |

No name is given for the speaking part of the Pasha. But Mr. Kramer and Mr. Dimond are not satisfied with Mozart's six singers and add three more parts:

| Alexis | Miss H. Cawse |
| --- | --- |
| Dr. O'Callagan | Mr. Power |
| Doris | ? |

Miss Hughes had, as we have seen, already sung Elvira in *Don Giovanni*. Miss Cawse is known as having sung the role of Puck in Weber's *Oberon* in 1826. Mr. Sapio was one of the sons of the fashionable singing teacher in London round 1800. Madame Vestris needs no introduction; since 1815, despite her modest abilities as a singer, she had been one of the darlings of the London operatic stage and therefore her role even in this *Seraglio* must have been considered at least as important as the Constanze of Miss Hughes.

The *Entführung* appears to have had a great success. The *Gentleman's Magazine* for December, 1827 (Vol. 97, II, 554), reports:

Covent Garden. Nov. 24. *The Seraglio*, an Opera, the music of which is adapted from Mozart's *l'Enlèvement du Serail*, was produced. The hero of the plot is a Sicilian nobleman, whose intended bride has fallen into the power of a Turkish Pacha; and the chief interest of the piece exists in his endeavours to reclaim her. The denouement closes with the discovery that she is the sister of the Pacha, who immediately gives her in marriage to her faithful lover. The music and scenery were admirable; and the piece was given out for repetition amidst universal plaudits.

Since we are interested to know the foundation for this success, we have no choice but to look closer into Mr. Christian Kramer's workshop. The man spared himself no labor and left, so to speak, not one stone standing upon another in Mozart's structure. He started in at once with the overture. To our astonishment the prelude to this "Turkish opera" begins with the solemn strains from the scene of the men in armour in the *Zauberflöte*, weakened by tied chords between the first and second measures. The choral melody is cut out and its place taken by an extension of the fugato, done with very dubious skill. Next follows the flute and drum solo of the trial by fire and water. Only after this does Mozart's *presto* get under way, shortened in the middle section—Belmonte's cavatina in the minor, for which Kramer substitutes a piece in E minor, apparently pizzicato, of his own free invention but related to Pedrillo's serenade.

Although Kramer begins the first act with Belmonte's cavatina, the delicate variations, the extensions, the free ending suggested by the "soft zephirs" of the text, give him no pause. Therefore he not only cuts the ritornello short but twists it horribly as if he were wringing the neck of a chicken. Pohl maintains that in place of Belmonte's aria Kramer wrote "a chorus that would be a better opening for the opera." But this is not correct; Kramer's chorus now follows the aria. Peasants enter, genuine opera peasants, free from the day's toil and celebrating their happiness in song.

> Away away neighbour,
> Light wakes us to labour
> And toil claims our day—

> But eve soon advances
> Then sport song and dances
> Cares sweetly repair. . . .

Into this pastoral roundelay "Alexis enters, beating a tabor" and, of course, singing, whereupon the chorus repeats its jingle. Belmonte is discovered, a stranger of manifestly peaceful intent, who gives himself out as a painter. In an arioso he greets the "grave matrons" and the "blooming maids," and through a dialogue between soloists and chorus, the scene works up to a Prize Song to the gentle god of wine.

Only then does Mozart have a chance to get in a few notes again: with Osmin's little song, garbled in the very first measure and a strophe stricken out; and with the duet which is grossly altered. Osmin's aria, "O these dandies hither roaming," is left out entirely, even the explosive ending that Mozart brought back at the end of the opera; but that, of course, Kramer will not do. Belmonte's next aria, of which Mozart was so proud, being cut out, there follow now the Turkish chorus and Constanze's aria, "Once sincerely," the coloratura passages much simplified for Miss Hughes, who was plainly no Catarina Cavalieri with her "*geläufigen Gurgel*." Then, after the dialogue, comes the final trio with bits cut out here and there, for in Kramer's fingers the red pencil strikes at the least detail with untamable passion.

Madame Vestris opens the second act, not, however, with Mozart's "By tenderness and kindness" but with an arietta of two stanzas in G, "Come girls with smiling faces," composed by C. Kramer. The melodic contour of the closing line proves that Kramer must have listened carefully to Weber's *Freischütz*, which had already been produced at the Lyceum in July, 1824, and at Covent Garden under the direction of

Weber himself in 1826. The duet between Blonde and Osmin is "adapted" but is on the whole one of the best preserved numbers. Likewise Constanze's recitative, "What a change." On the other hand her aria contains a wholly new section in D major. Her big aria, "Thou may'st learn to hate," is omitted here and transplanted to the last act. Then comes Blonde's "O what pleasure," not intolerably changed in the music but fitted by Dimond-Kramer with a text of no appropriate meaning (Dronish lover take to flight). Evidently Kramer's librettist or translator also suffers from an irresistible drive to reduce the text of arias or ensemble pieces arising out of a dramatic situation to any doggerel for a show piece. This is especially unfortunate because the *Entführung* was the first opera in which Mozart would have nothing to do with incidental show pieces, but had come to know himself as a dramatist and had taken the greatest pains in shaping the libretto according to his new dramatic sense. For the London taste of 1825, however, the second act—witness Weber's *Oberon*—was precisely the place for show pieces. So Mr. Sapio now gets his chance to show off in a song that begins with an unmistakable reminiscence of Tamino's Picture Aria.

Miss Cawse (Alexis) follows with a cheerful andantino un poco scherzoso in two stanzas with a refrain for the chorus; then come Miss Hughes and Mr. Sapio in a scarcely less cheerful duet (Joy hath tears) with an interpolated cadenza and a kind of stretto; and immediately thereafter, since Pedrillo's "Haste to battle" is struck out, the drinking duet. This however is here enlarged to a terzet, thanks to the introduction of a wholly new personage, Dr. O'Callagan, the Irishman so plainly drunk that he can only fill in with a few miserable notes from time to time. Later on in the opera this O'Callagan is given a rather ambiguous role as second lover to Blonde, whose feelings apparently vacillate between him and Pedrillo.

Belmonte's "When the tears of joy are flowing" is done away with, and we come immediately to the quartet, Mozart's masterpiece in the combination of music and drama that holds the situation so delicately balanced. This fortunately is only slightly altered, but in the London of 1827 no second act could be allowed to end with such a piece. Kramer therefore composes a grand finale with chorus and ballet (Hark! the joyous bells are ringing). The merry-making develops into a Bacchanal, as in Wagner's *Venusberg*, with "grotesque Dancing of Satyrs and Bacchantes"; and for the conclusion the pasha, here called Ibrahim, is seen coming from the distance with a full military band. Was Kramer himself perhaps at the head of it? A terrific noise in C major, fireworks, and end of second act!

As in Mozart's opera, Belmonte opens the third act, not however with Mozart's heroic aria but with a creation of Kramer's, "Love, lift thy torch." This piece is wholly unlike Mozart, not only in the choice of key (A flat) but in its commonplace sentimentality, more like Weber's 1820 manner.

Pedrillo's romance—"the celebrated ballad" as it is called in the pianoforte version—is "arranged expressly for Mad. Vestris" with spicy, peppery harmonies and is naturally finished off as a "number" or a show piece in a way that robs it completely of its dramatic function.

Well, now comes Kramer's weightiest contribution to Mozart's score, which he must have felt was sorely in need of padding. This is the "Elopement Scena" composed as a sort of pantomime music to accompany a lively recitative or arioso. The tension that Mozart had built up here precisely by the "naturalistic" spoken dialogue was simply not worth Kramer's consideration. So be it; the effect is the same. The two pairs of lovers are caught, although Osmin's aria is cut out as if he dared not give rein to his triumph. Then instead of her duet with Belmonte, Constanze sings her great "Aria a la Bravura" from the second act. At first sight this does not seem altogether bad, yet it is bad; because the big aria condemns all the other players to the role of mere onlookers while we are at a point in the action where everything presses towards a dénouement. The dénouement follows, to be sure; but before the horribly mutilated and altered Vaudeville, Blonde and O'Callagan (or Pedrillo) still have time enough for a jolly duet, by Kramer of course.

That is the form in which the *Entführung* was introduced to England. Plainly there is a long way to travel before we reach Edward Dent's production of the *Zauberflöte* in Cambridge (1st December 1911), or the productions of Mozart at Glyndebourne. But we had better be wary of casting too heavy a stone at Christian Kramer, Master and Conductor of His Majesty's Band. In its original form of a Viennese Singspiel of 1782 the *Entführung* would most certainly not have been understood in the London of 1827 and could have been nothing but a solemn fiasco. And granted Kramer's ruinous meddling with it, its predecessors from *Tito* to *Don Giovanni* had met with little better fate, although in the fifty years from 1780 to 1830 *opera seria* and *opera buffa* underwent far fewer changes than opera with spoken dialogue. This *Singspiel*, or *opéra-comique*, was meanwhile changing slowly into the Romantic Opera. The London *Entführung* is a sister work to Weber's *Oberon*, the "British" form of which Weber, who created it, by no means regarded as final. But again, no Pharisaical stoning of the British or London taste of the time. We know what happened to the *Zauberflöte* in Paris between 1801 and 1827, and to *Don Giovanni* from 1805 and on. We know the sad fate of *Così fan tutte* in all European countries, even down to our own day. We have but to read Berlioz's report on the first performance of the *Entführung* at the Théâtre-Lyrique (*A travers chants*, 19th May 1859):

> *The Abduction from the Seraglio*, according to the almost unanimous opinion of the music critics, was performed at the Lyric Theatre with the most *scrupulous fidelity*. All they did was to arrange in two acts a piece that originally had three, invert the order of succession of a few numbers, retire one great aria from the role of Mme. Meillet to add it on to Mme. Ugalde's, and place between the two acts the famous Turkish March so well known to pianists who play Mozart. Well now, indeed! Here is what is called scrupulous fidelity!

But even in Germany the record is not clean. In a long and arduous career as critic, I never heard Belmonte's third act aria. Everywhere "*von der Maas bis an die Memel*" the B flat aria from the second act was put in its stead, where it is ludicrously out of place. How says the Apostle?

For all have sinned and come short of the glory of God.

*Don Giovanni* was not performed on the 14th, and in fact it was not yet finished, lacking the overture and presumably also Masetto's aria, part of the second finale, and the opening duet of the second act. Either this duet was not in the first draft of the libretto, or Mozart originally wished to omit it.

For a long time this remarkable first libretto eluded discovery. Yet Sonnleithner's account, which was also reported in Jahn's and Abert's biographies of Mozart, was so definite that the existence of the libretto could not be doubted. Librettos of the 1787 Prague performance and the 1788 Vienna performance of *Don Giovanni* are great rarities—the only copy of the latter I know of is in the Library of Congress—but the Vienna curiosity of 1787 appeared for a long time to be lost entirely. It seems to have been unknown even to Gugitz, who in his edition of Lorenzo da Ponte's memoirs gave a complete bibliography of the Abbate's writings. It was only fifteen years ago that my inquiries brought it to light in the library of the Gesellschaft der Musikfreunde in Vienna. To be sure, it was mentioned by Eusebius Mandyczewski in the supplementary volume of *Die Geschichte der Gesellschaft der Musikfreunde* (1912, p. 73), but he did not make clear that this was not the 1788 Vienna libretto. For it is well known that *Don Giovanni* was not performed in Vienna until 1788.

It is an implausible little book, still in the old cover of colored paper, 54 pages in small octavo without a printer's announcement. The *scena ultima* of Act II is completed in old-fashioned handwriting; probably it never existed in printed form. Attached to the text are four pages of exact and intelligent notes in longhand by Leopold von Sonnleithner, from which I have derived the above dates of the Archduchess's journey. They also inform us that this unique copy is from the library of Carl Czerny (1791–1857). At the close of his remarks Sonnleithner says, "This libretto contains some deviations from the Vienna and Prague librettos, but these are not important; only certain differences in the changes of sets in Act I, Scenes 1, 4, and 5, and Act II, Scene 10 (11) and 11 (12) are to be noted." Evidently Sonnleithner discovered the libretto after 1865, since he did not consult it in preparing his printing of the Prague libretto (Leipzig, Breitkopf & Härtel, 1865), in which he noted the variants in the Vienna libretto and the Mozart autograph. Otherwise he would have noticed that the version of the text in Mozart's autograph is derived partly from our first libretto, while it also contains some alterations which, though they may not be "important," are significant and certainly follow Mozart's wishes.

But we are not concerned here with problems of textual criticism: they would be of prime importance only if we contemplated a new philological edition of the *Don Giovanni* libretto. We wish to pursue only one puzzling circumstance, namely, that this first libretto is not complete. Aside from the two end pages which are completed in longhand, probably having been left out on account of technical difficulties in the printing, almost the whole second half of Act I is missing; it breaks off in the middle of the quartet (No. 8 in the score).

What is the explanation for this peculiarity? It is impossible that the second act was complete and the first unfinished at the time of this printing. This would contradict the autograph of the score, which clearly shows that the second half of Act I was composed, understandably enough, before a large part of Act II. It would also be contrary to Mozart's practice; he would certainly not have begun to compose without being familiar with the entire libretto. Neither would it be compatible with da Ponte's facile, carefree way of working. The true reasons must lie elsewhere: in the fact that *Don Giovanni* was most unsuitable for a celebration honoring a royal bride, which must have been clear to both Mozart and da Ponte. Undoubtedly the imperial censor's or marshal's office demanded to see in advance the libretto of the work that was to be performed at the celebration. At this the authors must have been struck with terror, knowing it could not be approved in its totality. So we may suspect that it occurred to da Ponte to present only a partial libretto on the pretext that it was not yet finished. Thus he could leave out those scenes in which the "dissoluteness" of the hero is most drastically documented—the half confession of Donna Anna, the champagne song, and the attack on Zerlina—while presenting in its entirety the second act, in which morality appears to be restored.

Nevertheless, it did not happen that *Don Giovanni* was degraded to the status of a courtly *Festoper*, thanks, we may be sure, to Mozart's delicate sense of timing. Sonnleithner had arrived before us at the suspicion that Mozart "perhaps purposely deferred the completion of his work" in order to avoid difficulties. And so the concern this odd first libretto has caused us has been unnecessary, after all.

# XVII

# Recitatives in Don Giovanni

IT HAS often been said, and with truth, that luck was against
Mozart when he undertook the second versions of his
*Nozze di Figaro* and *Don Giovanni*. In his case the rule,
which nearly always holds good with other masters, that the
final version of a work is as a matter of course the definitive
one, does not apply. With *Fidelio*, with Schubert's songs, even
—in spite of a disturbing change in style—with *Tannhäuser*,
we hold to the last revision. Not so with Mozart: there the
first version alone shows the creator's intention at its purest.
The indifference with which Mozart sacrificed the original
form of *Figaro* and *Don Giovanni* to the caprices of singers
is inexplicable: it looks as though these two works, once they
had been finished in all their perfection, were nothing more to
him after their completion than playthings of theatrical routine and stage necessity. It is hard to understand how, in the
Vienna *Figaro* of 1789, he could replace a masterly aria like
Susanna's "Venite inginocchiatevi" by the wholly insignificant
arietta, "Un moto di gioia," during the singing of which the

Countess and Cherubino had nothing better to do than to become part of the audience; and it is even more incomprehensible that at the same performance the most magical number of the whole score, Susanna's "Deh vieni non tardar," was suppressed in favour of the rather colourless aria, "Al desio di chi t'adora."

But Mozart positively ruined the second act of *Don Giovanni* in the Vienna version of 1788. Nothing shall be said against the interpolated aria in the first act, Don Ottavio's "Dalla sua pace." It is a wonderful piece and may well be sung if Ottavio omits his "Il mio tesoro" in the second act; its position in Act I is dramatically not altogether unjustified; and above all it is very short. On the other hand, what happens in Act II of the 1788 version, between Leporello's escape from the clutches of the quintet of his opponents and the churchyard scene, becomes the more obscure the more one tries to make it clear to oneself.

Zerlina, knife in hand, drags Leporello back on the stage by the hair, with the aid of a peasant ties him to a chair in spite of his entreaties and cajoleries, and fastens him thus bound to the window frame. Whereupon the following long duet follows:

LEPORELLO: Per queste tue manine,
candide e tenerelle,
per questa fresca pelle,
abbi pietà di me!

ZERLINA: Non v' è pietà, briccone!
son' una tigre irata
un' aspide, un leone;
nò, nò, pietà non v' è!

&c.

It seems unlikely that this duet can ever have been sung since the performances of 1788, except, as we shall see in a moment, at the Prague performances of 1801: it has no true feeling of comedy, much less of tragi-comedy, and musically too it belongs to Mozart's less successful pieces, in spite of some ingenious realistic suggestions.

Two *secco* recitatives follow. Zerlina leaves the room. Leporello implores the peasant, who has remained behind, to bring him some water, doubtless in order to have his hands freed for the purpose of drinking; but the peasant departs with a grin. Leporello vainly tries to loosen his fetters by himself and, tugging violently at the rope that ties him to the window-frame, he pulls it out of the wall and escapes, with the chair clinging to his posterior and dragging the cross-bars after him. When Zerlina returns with Donna Elvira, she finds that the bird has flown. Elvira is of opinion that he must have been saved by his infamous master; Zerlina agrees and goes in search of Don Ottavio, to inform him of this latest accident and incite him to vengeance; and Elvira, without more ado, begins her *recitativo accompagnato*, "In quali eccessi, o numi," followed by her new aria, the most widely known of all these interpolated numbers: "Mi tradì quell' alma ingrata."

Quite apart from the fact that the whole succession of these scenes is merely episodic and quite superfluous—for why should Leporello be made to escape twice?—if not harmful, since it simply prolongs all this byplay from the opening of Act II to the churchyard scene without adding to the *musical* value of the whole, it is obvious that there is something missing here. Elvira's great scene remains unaccounted for, since it is inconceivable that she could have been so profoundly agitated by Leporello's second escape. Now if we glance at the libretto of 1788, we find that as a matter of fact the recitative that prepares Elvira's scene takes a completely different form. I shall quote the passage as it stands:

### SCENA XIII

ZERLINA, D.ELVIRA, poi MASETTO con due Contadini.

| ZERL.: | Andiam andiam Signora, |
| | Vedrete in qual maniera |
| | Ho concio il scellerato. |

| D.ELV.: | Ah sopra lui |
| | Si sfoghi il mio furor. |

| ZERL.: | Stelle! in qual modo |
| | Si salvò quel briccone? |

| MAS.: | No non si trova |
| | Un' anima più nera. |

| ZERL.: | Ah Masetto, Masetto |
| | Dove fosti finor? |

| MAS.: | Un' infelice |
| | Volle il ciel ch' io salvassi. |
| | Era io sol pochi passi |
| | Lontan da te, quando gridare io sento |
| | Nell' opposto sentiero: |
| | Con lor v' accorro, veggio |
| | Una donna che piange, |
| | Ed un uom che fugge: vo inseguirlo, |
| | Mi sparisce dagli occhi, |
| | Ma da quel che mi disse la fanciulla, |
| | Ai tratti, alle sembianze, alle maniere |
| | Lo credo quel briccon del Cavaliere. |

ZERL.:    E' desso senza fallo: anche di questo
          Informiam Don Ottavio: a lui si aspetta
          Far per noi tutti o domandar vendetta.
                                        (*partono*)

#### SCENA XIV
##### D.ELVIRA sola
In quali eccessi, . . . &c.

Here we have a perfectly plausible justification for Donna
Elvira's scene. Zerlina indignantly asks Masetto, who has just
arrived, where on earth he has been, and Masetto explains his
absence by relating a new offence on the part of Don Giovanni he has just witnessed: it had pleased Heaven that he
should intrude upon the villain's latest attack upon an innocent girl and save her. This story, which shows a new and
more serious side of Masetto, is the transition from the comic
scene between Zerlina and Leporello to Elvira's tragic out-
burst. Elvira is horrified at this new link in the endless chain
of her seducer's misdeeds: "In quali eccessi, o numi, in quai
misfatti orribili, tremendi è avvolto il sciagurato!" In the aria
that follows she complains that, in spite of all, she cannot
cease to feel compassion for him, and this in turn prepares for
her appearance in the second finale, during the supper scene,
which may possibly be regarded as the explanation why
Mozart set the whole of this additional scene without too
great a reluctance.

  The music for Masetto's narrative has so far remained unknown: to my knowledge it is to be found in none of the old
or new scores. But there is in the library of the Istituto Musicale in Florence a score (265), once among the effects of the
Palazzo Pitti, which exactly reproduces the 1788 Vienna ver-

sion of *Don Giovanni*. It is a manuscript from the workshop of the music dealer Lausch, who had at other times often acted as copyist for Mozart, and there are a hundred indications that his source for this copy was Mozart's autograph. An appendix to this manuscript, moreover, contains copies of the complete wind parts, which are no longer extant in the original, and thus proves that the three trombones in the second finale are authentic, although Mozart did not employ them in the overture.

This score contains Masetto's narrative, and not only that: it contains also the scene in which Leporello tries to break his fetters and takes to his heels, as well as the following scene for Zerlina and Elvira (with Masetto) in a version hitherto wholly unknown and, as we shall see, in Mozart's authentic form. The version hitherto known is not Mozart's own; to put it briefly and bluntly, it is forgery. This has been suspected before, as for instance by Bernhard Gugler, who says so in his edition of the *Don Giovanni* score (Leipzig, 1868), and by myself, as I said in my introduction to Eulenburg's edition in miniature score (p. xviii). To attribute to Mozart such faulty declamation as that of the word "legò" at the beginning of Leporello's recitative is impossible:—

LEPORELLO

A - mi-co, per pie-tà! un po-co d'a-cqua fre-sca o ch'io mi mo-ro! guar-da un po co-me stret-to mi le-gò l'as-sas-si-nal

Compare with this the genuine Mozart:—

pria che costei ri-tor-ni bi-so-gna dar di sprone al-la cal-ca-gna, e

stra-sci-nar, so oc-cor-re u-na mon-ta-gna.

### SCENA XIII

Zerlina, Donna Elvira, poi Masetto con due Contadini

ZERLINA

Andiam, andiam Signora,  Ve-drete in qual maniera Ho concio il scel-le-

-ra-to.  Ah so-pra lu-i  Si sfo-ghi il mio furor,  Stel-le!  in qual

mo-do Si salvò quel briccon? No, non si trova Un'a-ni-ma più ne-ra.  Ah Ma-

-set-to, Ma-set-to  Do-ve fo-sti fi-nor?  Un' in-fe-li-ce Vol-le il ciel ch'io sal

-vas-si.    Er-a io sol po-chi pas-si Lon-tan da te, quan-do gri-

da-rè io sento  Nell'op-po-sto sen-tie-ro:  Con lor v'ac-cor-ro,veggio U-na

don-na  chè pian-ge,  Ed un uo-mo che fug-ge:  vo'in-se-guir-lo

Mi spa-ri-sce dag-li oc-chi,  Ma da quel che mi dis-se la fan-ciul-la,  Ai

trat-ti,  al-le sem-bian-ze al-le ma-ni-e-re  Lo cre-do quel bric-

ZERL.
-con del Ca-va-li-e-re!    E' des-so sen-za fal-lo: an-che di

que-sto In-for-mi-am Don Ot-ta-vio: a lui si a-

-spet-ta Far per noi tut-ti o do-man-dar ven-det-ta.

A careful comparison will show how much simpler and yet more striking and effective is Mozart's treatment of all this. The difference between the conclusions of the second recitative is especially significant. The forger makes baldly for the key of B♭ major with which Elvira's *accompagnato* opens; Mozart closes in D major and so secures the explosion that follows its full force of expression.

But who was the forger? The clues point to Prague. The two spurious recitatives make their earliest appearance in the first full-score edition of *Don Giovanni*, which appeared, printed in set type, at Breitkopf & Härtel's in 1801 (Vol. II, pp. 587–88). The firm of Breitkopf & Härtel, already in those days intent on completeness in its editions, thought fit to print all the supplementary pieces of 1788 in an appendix to their score, although in a haphazard order. The material for this first edition was furnished by Mozart's earliest biographer, Franz Xaver Niemetschek, a professor at the Prague *Gymnasium*. A letter from Niemetschek to Gottfried Christoph Härtel, dated February 20th, 1801, gives full information. I am indebted for a copy of it to Dr. Wolfgang Schmieder, the keeper of the firm's archives, who kindly acceded to my request to make the necessary investigations. The following extract may be quoted:

> Here follows a supplement of recitatives to the two new extra pieces in the second act of *Don Juan*. My copyist tried to mislead me by assuring me that everything was now complete. But as fortunately this opera was given last week, I went to it in order to convince myself, and found that some recitatives were still missing, which I now send you herewith. I obtained them through a good friend of Guardasoni's. They cost, however, 1 thaler. So dear is Guardasoni. The 1st, i.e. the 8th scene, follows immediately upon the great sextet. Scene 9 follows on at once. Next comes Ottavio's aria in G. To that succeeds the 10th scene, which you have already received in an earlier supplement, namely where Zerlina brings back Leporello and ties him up during the duet in C. After the duet Zerlina goes to fetch the other victims, such as Elvira, &c., to show the captured rogue to them. And now follows the 11th scene, in which Leporello tears himself away; and where, as Zerlina returns with Elvira, they find the place empty. Where, too, Zerlina departs and Elvira sings the 12th scene, i.e. the orchestral recitative with the rondo in E flat, which I sent you the other day. On this follows the scene in front of the statue.
>
> And now you may be sure of having everything as complete as it is produced here. André probably referred to the old original, and thus not to these altered scenes. . . .

In other words, Niemetschek himself had already been deceived, either by the impresario of the Prague opera, Guardasoni, or by the latter's anonymous "good friend." Very likely the genuine recitatives, the omission of which at the Prague performance struck Niemetschek when he made a comparison with the Vienna libretto, were not found ready to hand, so that they were quickly composed afresh to satisfy the agreeable and highly-esteemed professor—for who cared what mere recitatives were like? A well-meant little swindle of that kind was no great matter in those days. And so it came about that for nearly a hundred and forty years the score of *Don Giovanni* has contained two spurious recitatives. It does not seem too soon to replace them by the authentic ones.

# XVIII

## *Mozart's "Adelaide" Concerto*

THE most beautiful performance I ever heard Yehudi Menuhin give was several years ago when he played one of Mozart's concertos of 1775, the Concerto in D major (K. 218). Menuhin played at once like a master and like a child, as if still in the state of innocence from which most adult violinists have long since fallen. No wonder that the number of Mozart violin concertos is too few for him. He has already had to resurrect the "last" Mozart concerto (K. 271a), which few violinists perform, rightly finding it somewhat uncomfortable because, although it was undoubtedly composed by Mozart, it is no longer in its original form. Having played this work, Menuhin now has to fall back on the first juvenile concerto, the "Adelaide." This was published under the editorship of Marius Casadesus and was first performed in London by Jelly d' Aranyi in one of the Courtauld-Sargent concerts.

Mr. Casadesus christened this work the "Adelaide Concerto" because the eleven year old Mozart is said to have composed it early in 1766 for the Princess Adelaide of France, writing it down in her presence. She was the eldest daughter of Louis XV; it was her younger sister Victoire to whom Mozart had dedicated his Opus I the previous year. The princess is described as having been "very fond of music and an excellent violinist." The original manuscript, it is said, "is only written on two staves, the upper containing the solo violin part as well as the tutti and the lower the bass part. The latter is written in E, the solo part on the other hand in D, the reason being that the instrument played by Madame Adelaide, a dainty 'ladies violin,' sounded better in a higher pitch than the usual one." From this we see that Madame, then a grown woman of thirty-four, played a "pochette," and if this was really the case perhaps she was not after all "so excellent a violinist."

This is all we learn about the autograph, except that it is "in a private collection in France" and "was not unknown to experts," namely to Saint-Saëns and Weckerlin, who are unfortunately both dead. I fancy myself somewhat of an expert on Mozart's handwriting, but I was not able to see even a line of the original or a photostatic copy. Even the great publishing house that brought out the work in splendid fashion in full score and piano reduction had to renounce all claim to such proof of the work's authenticity. Mr. Casadesus appears not to realize what a great discovery he has made here. For this would have to be not only Mozart's first violin concerto, but also the first of all his concertos; and what a remarkable one! Prior to 1766, namely in the autumn of 1765, in London, Mozart had adapted a series of Johann Christian Bach's piano works as piano concertos. In April 1767, nearly a year after writing the "Adelaide Concerto," he again adapted to his own purposes a number of concertos by other composers. His first original piano concerto was not written until December 1773. The more we consider, the more curious we become about the original manuscript of the "Adelaide."

In the summer of 1768 Leopold Mozart compiled a catalogue of his son's compositions from the age of seven onward "which can be shown in the original." Leopold was a very exact man. In the list he included even the smallest compositions of the little Mozart, and his sketchbooks as well. But unfortunately the "Adelaide Concerto" is missing. Leopold Mozart did not neglect to mention all the crowned heads and were dedicated. But he forgot poor Princess Adelaide and the even the court ladies to whom Opus I and II and III and IV violin concerto. Perhaps he realized how inadmissible it was, how contrary to eighteenth century custom, to dedicate an unpublished work to an important personage. What good was it to receive a dedication if the public did not know about it? Perhaps, then, Leopold was ashamed to list this concerto. For father Mozart was a man who understood very well what was appropriate for the eighteenth century. In the twentieth century we are no longer so sure.

According to Mr. Casadesus, little Mozart dated his dedication "Versailles, le 26. Mai 1766" and borrowed the style from the dedications of Melchior Grimm's first two works, laboriously fitting together turns of phrase from Grimm. Unfortunately, when he dated it, Mozart apparently did not realize that he was not in Versailles on May 26, 1766. Leopold—the pedant—kept a diary according to which the Mozarts arrived in Versailles two days later, on May 28. This archpedant also wrote letters; on June 1 the Mozarts were back in Paris, whence Leopold wrote on June 9: ". . . in the coming weeks we are to return to Versailles where we went twelve days ago and spent four days. . . ." Could anything be more pedantic? Now the reader may comprehend our longing to see the original manuscript of the "Adelaide Concerto."

We are far from wishing to cast the slightest doubt on the good faith of Mr. Casadesus or his publisher. But it seems clear that Mr. Casadesus has taken Mozart's cause upon himself with much devotion and to a very great extent. To such an extent, in fact, that he will not produce the original manuscript. A work of the form and scope that he presents to us could not have been written by Mozart in 1766. But even supposing Mozart had wished to write a concerto, then he would have written the work *as* a concerto and not on two staves. He was familiar with the handling of full score. The invention of the themes, particularly in the first movement, is Mozartian. But on looking more closely we find in many places both technical and formal turns "projected backward" from later concertos. Without the availability of musical examples, however, we do not wish to enter into a philological examination. One thought occurs to us: when Mozart was in Holland shortly before the second visit to Paris he sketched a notebook entitled "Capricci." Constanze was still in possession of this book in 1800; today there is no trace of it. Could a leaf of this "Capricci" notebook have strayed to Paris? Could Mr. Casadesus have had such a page before him? The odd notation in E and D major would be suited to the title "Capricci." Mr. Casadesus is in a position to satisfy all these doubts if he will only circulate a photostat of the manuscript. By so doing he can dispel our apprehensions and turn a doubting Thomas into the most faithful of all Mozart disciples.

*※→ ※→ ※← ※←*

# XIX

## Haydn, Mozart, and English Sea Heroes

I MIGHT have made the title of this article more comprehensive and called it "Haydn, Mozart, and English Victories"; but in that case I should have had to add Beethoven's name. Beethoven celebrated Wellington's victory at Vitoria with a martial fantasia for orchestra, Op. 91, which is today completely forgotten, although when it was first heard it excited wild enthusiasm—much more, in fact, than the Seventh and Eighth Symphonies (Op. 92 and Op. 93), which are still very much alive. But even if we are going to leave Beethoven out, it is a curious and interesting fact that each of the three great composers who form what the Germans call the "Classical Triad" should have given practical expression to his friendly feelings for England. It is particularly remarkable that both Mozart and Haydn should have devoted their art to the glorification of the exploits of English sea heroes.

In the case of Haydn, with whom I will begin in defiance

of chronological order, the facts are well known. Haydn's great *Mass in D*, which is known in England as the *Imperial Mass*, is in Germany called the *Lord Nelson Mass*. As Haydn was working on it in August, 1798, the news of the destruction of the French fleet at Aboukir reached even peaceful Eisenstadt, and he thereupon introduced trumpets and drums at the end of the Benedictus—an eloquent tribute to the victorious admiral.

It is less well known that Haydn also honored Nelson in another work. In September, 1800, two years after the battle at Aboukir, Nelson came to Esterház to stay with Prince Esterházy, accompanied by Sir William and Lady Hamilton. We know that Lady Hamilton was completely charmed by Haydn. She did not leave his side for two whole days and paid practically no attention to the admiral's illustrious host. Her companion, Mrs. Knight, wrote some stanzas entitled *Lines from the Battle of the Nile*, which Haydn set to music. The autograph manuscript is preserved in the family archives at Esterház and was first published a few years ago by Ludwig Landshoff. The work was originally written for voice and clavier; Landshoff also supplied an orchestral arrangement which shows a sensitive appreciation of the style of the period. The setting is only a *pièce d'occasion;* but it is not unworthy of the composer of *The Creation*. Indeed, the instrumental portion is magnificent. It begins with a slow introduction in C minor, which portrays by the simplest means the anxious oppression which hangs over nature and men in the grey dawn before the beginning of a fateful battle. Quietly moving passages in unison, sudden sforzandos on discords, impetuous outbreaks which are at once subdued—one seems actually to see the silhouettes of the warships behind the billowing mist.

Then comes a great battle picture in the form of the recitative, "Ausonia, trembling midst unnumbered woes," and a song of triumph written as an aria: "Blest, leader! Foremost in renown." Both recitative and aria are entirely in the style of *The Creation.* Haydn's most striking inspiration is the way in which he introduces the opening motive of the aria—a sort of idealized march—in the tumult of the recitative.

No one has yet properly studied the question of Mozart's contribution to the praise of English heroism, though it has been available in facsimile for the last eighty years. His work is to be found in Otto Jahn's *Life of Mozart* (Vol. II, Appendix II). The facsimile has appeared in every successive edition and has naturally got worse with each one, until in Abert's edition it is practically illegible. In Köchel's catalogue the work is included among the chamber music in the supplement (No. 25)—it was never finished. And the fact that it was never finished is what makes the story interesting.

I suppose every Englishman knows of the famous defence of Gibraltar by Elliot and the exploit of "Black Dick," otherwise Admiral Richard Howe. The fortress had been besieged by the French and Spanish for some years when Howe, by a bold surprise attack, managed to supply the besieged garrison with provisions and forced the enemy to raise the siege. The connection between this deed of heroism and Mozart's music is very curious. The deed first of all aroused the enthusiasm of a Hungarian lady (her name is unknown to me) who lived in Vienna. This lady commissioned J. N. C. Michael Denis, an ex-Jesuit who wrote under the name of the "German Bard," to write a stirring poem on the subject.

Denis was rather an exceptional man, who deserves to be

remembered with honor. He was born at Schaerding in Bavaria, though judging by his name he was certainly not a Bavarian. At the age of twenty he entered the order of the Society of Jesus at Vienna, and for twenty-five years was a teacher at the Theresianische Akademie. After the suppression of the Jesuits he first took charge of Garelli's library, and then in 1784 became curator of the court library. He was an enthusiastic admirer of Milton, and in 1762 he began to study English. In the course of the next ten years he translated the whole of Ossian and established himself as a bard under the pseudonym "Sined." He extolled the work of Klopstock, cultivated relations with the "Prussian Bards," and made a close study of all collections of Nordic poetry. Students of Wagner will find in his works a translation of a dialogue between Wotan and Erda from the *Edda* which is practically word for word the same as the Erda scene in *Siegfried*.

Denis celebrated the defence and relief of Gibraltar in a Bardic song, with the title, *Gibraltar, vom 11–18 Weinmondes, ein Bardengesang Sined des Oberbarden der Donau.* It consists of three pages of grandiloquent verse, first published separately in 1782. In 1784 it was reissued with an English translation by William Sanson under the title, *Gibraltar, from the 11th to the 18th of October, 1782. Translated from the song of Sined the German Bard,* and in 1792 the poem was included in the sixth volume of *Ossian und Sined Lieder.*

The same Hungarian lady also commissioned Mozart to set the song to music. We know this from Mozart himself. On December 28, 1782, he writes to his father:

> I am working at a very difficult thing—a Bardic song about Gibraltar by Denis. However, this is a secret, since a Hungarian lady wishes to pay this honour to Denis. . . .

He actually began to compose, but did not finish the piece, though there was undoubtedly the prospect of a comfortable fee. His letter gives us a clue to the reason why he later abandoned the work.

> The ode is noble, beautiful, everything you could wish for —only too exaggeratedly bombastic for my delicate ears. But what can you expect? The golden mean, truth in all things, is no longer known or prized. To win approbation one must write things which are either so intelligible that a coachman could sing them, or so unintelligible that they please people just because no rational man can understand them.

How much of Denis's text Mozart set or sketched in music is not certain. Only two pages of the manuscript survive, but there must originally have been more. What we have is only about a third of the poem set for soprano and a sketch of the orchestral accompaniment on two staves. That Mozart cannot have intended to give the work a piano accompaniment is obvious from the string tremolos and figurations which are specified. The voice part recites, and the orchestra inserts its illustrative or emotional commentary. There is an agitated picture of a deserted beach over which night falls. The quiet of the night is suddenly broken by the storm of a surprise attack. A single line is sufficient to show the picturesque energy of Mozart's setting:

Wo der blei-che Tod des Schiffers Kiele spal-tend sitzt

Mozart only gave his father half the reason why the piece was not finished. It was not merely too bombastic for his "delicate ears." The actual work of composition was "a very difficult thing." It offered him no structure, and hence no form. It did not give him a single opportunity to write a recitative and aria. It could only be set as an orchestral picture with a running commentary by the singer. It is strange that Mozart did not jump at the chance to use a form for which five years before he had conceived a sudden passion—melodrama. At Mannheim he had got to know some of Georg Benda's melodramas. He had actually seen *Medea* on the stage, and he certainly knew *Ariadne* from the piano score.

> I love these two works so much that I keep them continually by me. . . . You know, of course, that the text is not sung but declaimed, and that the music is a sort of *obbligato* recitative. Sometimes the words are spoken to musical accompaniment, which is a most marvellous effect.

In Sined's *Bardengesang* he had an opportunity to write a melodrama of this kind. If he had taken the opportunity, he would undoubtedly have finished his task and left us a work in rather a new style. However, by 1782 or 1783 he had apparently outgrown his enthusiasm for a hybrid work, which melodrama most certainly is, in spite of Beethoven, Schumann, and Strauss, all of whom cultivated it. In this case, as in others, Mozart's "delicate ears" guided him aright.

# XX

## Beethoven's Military Style

BEETHOVEN lived in a time of war. He was eighteen years old at the outset of the French Revolution, through which one of his first employers was to lose his electoral throne. The new French Republic had to defend itself against everyone until it produced an inspired commander who subjected all Europe to his warlike ambitions and even captured Vienna, Beethoven's second home. Bonaparte, it can be said, played no small part in both the outer and inner life of Beethoven. For the space of twenty-five years Beethoven could have heard, if he had listened, the alarms of war, and, politically interested as he was, there is no doubt that he did listen. It is quite logical that he should have celebrated in a great symphony the battle of Vitoria, June 21, 1813, which marked the beginning of the end for Napoleon. For Beethoven's admirers this work has remained a source of embarrassment, and if it were ever performed today it could only be played out-of-doors under the direction of the second-string conductor. Beethoven himself, however, took the work quite seriously, even dedicating it to George, Prince Regent of England, who, much to the composer's annoyance, took the gift somewhat lightly.

The Battle Symphony represents the lowest point in Beethoven's work, but not because it is an occasional piece, since for half a century prior to Beethoven music consisted of nothing but occasional works. Beethoven was the first example, and a dangerous one, of the "free artist" who obeys his so-called inner compulsion and follows only his genius. A hundred years before, this attitude of the composer toward his art and toward the world was quite unheard of; in the case of J. S. Bach it appears that he was afraid to come forward with his most intimate and lonely works, the *Inventions* and *Sinfonias*, and later the *Well-tempered Clavier* and the *Art of Fugue*, without having some special pretext. Therefore he disguised them as pedagogical examples "for the use and profit of the musical youth desirous of learning as well as for the pastime of those already skilled in this study." Music that did not have a religious or social function still needed some excuse. Even Haydn and Mozart hardly ever wrote music that did not have some such defined purpose. Beethoven, too, produced expressly occasional works, and these are by no means his worst. The two cantatas, the one on the death of Joseph II and the other on the coronation of Leopold II, are not only the last, but the best, of his youthful works. He wrote no more such pieces, although his *Missa Solemnis* must in the end be regarded as an occasional work that simply grew a little beyond its original motive.

It is not because of its occasional nature that the *Battle of Vitoria* did not take its place as a Tenth Symphony. Rather it is because it remains merely naturalistic, patriotic, and occasional, quite aside from our knowing that the man whose defeat it celebrates was greater than all his opponents. One is reminded of a passage from a letter written to James Morris, May 13, 1898, by Theodor Fontane, who assuredly was a patriot: "Whatever appeals to patriotism or chauvinism is worthless in art. There are very few exceptions to this rule." It is doubtful whether he thought of Kleist as one of these exceptions, and certainly not the Kleist of the *Hermannsschlacht*.

In Beethoven's work the military element plays a very important role, quite apart from his marches, such as the three "great" marches for piano written for four hands (Op. 45), and even the march from *Fidelio* which, though not great, is the most beautiful. The military element is a purely musical category for Beethoven, without any programmatic intention. He was not the first to use it so; long before the outbreak of the Revolution, in the winter of 1782–83, Mozart wrote his Piano Concerto in C Major with trumpets and drums (K. 415), the first to have so military an orchestral setting. Mozart then achieved an ideal expression of the military concept in the first movement of another piano concerto in C major (K. 467), which is perhaps the most beautiful of all his concertos. A youthfully warlike, youthfully vigorous work written at the height of life, its aggressiveness contains its own triumph. Whence did Mozart derive this type of concerto? From an Italian settled in Paris, Giovanni Battista Viotti. Mozart was well acquainted with Viotti, for in 1783 he had written richer instrumentation for a violin concerto of Viotti's and supplied it with a new slow movement. He simply transferred Viotti's concept from the violin to the piano concerto.

It was from Viotti, and presumably not from Mozart, that Beethoven derived the idea of a "military" first movement for all his concertos. Beethoven could have become familiar with Mozart's piano concertos only after his own concerto style had already been developed and molded, since Mozart's concertos were published rather late—not until after his death in fact. Viotti's concertos, on the other hand, were published forthwith and circulated internationally. I do not know whether anything has been written about Beethoven's relation to Viotti; if not, something should be. When one looks at Viotti's Seventh Violin Concerto, one notices how much Beethoven adopted from it. One also sees that Viotti was an insignificant forerunner, Beethoven a master who profited greatly from his work. How easy the great have it! They endure while lesser figures sink into obscurity; they receive all the credit for things whose origins have been lost to sight. In addition, their lifework stands before us as a totality in which the less important works illuminate the more significant and take on consequence from them. The secondary works of a great composer are more important to us than the principal works of a minor composer; and they *are* more important as a concrete manifestation of development, as a symbol.

Viotti had presumably not invented the "military" first movement of the concerto himself, but had met it in French music and developed it within this framework. His example was so powerful that the musical category of the military was used by both Mozart and Beethoven only in the concerto, nowhere else—perhaps a little in piano and violin sonatas (in Beethoven only in the C Minor Sonata), but neither in other chamber music nor in the symphony. It is unmistakable. One may characterize it as idealized quickstep: rapid four-four time, progressing boldly with growing intensity, with dotted eighth-notes and up-beat patterns, with ever-pulsating rhythm —although above this rhythm some cantabile, "feminine" melodies hover, and triplets and virtuoso figurations soar upward. It is a contribution of French genius to European music; the Italian concerto of Viotti has quite different characteristics.

All the first movements of Beethoven's concertos belong to this type, beginning with the Concerto in E♭ Major written when he was twelve, which starts out in the military manner with the winds (flutes and horns). The military element is even more apparent in the first two piano concertos, Op. 15 in C Major and Op. 19 in B♭ Major, whose chronology is not certain; the first movement of the first concerto, particularly, a revolutionary quickmarch, should have earned Beethoven, like Schiller, an honorary citizenship in the French Republic. Not without intention was the Third Piano Concerto in C Minor, Op. 37, later dedicated to the war hero and brother in Apollo, Prince Louis Ferdinand of Prussia. It is full of soft and even sentimental traits; but the dark determination of the initial theme is repeatedly emphasized, and it sounds especially military when, in the recapitulation not long before the cadence, it is intoned in D major by horns and trumpets under the sustained trills of the piano. The inner pulse, so to speak, of the movement is the drum motive in the third and fourth bars of the theme—a military motive, whose development is the typically Beethovian element in the movement.

Even the Fourth, the G Major Concerto, Op. 58, with its lyrical opening and its feminine charm, is not free of the military element, although it lacks trumpets and drums. The second theme is a march theme of Austro-Slavic coloring with an irresistible inclination to conclude in minor. It seems to me that this mixture of lyric and military elements is responsible for the character of this concerto—two opposing forces which are balanced within the framework of the piece.

The final Piano Concerto in Eb Major, Op. 73, is the apotheosis of the military concept. Not without reason is it called the Emperor Concerto: an emperor of military splendor reviewing the victory parade of his home-coming forces, Napoleon at the height of his power. It is both the troops, passing by with bands playing, and the man who dreams this dream of power and is able to bring it to fulfillment. This concerto is a sister work of the Eroica: the heroic element in the guise of the military.

The Triple Concerto, Op. 56, is the military concept in concerto form. The two themes are typical Beethovian march themes; it as if he were unable to direct his imagination away from these victory motives, with their full beats at the outset, dotted eighths, and pulse of marching rhythms; and in his most beautiful concerto, the Violin Concerto, a victory motive becomes the opening motto of the theme. It is the best and most sublime creative manifestation of the military element in music, so sublime that one is almost unaware of it unless one knows its origin. It is the fulfillment of what Viotti foreshadowed.

Yet it should not be thought that Beethoven's contemporaries did not understand the peculiar sublimity of this concerto and the uniqueness of his other concertos. They expected a first movement in four-four time of a "military" character; and they reacted with unmixed pleasure when Beethoven not only fulfilled but surpassed their expectations, not only broadened the limits but went beyond them. The enjoyment which is based on a knowledge of musical tradition disappeared in the nineteenth century; today we enjoy each work for itself, without sensing its relationship to works of its own and other genres. When Mozart wrote a first movement in three-four time (K. 413, 449, and 491), this was in itself daring, wholly aside from the inner audacity of the third work. In Haydn's Military Symphony (1794), there is a mixture of genres which, as such, arouses amusement, especially since the military element is so Austrian, entirely different from Beethoven.

Beethoven, with all his originality, was antipathetic to such mixing of genres. A concerto theme is a concerto theme, and as such is carefully distinguished from the themes for piano sonata, string quartet, and symphony. In the piano sonatas there is not one "military" movement in our sense, and in the ordinary sense there is perhaps only the "Marcia funebre sulla morte d'un Eroe" in Op. 26, the A♭ Major Sonata; but we know that this movement of a somewhat picturesque work owes its origin to Beethoven's vexation over the disproportionate praise with which his friends had received the funeral march in Paër's opera *Achilles*. Beethoven also strictly excludes military elements from his symphonies. I trust that no one will maintain that the first movement of the First Symphony is of a military character. The finale of the Fifth Symphony is not a march but a hymn, and it is written in a different time from that of all the Beethoven concertos, with the single apparent exception of the C Minor Concerto: the military measure is four-four time. (Surely it was by mistake that Beethoven marked the finale of the C Minor Symphony four-four time rather than *alla breve*.) In the last movement of the Eroica there is the beginning of a quickmarch; but it is evident that to Beethoven the military is a separate category from the heroic. And the Funeral March? It is not military; the second movement does not supply what might have been expected from the first movement. The Funeral March is a threnody; to use it for practical purposes, such as playing it in memory of a soldier, is to misunderstand it completely. In the Agnus Dei of the *Missa Solemnis* the military element is altogether a concrete symbol; it betokens war, it is gloomy, and its effect is gloomy. In the choral finale of the Ninth Symphony, the military element is orgiastic, and the tumult is so exaggerated that only the trivial remains as a climax. In Beethoven the military concept in its particular musical sense is exaltation, that highest exaltation of an heroic soul which also includes the depths.

# XXI

## Strauss and Hofmannsthal

"I consider it quite right and proper that you should expect a great deal of yourself. Who should make great demands on himself, if not the man whom the world calls a master?" Hofmannsthal to Strauss.

I HAVE been reading once more after several years the correspondence between Hugo von Hofmannsthal and Richard Strauss, which was published in 1926 under the not quite correct title *Richard Strauss. Correspondence with Hugo von Hofmannsthal*. Appearing as it did during the lifetime of both correspondents, it was an astonishing publication; and its importance has never, to my knowledge, been rightly appreciated. For it calls for, not the usual friendly occasional criticism, which passes over depths and shallows alike, but a criticism of the two "ideal" personalities, who have co-operated in the creation of the most problematic, the most difficult, the most questionable of all works of art—opera. Today, perhaps for the first time, this criticism can be attempted. Hofmannsthal is dead; Strauss is 70 [1934]. He has finished his work, and he will not change much now, even if he reaches the age of Verdi or Methuselah. One should not prophesy, of course, in matters of art. I know the fine speech made by an Italian scholar on the occasion of Verdi's seventieth birthday, a speech which assumes, as I have done with Strauss, that Verdi's work was finished, and which regards *Otello* as crowning and completing his lifework. But after *Otello* came *Falstaff*, which shed a new light on everything that Verdi had written before. Strauss too has written several operas after *Arabella*, the last one in collaboration with Hofmannsthal.

I have said that the title *Richard Strauss. Correspondence with Hugo von Hofmannsthal* is incorrect. It should have run: *Letters from Hofmannsthal on the Problem of Writing Opera Librettos for Richard Strauss, with some Answers from the Composer*. Hofmannsthal's share in the general and particular expression of views is much the more considerable. That is naturally due in part to the fact that Hofmannsthal was a poet, a great writer, a passionate lover of the discussion of aesthetic questions; he knew how to handle words professionally, whereas Strauss's letters, for the most part, are by no means remarkable as literature. Strauss is a practical musician who sees, and must see, things from his standpoint; he tells the poet his requirements as a composer, and is able to elucidate for Hofmannsthal any number of points in connection with the music. Hofmannsthal was, in the most usual sense of the word, "unmusical"; actually he was one of the most devoted servants of the Muses that has ever lived. At the beginning of his collaboration with Strauss he worked without paying any attention to the music, which he was quite unable to imagine. His libretto is complete in itself as poetry; it is self-sufficient. "For me," he writes, "your music only adds something very beautiful, something which is naturally far more than actors or the designer of the scenery could ever offer me."

Thus originated *Elektra*, the first work in which Strauss and Hofmannsthal collaborated. The composer took over the complete poem, as he had previously taken over the complete poem of *Salome*, and "swallowed it whole" ("*mit Haut und Haar gefressen*"). It is one of the most grandiose of Strauss's works. It is also one of the most unevenly proportioned, since the climax comes at the beginning, in Electra's first monologue. It is one of the least satisfying, since from the moment of the murder of Clytaemnestra it is no longer Electra who is the principal figure, but the matricide Orestes. Hofmannsthal realized this. One day he proposed to Strauss a mime drama, a ballet on a larger scale, on Orestes and the Furies. He constantly felt it necessary to continue *Elektra* in some other form, a form independent of words. It is obvious that Strauss could not make up his mind to set this gigantic subject, while different plans were taking shape in different forms. A *Semiramis* led to *Die Aegyptische Helena;* a *Steinernes Herz* (Heart of Stone) to *Die Frau ohne Schatten* (Woman Without a Shadow); the Casanova comedy *Cristina* was transformed into *Arabella*. The partnership was marked throughout by cordiality and appreciation, on Strauss's side as well. We know the milestones on the road which they trod together —*Der Rosenkavalier*, *Ariadne*, *Josephs Legende* (for which Hofmannsthal was not wholly responsible), *Die Frau ohne Schatten*, *Die Aegyptische Helena*, *Arabella*. Everything that Strauss wrote without Hofmannsthal, everything in which he depended on his own resources—*Schlagobers* (Whipped Cream), *Intermezzo* and other works—was an absolute failure and a catastrophe. Everything that Strauss has written since *Elektra* outside the field of opera is not only work of secondary importance, but second-rate, from the *Alpine Symphony* to the piano concerto.

What Hofmannsthal meant to Strauss, Hofmannsthal at any rate knew quite definitely. He realized that without him Strauss would long ago have reached the viewpoint of the public. He always lifted Strauss up above himself. (It is also true that Strauss on many occasions did the same for Hofmannsthal.) What Strauss secretly wanted was the conventional, the "operatic." Hofmannsthal was always trying to get beyond it, but Strauss always managed to smuggle it in again. Hofmannsthal admired Wagner and was envious of the Wagnerian unity of conception of poetry and music; but he was the very opposite of a Wagnerian. It was only gradually that Strauss surmounted the Wagnerian style. Perhaps it is truer to say that he never did; even in August, 1916, he wrote: "I promise you I have now definitely laid aside Wagner's coat of mail" ("*Musizier-Panzer*"). At the time of *Rosenkavalier* he still talks of "symphonic unity." Hofmannsthal quite consciously provided the stimulus for a new tempo in opera as a change from "Wagner's perpetual slow and solemn andante" and Strauss realized it in practice. Will a future history of opera recognize in this the proper achievement of the poet and musician? Throughout his life Hofmannsthal fought against the danger that Strauss "in matters of art may decide in favour of what is more comfortable in contrast to what is higher and richer in possibilities." He continually appeals to Strauss's "truly artistic, revolutionary nature" ("*anarchische Natur*"). There was none. Without Hofmannsthal, Strauss would have continued to be even more the "composer of the day" ("*Gegenwarts-Musiker*"), the composer of the bourgeois period between 1896 and 1914, than he actually was.

In spite of all Hofmannsthal's affection and admiration for him, Strauss never really came up to Hofmannsthal's expectations. There were differences on single and quite decisive points, as when, for instance, Strauss allowed Ochs's philosophy of love to culminate in a fortissimo a yard long, instead of "whispered with his hand in front of his mouth." But the poet found *Rosenkavalier* "certainly very satisfying as a whole of text and music, but not completely so." Hofmannsthal is forever striving after what is not present, and is burdened with all the riches of the past. Strauss is much more carefree; more trivial, but more vigorous. Hofmannsthal lifts him to realms which he had never thought of and would never have reached by himself. But Strauss leads the poet into the region of immortality, which Hofmannsthal would never have reached without the composer's energetic vitality. It is true that at the end of their partnership, after *Die Frau ohne Schatten*, in which Hofmannsthal had expected much too much of the opera public of his time, and after *Die Aegyptische Helena*, in which he had expected too much of Strauss himself, Hofmannsthal gave way. He wrote *Arabella* for Strauss, and brought himself down to Strauss's level. It is a work of the most refined technique, but it is also, to a certain extent, the "pretty story of love and intrigue" which Strauss had once asked him for.

What is the most successful work produced by these two very different artists? The answer is *Ariadne auf Naxos*. It did not at first look as though it were going to be. Strauss accepted the poem without understanding, with a cruel indifference. The work in its original form—as a pendant to one of Molière's comedies—was a troublesome infant; it was only after some years that it reached its final shape. This interlude in their labours is their masterpiece. What is the reason? Why do we find in it the perfect encounter between the poet and the composer? It is a question which can only be answered with difficulty. The reason is that the poet, lagging behind and heavy laden, represents everything in the mirror with the baroque frame, in the frame of an almost inconceivable mixture of styles, which makes it possible to say with impunity what is most serious, most profound, and most exquisite; and also that the piece called forth the best in the composer—his superabundant technique, his most delicate sensuousness, his delight in parody. Not coarse, but refined parody. It has often been remarked that Strauss is in a special sense a Bavarian, an Upper Bavarian. Anyone who knows the Bavarian (and I am myself, to some extent, a near fellow-countryman of Strauss), knows his ironic talent for mimicry, his mastery of parody. The Upper Bavarian is a born actor. Indeed, despite Oberammergau, he really makes his effect on the stage only in comedy and parody, never in emotion, which with him turns only too easily into sickly sentimentality. Do people realize that Strauss is an Upper Bavarian? Do they guess why *Ariadne* is his masterpiece? Do they realize that he mistook the sublime conclusion of this "flower in song" (as Hofmannsthal saw it), that he emptied it of its true content, Wagnerized it, and covered it with ornament?

# XXII
## Wagner and Ludwig II

SOME thirty years or so ago in the Archives at Munich I asked the Keeper about Wagner's letters to King Ludwig II. The Keeper told me then that I must not be inquisitive, that the letters were "unpalatable." He was right. They are unpalatable; but they are something worse still. Combined with all the other evidence from every source they give us a most sobering and damaging picture of Wagner's character. Anyone who has read through the four beautifully printed volumes of the letters, published in 1938 [1]—described in the advance notices as "the crown of Wagnerian literature" —will know fairly well what Nietzsche must have felt in 1876 after Bayreuth, the "crown of Wagner's life." What could have induced Bayreuth (since the Wittelsbacher Ausgleich-Fonds has no moral interest in Wagner's memory) to publish this correspondence? There are two reasons. The first is that

[1] *König Ludwig II. und Richard Wagner. Briefwechsel. Mit vielen anderen Urkunden in vier Bänden, herausgegeben vom Wittelsbacher Ausgleich-Fonds und von Winifred Wagner.* Edited by Otto Strobel. Karlsruhe: Braun, 1938.

Wagner had nothing whatever to fear in Germany between 1933 and 1945, as the extracts added to the fourth volume from reviews in the *Völkischer Beobachter*, the *Bayrische Ostmark*, the *Westfälische Zeitung* and the *Frankfurter Zeitung* plainly show. The second reason stems from the fact that in 1933, exactly ten days after Hitler came to power, the firm of Knorr and Hirth in Munich published a small volume which is as modest in appearance as the other four are magnificent. It was called *Richard Wagner in München, 1864–1870*. The author was a professor of good old Bavarian stock named Eduard Stemplinger, who proved that the official story—that Wagner in 1865 and later was sacrificed to the Munich bureaucracy, the priests and Jesuits, and the organized fury of the mob—was an absolute fiction. Wagner was himself the architect of his misfortune and had only himself to blame for his "expulsion."

The four volumes of letters, in which, incidentally, a few actual errors in Stemplinger's work are controverted, are on the whole an overwhelming justification of his book and present a collection of documents which precisely confirm his account. It is not a complete collection, abundant as it is. From the point of view of the expert, a number of sources are still lacking. But in spite of that, we owe the publishers and the editors a debt of recognition for having been so assiduous and conscientious in reproducing letters from both sides and for having shown such respect for truth. One must not blame the editor if the dominant note of both introduction and commentary is generosity and pious devotion to Wagner's memory. But there will be an end of the conspiracy of silence, palliation, and falsification, at least in Bayreuth; and the days of Glasenapp, Golther, and Du Moulin Eckart (a "historian" whom I myself was able to watch "at work") seem to have gone forever.

Everyone knows how Wagner's relations with the King began. Deep in distress, both economic and spiritual, Wagner had himself suggested the "sublime miracle" of his invitation when, in the preface to the publication of his *Ring* poem, he had put to the world the pathetic question whether some prince would not arrive to make possible the performance of his work. Ludwig, converted by a performance of *Lohengrin* into an ardent admirer of Wagner's, read the passage and felt himself destined to be that prince. On May 4, 1864, a few months after the young man's accession to the throne, Wagner was at Munich. What then developed was a bond of friendship of an intensity rare in Wagner's life. There were, in fact, none of his friendships he did not survive, except those with Liszt and the King. Even in these relationships desperate crises occurred, which were weathered but never really solved. Crises were inevitable between Ludwig and Wagner: the causes lay deep in the nature of each. The King—a poor unbalanced lad of eighteen years, without any particular intellectual gifts, superficially educated, badly brought up, tainted with a hereditary disease, and morbidly high-strung—set the tone for their intercourse. Wagner took it up with shameless unscrupulousness, though he, a man of the world, must have known at the first encounter what kind of puerile creature he had before him.

The falsity of the tone strikes us from the first. Look where one will in the King's letters, he is always found echoing Wagner, filling his paper with quotations and reminiscences of the opera librettos,[1] with memories of "rapturous hours," and with assurances of boundless love and unalterable loyalty. It is like a parody of a scene in Wagner's theatre: the King is Lohengrin or Parsifal, Walther von Stolzing or Siegfried, while Wagner plays Hans Sachs, Gurnemanz, or Wanderer-Wotan. It is only necessary to read a few of Wagner's addresses and formulas of devotion to understand what the worthy old keeper of the Munich archives meant by "unpalatable": "Beloved, unique friend! Supreme beauty of my life!"; "His own true subject and deeply gladdened protégé"; "Of my dear, noble friend, of my adored"—ad infinitum. Only Cosima showed a more fertile invention. Again and again the King assures Wagner that he will accompany him through the portal of death, though, as a matter of fact, when it came to February 13, 1883, the idea was abandoned.

For in the meantime each had disappointed and deceived the other a hundred times. The King never had the smallest understanding of Wagner's true greatness; for one thing, he was utterly unmusical. It is not *Tristan* or *Meistersinger*, or *The Ring*, or *Parsifal* that represents Wagner's true musical relation to the King, but the bombastic and jejune *Huldigungsmarsch* for military band. All that the King sees in Wagner's work is a kind of intoxicating theatrical stimulant which he can procure against the composer's will, as an addict gets hold of a drug behind his doctor's back. Profound disagreements arise between the patient and the medicine man who is secretly encouraging the progress of the disease, as when at a performance of *Lohengrin* the King simply sends home the

[1] "When a few hours ago I saw the Rhine close to for the first time, and the sun's gold was mirrored so brightly in its waters, ah, how I thought of my beloved *Rheingold*."

elderly tenor Tichatschek whom Wagner had invited to sing, or when he asks to see *Rheingold* and *Walküre* against Wagner's wishes and actually does manage to see them, as the scores are his property. Wagner conceals the completion of *Siegfried* from the King merely to stop the same thing happening to this part of the tetralogy as well. The King is quite capable of expressing himself contemptuously about Wagner, or of acting against his wishes—and in the same hour writing to assure him of his eternal fidelity. He was irresponsibility personified, and Wagner knew it. What he actually thought of the King can be seen to some extent from a letter he wrote to the politician Constantin Frantz on March 19, 1866:

> I regard the young King Ludwig as quite uncommonly able, as the first sight of his very striking features would convince you. How the characteristics of a ruler will develop in him is now the great question. An inconceivably thoughtless upbringing has had the effect of arousing in the young man a deep-seated disinclination, which does not yet appear to be invincible, to occupy himself seriously with state affairs, which, with a contempt for all the interests involved, he allows to be dispatched merely in accordance with existing routine and through the existing officials, as though he loathed the whole business. His family and the whole court are repugnant to him, the army and the soldiery detestable, the nobility ridiculous, the mass of the people contemptible; as far as the priests are concerned, he knows his own mind and is without prejudice; in matters of religion he is serious and fervent. There is only one way to arouse the sympathetic powers of his soul and that is myself, my work, my art, in which he perceives the real world, while all the rest seems to him a foolish fantasy.

But even in this last persuasion Ludwig II sadly disappointed Wagner—most sadly of all when he refrained from attending the performances of *Parsifal* in 1882. Cosima's final opinion of the King appears in a passage in her diary where she speaks of the "strange crotchets in the King's brain." The King, with a weakling's cunning, knew how to evade many of Wagner's inconvenient demands, and when a crisis arose, he was always "very busy." In later years Wagner hardly ever saw him at all, apart from a few official appearances.

The disillusions and deceptions which Wagner suffered he paid back in full measure—most fully by the concealment of his relations with Cosima Bülow, the wife of his most devoted henchman. The King, perhaps in consequence of his own unhappy disposition, held strong views on moral remissness. Adultery, which within Wagner's first few weeks at Munich was an accomplished fact—and no secret at all in the circle of intimates—had to be carefully concealed from him. Abysses yawned. The climax of the intrigue was reached in May, 1866, when Cosima, Wagner, and, alas! Bülow, too, who cannot have been without his suspicions, obtained from the King an official rehabilitation of Cosima's honor, which had been impugned by attacks in the press. The letter which Cosima wrote at that time to the King—"I sink on my knees before my King and beg him in humility and distress to send the letter to my husband, so that we may not have to leave the country in disgrace and ignominy. . . . I have three children, to whom it is my duty to pass on unspotted the honored name of their father"—can hardly be surpassed in unscrupulousness. One of these children, Isolde, was actually Wagner's daughter! And *Parsifal* did not forsake his own.

When Ludwig learned the truth he was furious, and serious discord ensued. Over and over again Wagner had grounds for withdrawing altogether. But it was not so easy for him to leave a King who, in the truest sense of the term, had rescued him and was always rescuing him again. After the 1866 war took a turn unfavourable to Bavaria, and Ludwig talked of abdicating, there was consternation at Triebschen. Of what use to Wagner is a King without a civil list? Old friends were pitilessly cold-shouldered if they offered any threat to Wagner's claims on the King's generosity, and Wagner himself turned down a scheme for the building of a Wagner theatre in Munich when Ludwig took too strong a fancy to Gottfried Semper's model. There was only one right place for the money.

And Wagner kept his eye not only, though principally, on money for his work and for himself. He also had an eye to power. Along with the letters to the King there is a diary, kept for a time in 1865, which was intended to influence the King politically; and Cosima also worked privately to the same end. It would take us too far to go into Wagner's political views and projects, which are often fantastical, and on behalf of which he enlisted the aid of a Munich fortuneteller, Frau Dangl. This "mysterious old woman of the people," as he calls her, came to him one evening and revealed to him that Ludwig was destined—for so it was written in the stars—to be called to great deeds. On the strength of this Wagner for a time saw in Ludwig "Germany's Redeemer"—a view of the monarch which Bismarck notoriously failed to share, although, like Wagner, he had no scruples in exploiting Ludwig's weakness. Wagner hated Bismarck and the Prussians, as later he hated the "Reich." Not that this prevented him from adding a *Kaisermarsch* to the *Huldigungsmarsch* in 1871.

After the dramatic agitations of the Munich and Triebschen period came the ten outwardly tranquil Bayreuth years. The King presented Wagner with "Wahnfried," made the first festival possible by his financial and artistic aid, helped again and again when needs were pressing, and from time to time wrote a letter expressing enthusiastic interest in Wagner's work, person, and family, which Wagner answered expansively. All this material is of the greatest value for the history of those last years; and the important thing is that here nothing is suppressed and nothing added. It must have been a sorry grief to the Nazi regime in Germany to know that Wagner showed as much anxiety about trying to save his son from ever having to die for the Fatherland as he had in keeping himself at a safe distance from the bullets of the government troops in the Dresden revolution.

Even in his prejudices Wagner is not quite so consistent as one could wish. He regarded the whole of Germany as being in the grip of the Jewish bankers; but when one fine day in 1865 he came into the possession of 40,000 thalers from the King, he lost no time in begging his friend August Röckel to find a banker who would take this "little capital under his wing, preferably one who would invest it for me profitably, at a good rate of interest"; and Röckel found this money merchant in the banker Hohenemser of Frankfurt-on-Main, who was decidedly not an Aryan.

The man who wrote all these letters was also the creator of *Tristan*. Among the great musicians there is none who requires that we shall so extensively forget the man if we are to apprehend the pure artist. Nowhere is the problem of the unity of the man and the artist so difficult to solve as in the case of Wagner. Nietzsche put it best when he wrote: "It is hard to impugn Wagner in details and not to win one's case; his art, life, and character, his opinions, his likes and dislikes, all have weak spots. But as a whole the phenomenon can withstand every possible assault."

In the fourth volume of this edition there are one or two documents which afford welcome relief. There a few letters from the Duchess Sophie Charlotte, the King's fiancée, to Wagner, written with charming feminine grace and sweetness. There is the answer of Wagner's old friend August Röckel to the reproach that he had not been sufficiently energetic in fighting Munich gossip—an answer so excellent, so virile, so smashing that Wagner had nothing more to say. Finally, there is a letter from Nietzsche to Wagner, dated May 24, 1875, which shows such purity of thought, intellect, and diction that one can scarcely bring oneself to read any more of Wagner's fussy bureaucratic German. This letter, sent to the King in a copy, apparently escaped the holocaust of all the originals of which Cosima boasted. (Even today I cannot believe that a man would be capable of this heroic strategy. But, of course, a woman . . .) Bayreuth once assured the son of the poet-musician Peter Cornelius—except for Liszt, Wagner's most important friend among musicians —that his father's letters were no longer in existence. Yet they were in existence all the time; so, perhaps, Nietzsche's are, too. It would, indeed, be the "crown of Wagnerian literature" if the correspondence between Wagner and Nietzsche, and Wagner and Cornelius were to follow the letters from Wagner to Ludwig.

# THE NORTON LIBRARY

PB 21777